The Shield of the Weak

Pedro Figari, *La Pulla* (*Sharp Tongue*) (detail), ca. 1934, Museo Histórico Nacional, Montevideo, Uruguay. Reprinted with permission.

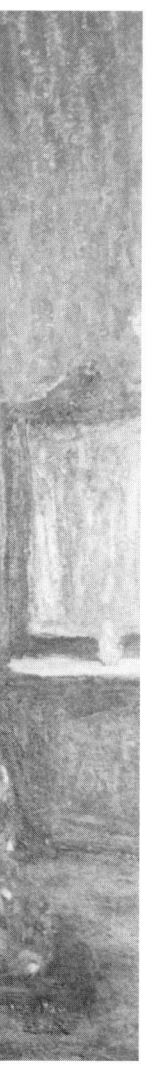

The Shield of the Weak

Feminism and the State in Uruguay, 1903–1933

Christine Ehrick

University of New Mexico Press
Albuquerque

© 2005 by the University of New Mexico Press
All rights reserved. Published 2005
Printed in the United States of America

09 08 07 06 05   1 2 3 4 5

Library of Congress Cataloging-in-Publication Data

Ehrick, Christine, 1967–
  The shield of the weak : feminism and the state in Uruguay, 1903–1933 / Christine Ehrick.— 1st ed.
      p. cm.
  Includes bibliographical references and index.
  ISBN 0-8263-3468-7 (cloth : alk. paper)
  1. Women in politics—Uruguay—History. 2. Feminism—Uruguay—History. I. Title.
  HQ1236.5.U8E47 2005
  305.42'09895'09041—dc22
                                        2005002484

Book design and composition by Damien Shay
Body type is Trump Mediaeval 9.5/13.
Display is Typo Upright and Novarese.

Table of Contents

List of Illustrations — vi

Acknowledgments — xi

Introduction — 1
    Women and Politics in "The Model Country"

Prologue — 21
    The Nineteenth-Century Roots of Batllismo and Feminismo

Chapter One — 33
    The First Feminisms: State Building and Women's Organizing, 1880s–1915

Chapter Two — 69
    Batllista Ideology and Policy: Gender, Class, and the Politics of Compensation, 1910–1933

Chapter Three — 91
    Women and the "National Family": Education, Social Assistance, and the State

Chapter Four — 127
    Liberal Feminism, 1916–1932

Chapter Five — 161
    The Catholic Ladies' League after Batlle, 1916–1932

Chapter Six — 181
    Socialists and Communists, 1916–1932

Conclusion — 205

Notes — 215

Bibliography — 255

Index — 275

List of Illustrations

Figure 1: 51
Feminismo Cristiano (Christian Feminism), 1907.

Figure 2: 56
Belén Sárraga, c.1913.

Figure 3: 59
Otilia Schultze de Galarza and her husband Pablo Galarza.

Figure 4: 62
María Collazo, Buenos Aires, 1907.

Figure 5: 73
José Batlle y Ordóñez, c.1920.

Figure 6: 78
The *Escuela de Aplicación de Señoritas* (Young Women's Applied School), Montevideo, 1914.

Figure 7: 79
Experimental Chemistry Class, Women's University, c.1915.

Figure 8: 80
Professors at the Women's University, c.1918.

Figure 9: 97
Paulina Luisi and the first-year medical school class of 1901, Universidad de la República, Uruguay.

Figure 10: 109
National Public Assistance and programs assisting women and children: the first *Gota de leche* ("Drop of Milk") office in Montevideo, c.1913.

Figure 11: 114
Lottery ticket supporting the *Asilos Maternales*, 1924.

Figure 12: 121
Laura Cortinas, late 1920s.

Figure 13: 135
The Uruguayan National Women's Council during the 1920s.

Figure 14: 137
Paulina Luisi, 1918.

Figure 15: 141
Fanny Carrió de Polleri, c. 1918.

Figure 16: 147
Political Cartoon: The Uruguayan Woman Demands her Political Rights, 1929.

Figure 17: 165
Margarita Uriarte de Herrera.

For Mom and Dad

Acknowledgments

This book took a long time to complete—too long actually. The manuscript, and my life, underwent many changes along the way, including moves from California to Iowa, back to California, and now to Louisville, Kentucky. Throughout this process both the book and the author have benefited from immeasurable support and assistance from many people, without whom I would never have gotten to this point. Thanks to the Fulbright Commission, and to Director Mercedes Jimenez de Aréchaga, whose generous support and flexibility allowed me the time to complete my research. Additional assistance from the University of California, Los Angeles, the University of Northern Iowa, and the University of Louisville allowed for preliminary and follow-up research trips to Uruguay over the years. David Holtby at the University of New Mexico Press was endlessly patient with my many revisions of this manuscript. I am grateful for his many suggestions and advice, and for his support for this project.

Michael Monteón, my senior honors thesis advisor at UC San Diego, first suggested studying Uruguay. In graduate school at UCLA, Ellen DuBois, Fernando López-Alves, Brad Burns, Adriana Bergero, and Robert Brenner encouraged me to pursue this project, against the general perception that "minor country" studies at the doctoral level was a professional dead end. I particularly owe the development of my thesis to my advisor, José Moya, who spent many hours helping me to define and narrow the focus of my research.

I am grateful also for the encouragement and friendship of so many people in Uruguay who made the research for this book possible. Thanks especially to José Pedro Barrán, Gerardo Caetano, Luce Fabbri, Fernando López D'Alesandro, Oscar Padrón Favre, Amalia Polleri, Dardo Ramos, Universindo Rodríguez Díaz, Siliva Rodríguez Villamíl, Graciela Sapriza, and Enrique Saracini. Ana Pacini generously opened her home to me, as well as the archives of the Uruguayan National Women's Council, and enthusiastically supported this project. The staff at the Biblioteca Nacional, the Archivo General de la Nación, the Registro Civil, the Uruguayan Anti-Tuberculosis League, and the Asociación "La Bonne Garde" provided assistance and access to documents and archives far beyond the call of duty. My Uruguayan family

Acknowledgments

and friends always made every visit to Uruguay a sincere pleasure, and they are the reason that Montevideo always has, and always will, feel like home. Thanks first and foremost go to my Uruguayan "familia"—Elsa Despouey, Lourdes Sena, Javier Bentancor, Ercilia Sheppard, *y los demás*—for all your *cariño* and for never a dull moment. Beatriz Abramián, David Altman, Rossana Castiglioni, Matthew Corey, Anthony Fletcher, Steven Kay, Veronica Pamoukaghlián, Francisco Pucci, Estela Retamoso, Susana Roda, Vartán Saravia, and Aimee Verdisco provided friendship and support, and were always there to drag me away from my research when it was most necessary.

My sincere thanks also to all of those who read and commented on parts or all of this manuscript: Ann Allen, Jeremy Beck, Eileen Boris, Andy Burstein, Manali Desai, Carolyn Eichner, Tina Escaja, Van Gosse, Donna Guy, Elizabeth Hutchison, Nancy Isenberg, Sofia Martos, Sandra McGee Deutsch, Corinne Pernet, Karen Spierling, Dolores Trevizo, Ericka Verba, and Aimee Verdisco. Thanks also to Däch and Lee Keeling for their assistance in preparing illustrations, and to Floyce Alexander for his careful copyediting.

My parents, Steve and Barbara Ehrick, always believed in me even if they thought what I was doing was a little odd, and my sister Alison's cynical sense of humor (putting mine to shame) could always brighten my day. Dolores Trevizo, Jeffrey Harold Burgett, Manali Desai, and Helen Petroff helped keep me sane during some difficult times. Tim and Tom Bedore were a big part of my family for many years, and I cannot imagine where my life would be right now without them. And finally, my thanks to Jeremy Beck, who has always believed in me and kept me focused: Your love and support have meant more to me than I could ever express. Our son Samuel arrived as this book was in its final stages, a most welcome interruption.

Introduction
Women and Politics in "The Model Country"

> José Batlle y Ordóñez governs in defiance of the powers of heaven and earth. The Church has promised him a nice place in hell...and the Devil will avenge his offences against male-supremacists.
>
> *"He is legalizing licentiousness,"* say his enemies when he approves a law permitting women to sue for divorce. *"He is dissolving the family,"* they say, when he extends inheritance rights to illegitimate children.
>
> *"The female brain is inferior,"* they say, when he creates a women's university and announces that women will soon have the vote so that Uruguayan democracy need not walk on one leg, and so that women will not forever be children passing from the hands of the father to those of the husband.
> — Eduardo Galeano, Memory of Fire[1]

For much of the first half of the twentieth century, the Southern Cone nation of Uruguay was held up as a model democracy and as home to the region's most advanced welfare state. Prior to the military dictatorship of the 1970s that shattered its image as an exceptional oasis of democracy, writers hailed this small country as "one of the most progressive states in the world."[2] The construction of that state is associated with José Batlle y Ordóñez, president of the republic from 1903 to 1907 and from 1911 to 1915 and a leader of the ruling Colorado Party until his death in 1929. During this era, Uruguay became the first nation in Latin America to legislate the eight-hour day, the first to guarantee health care to the poor, and the home of a social security system that became a model for the rest of the continent. Legislative changes also made it easier for women to divorce and gain access to higher education and social services, and in 1932 Uruguay became one of the first Latin American nations to grant women the vote in national elections. Contemporary Uruguayan author Eduardo Galeano underscores Batlle's reputation as a radical and a visionary, and as a perceived threat to the Catholic Church and other traditional powers. That he and other observers focused on the position of women in Uruguayan society speaks to the central place that the "woman question" occupied in Batllista ideology and policy. Russell Fitzgibbon, in his 1956 *Uruguay: Portrait of a Democracy*, wrote that the Uruguayan woman "now enjoys a greater degree of social and economic emancipation in Uruguay than in any other Latin American country."[3]

But what is the relationship between this image and the reality for Uruguayan women during this era? Do we find a feminist utopia, or something of a patriarchal smokescreen, where illusions of advancement were projected over traditional gender relations? The Batllista state did challenge many pillars of Spanish American orthodoxy, including those sanctioning the subordination of women; but it was never as revolutionary as its biggest champions or critics painted it to be. Batlle defined his project and his party as *'el escudo de los débiles'*, or the shield of the weak, where the "weak" were generally understood as women, children, and the poor and working classes.[4] This was a limited welfare state that, like so many others, provided benefits to the socially and economically disenfranchised, without truly challenging the roots of social inequality. Either despite or because of these limitations, Uruguay was a model for many, viewed as proof that Spanish America could achieve a limited but functional democracy and substantial social reform without provoking political instability or civil war. It thus stands as an important case for those interested in the historical intersections of gender, feminism, and state formation in Latin America.

The first wave of Uruguayan feminism coincided chronologically with the Batllista era, and this study highlights the connections and the dialogue between these two processes during the first third of the twentieth century. Ideas about woman's new place in society interacted with class, political ideology, and party affiliation to give rise to a wide spectrum of multiple and diverse feminisms that were also, in their own ways, responding to the challenges and opportunities presented by Batllismo and the Batllista era generally. The overall goal of this project has been to write women into the history of the *época batllista* in an integrative way, providing both a gendered analysis of state formation and a comprehensive overview of the history of feminism in

Uruguay during this formative era. Following a brief overview of the colonial and postindependence periods, this study begins in the late nineteenth century, with the first real attempts at consolidation of a liberal state and the precursors of feminist organizing. It concludes in the early 1930s, with the December 1932 law that gave Uruguayan women full voting rights and the March 1933 military coup that effectively put an end to a political era in the country.

Theoretical Perspectives

Much of the now substantial body of work on gender and the welfare state has engaged—implicitly and explicitly—the debate over the historical relationships between public and private patriarchy, capitalism, and the modern state. Some earlier literature centered, for example, on issues of private (family-based) patriarchy vs. state-based patriarchy, and the question as to whether the welfare state has historically acted to reinforce patriarchal control over women or has, instead, offered women a means to free themselves from the oppression of the traditional family and dependence on an individual man.[5] Recent scholarship has moved away from this quantitative focus (i.e., did patriarchy increase or decrease with the welfare state?) to a more nuanced, qualitative analysis of what changed and what remained the same during these transformations. As Ann Orloff has noted, "[m]ale dominance is not necessarily reproduced; indeed, it is often transformed."[6] This perspective also moves us away from teleological arguments equating modernization with increasing equity in gender relations. The impact of state formation is often more complex, and its record in terms of gender relations more mixed.

Scholars of twentieth-century Latin American states have engaged this "modernization of patriarchy" framework, carefully demonstrating the ways in which unequal social relations—for which gender was a major signifier—were updated and remodeled to shape the needs of the state, the economy, and the social order.[7] Studies of twentieth-century Brazil and Mexico by Susan Besse and Mary Kay Vaughan, respectively, offer a useful framework, in that they trace the reformulation of patriarchy without any fundamental alteration of unequal social relations.[8] In the Puerto Rican and Chilean cases, Eileen Findlay and Karin Rosemblatt concur that discourse aimed at forging a "national family" tended to reproduce, and in some cases reinforce, gender inequalities and dependencies, via the family wage and other policies.[9] In addition to their theoretical contributions, these studies'

3

detailed focus on the specificities of local context help us to better understand where Latin America fits within this broader literature on gender, class, and state formation, and we can begin to forge comparative connections between national cases within the region. Batllismo was an early example of this national family discourse that simultaneously reified gendered hierarchies and incorporated women into the public sphere. While the "compensation feminism" at the center of Batllista gender ideology was premised upon women's immutable dependence and biological disadvantage, the Uruguayan welfare state also provided some women with new resources to gain leverage or to free themselves from oppressive circumstances. This was most true for middle-class and affluent women, who were better able to avail themselves of these opportunities than their working-class sisters. But even poor women were occasionally able to use the state apparatus to gain—albeit incrementally—improvements in their circumstances.

The present project differs from much of the recent scholarship on gender and the state in Latin America in that it maintains a central focus on feminists and feminist politics in the early decades of the twentieth century.[10] Starting in the 1970s and continuing through the early 1990s, there was an explosion of English-language material published on the history of feminism in Latin America, contributing to the much-needed task of reviving and reconstructing women's historical narratives.[11] These works also contextualized women's politics in ways that allowed us to better understand Latin American feminisms' similarities and derivations from U.S. and European models.[12] The most important English-language work on Uruguayan feminism specifically is Asunción Lavrin's *Women, Feminism, and Social Change in Argentina, Chile, and Uruguay, 1890–1940*. Lavrin compiled large amounts of data on the history of feminism in the Southern Cone, alongside information on gendered policies during the same era. This is a project of tremendous scope and ambition, but Lavrin does not connect her studies of feminist politics to the process of state formation. While I offer certain correctives to Lavrin's narrative and analysis, my primary goal is to link Uruguayan feminisms and Batllismo in ways that lie beyond the scope of Lavrin's comparative project.

This book seeks to utilize new gendered understandings of state formation, as well as social historical methodology, to take a new look at feminist activism in Uruguay. The history of Uruguayan feminism during these years, for example, is inseparable from the figure of Paulina Luisi (1875–1950), the nation's first female physician and the founder of the two main liberal feminist organizations of this era. A still controversial figure claimed by competing feminist and partisan factions in Uruguay, a sense of her political activities, views, and alliances is crucial to understanding this history. But if we want to really understand feminist politics in local context, it is important to consider, as much as the historical record permits, all of the women who led or joined these groups. To that end, this project utilizes a large database of biographical information on leaders and members of feminist organizations. By collecting published and unpublished membership information, and then using that information to compile information about specific individuals through the Civil Registry and other sources, I was able to construct a database with varying degrees of information on more than five hundred politically active women in Uruguay during the years under examination. This data provides a sense of who these women were in class and political terms, and allows us to compare memberships of different organizations and to trace change within those organizations over time. Available information on family, neighborhood, age, ethnicity, and professional status provide insight into the impact of immigration, education, and state formation on women's political activity and affiliation. This database is unavoidably uneven: much more information was available for liberal feminist groups than for either the Catholic Ladies' League or women in the Socialist and Communist parties, for example.[13] Additionally, more information was available (and far more activity recorded) in the capital city of Montevideo than in the provinces. Thus, although women were active in the Uruguayan interior during this time, and evidence suggests somewhat distinct patterns of political involvement than in the capital, this project largely focuses on feminist activity in Montevideo.

How did Latin America's first welfare state come to emerge in a place where political institutions had been nearly nonexistent only decades earlier? Scholars of nineteenth-century Uruguay have sought to explain this apparent paradox. Francisco Panizza has written that the Batllista era in Uruguayan history is best understood as a convergence of "late institutionalization" and "early modernization": that the frontier conditions of the nineteenth century in fact facilitated the state-building projects of the twentieth. The region's fringe status during the colonial period and beyond meant that neither state, church, nor oligarchical elites gained a foothold in the ways observed in more central parts of the Iberian empires. The resulting weak colonial legacy facilitated the state-building process of the late nineteenth and early twentieth centuries because, in simple terms, many of the traditional obstacles to liberal modernization were too weak and ineffectual to mount a meaningful resistance. Specifically, the lack of an effective state infrastructure was both a cause and an effect of a weak and disorganized oligarchical sector; both Panizza and Fernando López-Alves have argued that this lack of elite class consolidation was a key factor in explaining the success of early reform in Uruguay. López-Alves has elaborated on the political dimension, arguing that the economic elites' general disconnect from politics and the strength of political parties in postindependence Uruguay made it possible for the country to take a more democratic road to development than, for example, neighboring Argentina.[14]

The work of both of these scholars has made enormous contributions to our understanding of the particularities of both political party and state formation in nineteenth-century Uruguay. But they do not, by and large, take up questions of gender, nor do they examine the consequences of these particular historical circumstances for women in postcolonial Uruguayan society. What did Uruguay's combination of late institutionalization and early modernization mean for women of varying social classes, for example? Other Latin American scholars have argued that the virtual dissolution of the state following Spanish American independence brought a temporary loosening of gendered boundaries of activity and standards of behavior. In her study of women in Colombia's independence wars, for example, Rebecca Earle concluded that "the war provided women with an unusually protracted opportunity to act publicly," an opinion seconded in Ariel de la Fuente's study of postcolonial Argentina.[15] In Uruguay, where conflict was prolonged and parties strong, women's public participation may have been extended, and their partisan alignments reinforced. Elizabeth Dore and others have argued, on the other hand, that the process of liberal state building, which generally coincided with a winding down of armed conflict, represented a significant reversal for women, as the church and other traditional sources of paternalistic support were shunted aside. How did the weakness of the church and frontier conditions in Uruguay affect this equation? While much more research is required on this issue, and I would in no way assert that the violence and chaos of the Banda Oriental created an oasis of freedom for women, I do argue that late institutionalization—in the form of a weak colonial state and prolonged postindependence civil wars—forged a strongly partisan template for women's public activity which would influence the shape and direction of feminist politics in the twentieth century.[16]

The combination of late institutionalization and early modernization also meant that, in contrast to many other welfare states in Latin America and elsewhere, the Batllista state anticipated, rather than responded to, the emergence of an organized civil society and a vocal middle class. Essentially picking up where Panizza and López-Alves left off, Gerardo Caetano's study of Uruguayan politics during the years 1916–1929 analyzes the changes that brought the traditional disarticulation between economic elites and Uruguayan politics to an end. He argues that Uruguayan civil society was born in the context of a "great antireformist reaction" that emerged toward the end of Batlle's second presidential term (1911–1915). Unlike the original reformism, which came largely from above without any mass mobilization compelling or supporting it, the *alto* ("halt") to reforms was in response to newly cohered business interests and middle sectors that felt the Batllista experiment had gone far enough. But the conservative counter-impulse was not able to turn the clock back entirely, with the result that many of the fundamental tenets of Batllismo became institutionalized in Uruguayan politics and society.[17] Once again, Caetano's study has almost nothing to say about women's changing political roles. Yet the civil society that emerged during those years was not solely masculine, and liberal and other feminist organizations need to be included among the list of political "pressure groups" that began to make their appearance on the Uruguayan scene during the 1910s and 1920s. Uruguayan feminisms, whatever their ideological or partisan stripe, developed concurrently with the Batllista welfare state, and positioned themselves along varying axes of opposition, support, or challenge to that process of state formation. In this way, Uruguayan women took part in the debate and dialogue over reform and its limits, especially in the struggles over the parameters and definitions of citizenship that characterized this era, and thus they played an important role in the construction of the Batllista state.[18]

Understanding both the innovations and limitations of Batllismo calls for an intersectional analysis that considers class/gender relations as a unified whole. For that reason, I argue that this history is best understood as a modernization of paternalism (rather than a modernization of patriarchy), a paradigm which allows us to engage in a broad analysis of power and inequality. Gerda Lerner defines paternalism as "the relationship of a dominant group—considered superior—to a subordinate group—considered inferior—in which the dominance is mitigated by mutual obligations and reciprocal rights."[19] This conceptualization is echoed in Sandra Lauderdale Graham's study of masters and servants in nineteenth-century Brazil, where she describes relationships based on unequal interactions of "protection and obedience," relations not limited to master/servant interaction, but diffused throughout Brazilian society.[20] Paternalism, in other words, captures the idea of a stratified society constructed around the idea (if not always the reality) of interlocking hierarchical relationships and mutual obligation. The concept of paternalism has unequal gender relations as its central metaphor (some would say at its historical origin, arguing that paternalism is in effect derivative of patriarchy), but it is more flexible in encompassing unequal relationships based on class, ethnicity, gender, or other factors, alone or in intersection. As the principal paradigm for relations between social unequals, paternalism is the key framework through which Uruguayan policy regimes were refracted. In this study, I use the term *patriarchy* to refer specifically to inequalities and hierarchies of gender.

Examining the Uruguayan welfare state through the lens of paternalism provides for a clearer understanding of Batllismo, and allows us to better distinguish between different groups of women and thus evaluate the variegated impact of reforms on differing sectors of society. Elite *damas de caridad* (ladies of charity), for example, were on both sides of this paternalistic equation. On the one hand, as the administrators of beneficent societies, elite women assumed the dominant position of protectors of their working-class clientele. As Félix Matos Rodríguez makes clear, in nineteenth-century Puerto Rico elite women, via "ladies' committees," were active participants in constructing bourgeois hegemony. Beneficent and other work raised elite women's profile in the second half of the nineteenth century, while poor women were increasingly marginalized. On the other hand, these same women were relegated to second-class status vis-à-vis males of their same class. It is from this contradiction, where women were enlisted to uphold social hierarchies and accept their own subordinate status, that a form of paternalistic liberal feminism emerges. These ladies' committees, Matos Rodríguez tells us, became an entry point for early liberal feminist activity in Puerto Rico, and a similar pattern is observable in the Uruguayan case. It is via this ambiguity that we can best understand feminisms and feminist politics during this era.[21]

Feminisms in Uruguay

While feminism was one of two great internationalist movements of the late nineteenth and twentieth centuries (the other being socialism), it was shaped by local and national realities in profound ways. With regard to feminism and feminist politics in Batllista Uruguay, I emphasize four main points. First, feminism was plural: liberal feminists were not the only, or even the first groups to identify themselves as such, and as historians we need to adopt a broad definition of feminism in order to understand a broad phenomenon. The second characteristic, connected to the first, was that Uruguayan feminism was partisan: in addition to class divisions and other factors that shaped feminism's pluralism, party politics assumed an important role in inter- and intra-organizational interactions, disputes, competitions, and coalitions. These characteristics also allow us to specify the local aspects of Uruguayan feminism, the third area of emphasis. While they were affiliated with international organizations, local conditions and circumstances exerted important influences on feminist politics and interactions, underscoring the fact that we cannot understand Latin American feminisms without first understanding their particular and distinct social, political, and historical context. Finally, I argue that certain aspects of Batllista state formation helped politicize and shape the ideological outlook of certain groups of women, who generally gravitated toward liberal feminism. The politicization of certain groups of women, I argue, was linked to the fact that many became agents of the state, in direct and indirect ways, during this era, providing a platform that both catalyzed their feminism and gave that feminism a particular orientation toward the state as a locus of reform.

Many early studies of Latin American feminism focus exclusively or near-exclusively on liberal feminists: those middle-class women's groups that fought for women's suffrage, expanded education, equality in the civil codes, etc., within a largely secular and capitalist framework.[22] More recent scholarship examining the activities of right- and left-wing women and the gender politics of their respective movements and organizations has provided important correctives to this earlier perspective, underscoring the fact that middle-class liberal feminists were not the only politically active women on the scene during this era.[23] Yet, with the prominent exception of Susan Besse's *Restructuring Patriarchy*, little has been done to integrate new understandings of right- and left-wing women with scholarship on liberal feminism, which would allow for the construction of a broader analysis of women's mobilization across the political spectrum during this formative era. As Besse has observed, "What it meant to be a 'feminist' was an issue of great contention in late 1910s to 1930s Brazil."[24] This was absolutely the case in Uruguay where, for example, the first liberal feminist organization was founded ten years after the Catholic Ladies' League, a conservative elite group that identified itself with "Christian feminism." The birth and growth of liberal feminism also had its parallel within the labor movement and the left, as anarchists, Socialists, and later Communists attempted to integrate women into their ranks, albeit with only moderate success.[25] Moreover, groups like the Catholic Ladies' League and women's organizations within the Socialist and Communist parties competed with, challenged, and criticized the liberal feminists, and in so doing influenced and shaped liberal feminist strategies and campaigns, and vice versa. This was an era, in sum, whose feminist awakening was broad-based, crossing class and ideological lines, and when women from various sectors of society struggled to define *feminismo bien entendido* (feminism properly understood) and to open doors for women's integration into the public sphere in the ways they saw as most beneficial.

A study that highlights the plurality of feminisms begs the question of what we mean by feminism for this place and time. It is, of course, a term that resists simple definition. Nancy Cott's classic definition is based on three criteria: a belief in sex equality or opposition to sexual hierarchy; a belief that woman's condition is socially constructed; and a perception of women as a distinct social grouping.[26] These definitions/criteria are quite broad, and could comfortably coexist with a variety of political ideologies, from Catholicism to Communism. Karen Offen has offered a more specific taxonomy. She identifies two distinct—yet often overlapping—tendencies within feminist thought and practice: "individualistic" and "relational" feminism. "Individualistic" feminism, most dominant in the United States and Britain, emphasizes the individual, rather than the larger community, and highlights the similarities, not the differences, between men and women. In contrast, "relational," or "maternalist" feminism—strongest in Catholic Europe and also in Latin America—emphasizes women's differences from men, particularly their roles as mothers, and posits an "egalitarian" vision based on gender difference.[27] Koven and Michel define maternalism as "ideologies and discourses which exalted women's capacity to mother and applied to society as a whole the values they attached to that role: care, nurturance and morality."[28] While conservative groups like the Catholic Ladies' League could comfortably fit under the relational/maternalist feminist umbrella, the activism of working-class and leftist women is still in the balance. Offen, for one, is more circumspect when it comes to socialist and other left feminisms. Placing class interests before gender interests, and generally refusing to work in broader "feminist" coalitions, most Socialist and Communist women were not really feminists at all, she has argued. Yet this characterization implies that liberal (and Catholic) feminists did not (occasionally, often, or always) do the same thing. Her criticism of the "Marxist-socialists' attempt to thrust the wedge of class into the growing feminist sisterhood" rests on the notion that such a "sisterhood" above classes existed in the first place.[29] Others who have studied liberal feminisms in Latin America during this era have clearly demonstrated that the "wedge of class" was present in the theories and practice of all of these feminist groups.[30] And while much of women's activity on the left should not properly be considered feminist, there is nevertheless an identifiable strain of what Elizabeth Hutchison calls "worker feminism," which develops in the anarchist-dominated labor movement of the late nineteenth century and persists (in modified form and not without difficulty) into the later Socialist and Communist eras. For this history, in sum, I believe it is useful to adopt Sonia Álvarez's characterization of feminism as a "partial ideology that can prove compatible with liberal, conservative, radical and socialist ideologies."[31]

In defining what feminism was, it is also important to define what it was not. I do not use the term to define, in Cott's words, all of "what women did," and there are women's movements in this study that I would not identify as feminist. I do not think the telephone workers' strike of 1922, for example, or the activities of the ladies' committees in state-sponsored social-assistance organizations were in themselves feminist movements or activities. Some of these actions or activities were potential catalysts for the development of feminist consciousness and entry points into the world of feminist activity, however. Struggling for "practical gender interests," in Álvarez's words, can be a springboard into broader struggle oriented around "strategic" gender interests.[32] In this case, events set in motion by the Batllista state itself created new places and roles for women and shaped Uruguayan feminism.

Few women's historians have systematically addressed the role of party politics in pre-suffrage feminist activism. Rebecca Edwards's study of gender and party politics in the United States, for one, has demonstrated that U.S. women's suffrage activists had strong partisan sympathies, and that party politics were a divisive element within the movement.[33] Within the Latin American context, Corinne Pernet's study of Chilean feminism in the 1940s concludes that "most leading feminists, despite their claims to the contrary, were strongly involved in and affected by party politics."[34] Her work charts the conflicts and competition between Radicals, Socialists, and Communists during and after the Popular Front period, attributing the movement's weaknesses in part to the failure to overcome partisan divisions.[35] In the Uruguayan case, it is clear that women were political actors—many with strong partisan feelings—long before they won the vote. Even though formal politics was "man's business" before the 1930s (and beyond), we should not assume that women were above or indifferent to party politics, or that political "color" was not part of their identity. Partisan identification was indeed a central force shaping the centripetal and centrifugal forces that operated within and between different feminisms in Batllista Uruguay, and as such should be considered seriously as a factor of analysis.

The influence of party politics was one way that local conditions shaped these international organizations and movements. Weighing the relative influence of local and international influences leads us to a discussion of the role of immigrants in Uruguayan feminist organizations. In analyzing the relative strengths and weaknesses of (liberal) feminist organizing in comparative context in Latin America, Asunción Lavrin and Francesca Miller take different approaches. Identifying overall social structure as a primary variable, Miller has argued that building a liberal feminist movement was easier in more mesocratic and homogenous societies like Argentina and Uruguay than in a place like Peru, with its small middle class and higher degree of racialized class stratification.[36] In her study of feminism in the Southern Cone, on the other hand, Lavrin sees European immigration as something of an independent variable. The relative strength of feminist movements in Argentina and Uruguay, she posits, can be attributed in part to the fact that European immigrants were a more important demographic factor in these countries than in places like Chile and Peru. Data for Uruguay, however, points away from Lavrin's thesis. While it is of course true that Uruguay received relatively more immigrants than Chile, for example, this pattern does not hold for Uruguayan feminists themselves, who were overwhelmingly native-born, making immigration at best a dependent variable in this story. While most elite and middle-class Uruguayan feminists were part of an intellectual and political elite that saw Europe as the model of modernization, they were nevertheless generally *criollas* doing politics at home, and had to work within a local context to be successful. In no sense am I arguing that Uruguayan feminism was a fully homegrown, autochthonous development. Nor am I arguing that international forces and networks did not exert tremendous influence over all of these movements and organizations. Paulina Luisi, for one, spent many of the years in question in Europe, and she and others maintained important connections and correspondence with their European and Latin American counterparts and closely followed events abroad.[37] But returning to Miller's thesis, I suggest that the fact that Uruguay was both home to a strong liberal feminist movement and a popular destination for European immigrants are both products of the region's particular historical, political, and economic trajectory.

Feminism and the State: Civil Society and Parastatal Actors

Batllismo did more than create a friendly environment for feminist activism. During the course of my research, I became specifically interested in how Batllismo and earlier state-building projects integrated women into the public/political sphere, and how that incorporation helped create conditions for particular forms of feminist political development and orientation. Women had a role to play in Batllista modernization, and this in turn effected changes in the boundaries of women's citizenship. Women of varied class and political backgrounds sought to take advantage of openings Batllismo provided and asserted their right to participate in public discourse. It is no coincidence that many of liberal feminism's affiliate organizations were, directly or indirectly, agents of the Batllista state. Women's labor was vital to the process of state building, and women were incorporated into the "parapolitical sphere"—in education but also in social assistance—in growing numbers. Scholars of liberal feminism have recognized the state as a key factor in feminist mobilization, especially in identifying the rise of secular public education as an important foundation for early feminist activities. Miller, for example, notes that "it was female schoolteachers who formed the nucleus of the first women's groups to articulate what may be defined as a feminist critique of society."[38] She attributed this to the fact that schoolteachers were educated, middle-class women whose professional work brought them into contact, creating a community of ideas and shared experiences. I would add that schoolteachers were also economically (semi)independent public employees with a sustained and direct relationship to the state. Their position as agents of the state would likely have enhanced their sense of citizenship, and given them a stake in enhancing women's accomplishments and highlighting their contributions to the modernizing project.

In some cases, this positionality led women to challenge the system from within in order to defend and expand their professional and civic territory. Perhaps the best example of this is Paulina Luisi herself, who was very much a product of the liberal state. Like schoolteachers, women professionals—physicians, lawyers, and the like—were products of institutions of higher education and were enlisted, directly or indirectly, in the job of modernizing Latin American societies. In this, Luisi fit the profile of many liberal feminist leaders in South America. As Uruguay's first female physician, she represented the pinnacle of feminine educational achievement, and was catapulted to the head of the feminist struggle.[39] In subsequent years, she maintained close ties with the Uruguayan state, serving in various diplomatic and other official and semiofficial capacities. As we will see in Chapter 3, Luisi's educational and professional background and training had an impact on both her engagement in feminist politics itself and the specific nature of her feminism.

Charitable activities and/or philanthropy have also been identified as an important platform for women's politicization.[40] Like teaching, philanthropy and other advocacy work brought women into the public sphere in ways that were acceptable because it was seen as being in keeping with women's traditional maternal role. Charitable activity brought more affluent women into direct contact with the poor and working class and created communities of like-minded women with shared experiences. Gisela Bock, writing about middle- and upper-class European women, observed: "actions to aid the poor and the oppressed...became the preliminary step and vehicle for the engagement on behalf of their own sex."[41] In many European and a number of Latin American countries, what began as private and church-based activity was increasingly incorporated into expanding welfare states in the late nineteenth and early twentieth centuries. Linda L. Clark's work on French inspectresses, for example, illustrates that incorporation into expanding states could also act to catalyze feminist activity and thought.[42] Women were brought into the French state, Clark argues, because of their perceived "maternal" qualities, and to bolster the protective, nurturing aspects of the welfare state. But as motherly agents of a paternalistic state, the inspectresses' position was ambiguous and multifaceted: the state "expected them to help moralize and discipline the lower classes" yet remain subordinate themselves. Like schoolteaching and medical school, this professional vantage point afforded women a more direct line of sight to feminist ideas. Many came to understand that without the vote and other rights, their possibilities for employment and expanded authority were limited. Political enfranchisement and full citizenship were also about obtaining respect and recognition for women's vital role in forging a modern nation. The result in France was that "many school inspectresses joined feminist ranks." Thus not only the fact of feminist involvement, but the nature, orientation, and goals of that involvement were shaped in part by women's relationship to the state.[43] In Uruguay too liberal feminist groups had strong ties to various aspects of the Batllista state, and those ties helped to define the organizations' orientation and priorities. Additionally, by examining the relationships between individual members of liberal feminist organizations and state entities, we can further reconstruct the specific connections between feminism and state formation in the Batllista era.

Understanding this transitional phase of the Uruguayan welfare state—and its implications for Uruguayan feminism—necessitates an expanded, more nuanced understanding of the state and state agents. Questioning any strict division between state and society, recent theories have expanded the boundaries of the state and policy to encompass a broader cultural and discursive construct.[44] This allows us to better understand the roles of non-state and parastatal actors, including those entirely in the private sphere and those subsidized or overseen by state agencies, in policy formulation and implementation and the myriad constraints and legacies that acted to shape social policy. The Batllista state, like the French welfare state described by Janet Horne, was a "hybrid" state that encompassed a large "parapolitical sphere" of ostensibly private institutions under effective state control.[45] In the Uruguayan case, as elsewhere, this "parapolitical sphere" was gendered: largely administered by women, and mostly oriented toward providing assistance to women and children.[46] Like the middle-class French inspectresses of Clark's study, feminist activism in Uruguay can be understood as a tool to preserve (or hopefully expand) these women's place in state programs. In the Uruguayan case, the participation of elite "ladies of charity" in the early, most conservative phases of liberal feminism in Uruguay should be understood in this

Introduction

light. That upper-class women were the pivot point between state-sponsored social assistance and liberal feminism is significant. By the era of the Popular Front in Chile (1938–1952), for example, elite women were largely irrelevant or retrograde elements in the story of both feminism and social assistance. In Batllista Uruguay, however, the particular convergence of state formation and feminism meant that the shifts in social assistance that brought many elite women into direct contact with state apparatus for the first time, transforming them into agents of the state, had the effect of politicizing an important minority of these women, who formed a significant core catalyst of Uruguayan liberal feminism.[47] They would leave a defining mark on the movement. Returning to Batlle's metaphor of the state and the Colorado Party as the "shield of the weak": the state defined women as "weak" and in need of the state's "shield" to protect them, but in so doing it also provided women with some limited opportunities to direct which way that shield would be wielded, and even more rarely, provided them with the chance to take up that shield in their own defense.

The roots of both Batllismo and feminism in Uruguay can be found in the region's postindependence nineteenth-century history. An opening prologue traces the historical roots of both Batllismo and women's activism from independence through the end of the nineteenth century. An examination of the region's colonial and nineteenth-century history highlights the unique features of Uruguayan historical development, and the way those features shaped gender relations and patterns of women's political involvement. Chapter 1 discusses women's political activity in the early years of the *época batllista*, from the late nineteenth century to 1915. Catholic and liberal women's organization became more defined via the Catholic Ladies' League and the Liberal Party, and working-class feminism split into anarchist and Socialist factions during these years. The Uruguayan state was in development, but reform had not yet become institutionalized. This was an optimistic era when gender relations were very much in flux and malleable, and had not yet been directed into more official state- and party-disciplined channels.

Chapters 2 and 3 look at the process of Uruguayan state formation during the Batllista era, focusing specifically on the reshaping of paternalism that took place during these years. Chapter 2 provides an overview of Batllista ideology and policy from the 1910s to the early 1930s. The first section discusses the gender ideologies of Batlle himself and one of his principal advisors, Carlos Vaz Ferreira, whose theories of compensation feminism are key to understanding Batllista social policy. The second section deals with some of the more important pieces of Batllista legislation affecting women, including divorce, women's education, paternity investigation, labor legislation, and the vote. Chapter 3 looks at two important groups of women who developed new relationships with the state during this era: university-trained professionals (especially physicians) and those involved in social-assistance organizations. The first section focuses on Paulina Luisi, herself a product of the state's changing policy toward educating women. As a teacher, physician, and sometimes diplomat, she maintained an important relationship with the state over the course of her career, a factor that cannot be overlooked when examining her ideology and political activity. The second part looks at the 1910 National Assistance Law and the role that the ladies' committees played in implementing new expanded social services to the poor and disenfranchised.

Chapters 4 through 6 tell the story of feminism and women's organizing from 1916 to 1932. Chapter 4 looks at the history of liberal feminism in Uruguay, focusing on the two most important liberal feminist organizations, the National Women's Council of Uruguay (Conamu) and the Uruguayan Women's Suffrage Alliance (Alianza). In addition to a general overview of these groups' campaigns and activities, this chapter also compares the two groups of women who populated these organizations. Among other things, the changing membership base of both Conamu and the Alianza reflected the growing presence and influence of the female middle class in Montevideo especially, and the changing class structure of the society more generally. This chapter also analyzes the class politics of the organizations, underlining the ways in which working-class and poor women were largely marginalized and relegated to second-class status by groups that reflected the positions of middle-class and affluent women. Chapters 5 and 6 look at the activities of right and left feminisms from 1916 to 1932. The *Liga de Damas Católicas* (Catholic Ladies' League) remained active during these years, and continued to compete with the liberal feminists for the hearts and minds of legislators, working-class women and female university students. Chapter 5 explores the evolution of the Catholic Ladies' League in the 1920s, especially the changes engendered by the growing popularity of right-wing nationalisms in the latter part of that decade. Chapter 6 continues the story of left feminisms in Uruguay. Following a discussion of Socialist party politics after 1915, this chapter will look at the woman question within the Communist Party. As a party whose focus was never purely electoral, Communist women had a more official status than their Colorada and Blanca counterparts. Nevertheless, the party's rigid class analysis meant that women were almost always seen as others and relegated to secondary status within the organization. By the late 1920s, all of these groups saw women's suffrage as inevitable, and sought to modify their strategies accordingly. While all sides held their breath to see who would most benefit from these new votes, a coup d'état in March 1933, four months after women won the right to vote, rendered the question moot by suspending all elections until 1938. Finally, the Conclusion briefly summarizes the findings of the previous chapters, and seeks to situate the Uruguayan case within the broader literature on gender and the state in Latin America.

Prologue
The Nineteenth-Century Roots of Batllismo and Feminismo

> With light hearts the people then proceeded to divide themselves into two political parties—Whites and Reds.... But of these wars of crows and pies it would be idle to say more, since after going on for three-quarters of a century they are not wholly ended yet.
>
> — *W. H. Hudson*, The Purple Land, *1885*

> The parties have become largely hereditary; a child is born a little Blanco or a little Colorado, and rarely deserts his colour. Feeling runs so high that in Blanco districts it is dangerous for a man to wear a red necktie.
>
> — *James Bryce*, South America: Observations and Impressions, *1912*

*I*t is in Uruguay's postindependence era, when partisan loyalties were first taking shape, that one sees the roots of women's activism in Uruguay and its links to the overall process of national development. By the late nineteenth century Uruguay was deeply divided along party lines, and that partisan affiliation was at least as much about family, regional, and patronage ties as it was about ideology. Postcolonial Uruguay was an eminently masculinized world, demographically and symbolically, but this did not mean that women remained outside of or indifferent to party politics and conflicts. Although much more research on women and politics in nineteenth-century Uruguay is needed, it seems clear that women indeed played a significant role in forging postindependence communities. I suggest that this early politicization, in turn, helped shape the parameters of women's engagement in the political process well into the twentieth century. More precisely, early Blanca and Colorada activism formed a foundation and a legacy upon which, merging with other ideas and nourished by outside influences, feminist traditions of subsequent generations would grow.

Like the rest of the Río de la Plata region, the territory that is now Uruguay was a remote backwater of the Iberian colonies until the eighteenth century. Uruguay's fringe location meant that European settlement was late and sparse, resulting in a "weak colonial legacy" that has had a lasting impact. Both church and crown had trouble making their presence felt: clergy were scarce, and officers of the court even more so. Outside of Montevideo, frontier conditions were even more pronounced. While the same was true for many rural areas of late colonial Latin America, there is little doubt that the grip of state (and church) control was especially slack here. Uruguay's colonial period was also relatively short: Montevideo had not yet celebrated the centennial of its foundation when the wars for independence were launched in Buenos Aires in 1810. Uruguayan independence was shaped by ongoing rivalries between Buenos Aires and Montevideo, continued Portuguese (and later, Brazilian) designs on the territory, British commercial aspirations for control over the Uruguayan port, and gaucho uprisings in the interior. Following two tumultuous decades of occupations, interventions, and revolts, the *República Oriental del Uruguay* became an independent nation in 1828. As with much of Spanish America, liberation from colonial status did not bring internal peace and stability. Despite its small size, the young nation had difficulties achieving anything resembling national rule. Continued Argentine and Brazilian interventions in the region only exacerbated the problem, making it difficult to speak of a nation at all in the first decades after independence.

During this era of postindependence civil war, the two traditional political parties that dominated the Uruguayan political scene until recently were born: the Colorados (Reds) and the Blancos (Whites). The founding leaders were two heroes of the independence era, former allies who later became rivals: Juan Antonio Lavalleja and Fructuoso Rivera. Lavalleja led the reinitiation of the independence campaign in 1825, and became provisional governor of the Oriental Republic in 1828; Rivera became its first president in 1830. This unity was short-lived, however, and in 1832 Lavalleja and his followers revolted against Rivera. From here two factions emerged, although Manuel Oribe soon took up the leadership of Lavalleja's group. Each side came to identify itself by the wearing of the *divisa*, a hatband or other piece of cloth that announced one's party affiliation: red for the Riveristas and white for the Oribistas, laying the foundations for the Colorado and Blanco parties, respectively. Uruguay's borderland status meant that political factions also reflected the ongoing tug-of-war between neighboring powers. Generally speaking, the Blancos were considered *aportenados* (Buenos Aires-identified) and the Colorados *abrasilerados* (Brazilianized). But Caetano and Rilla assert this caveat: "[T]o speak of *national parties* in the fifty years following independence is to speak in approximations... they were not really parties, nor were they completely national."[1] Nevertheless, much of the country was soon divided along party (or at least color) lines, which often confronted each other militarily, and which became key components in the construction of identity and citizenship. While the Colorados tended to be more liberal and secular, and the Blancos more conservative and Catholic, it would be a mistake to see these partisan divisions (especially at this point) as fundamentally programmatic or ideological. For the most part, men took up a divisa, or political color, because of family loyalty, region, revenge, patronage, or simple self-preservation. "The primacy of partisan loyalty for its own sake was an Uruguayan truism of the day," John Chasteen wrote.[2]

Party politics were, to be sure, a masculine enterprise. This was an era defined by the caudillo and his loyal gaucho followers, where bravery, loyalty, and prowess on the battlefield were the preeminent markers of masculine valor. While most Uruguayan women maintained a decidedly auxiliary, nonmilitary role, they were not uninvolved or unconcerned with the political and military conflicts that characterized the postindependence era. Women's own physical and economic security could be dependent on victory for their side, and they were surely moved by the same partisan and family loyalties, as well as material self-interest, that drove men to take up the divisa in defense of their party. Thus, while it was largely men who fought and died for their respective parties, the sentiments and forces that motivated those actions were shared by men and women alike. Foreign observers occasionally noted the presence and participation of women in postindependence struggles. Sometimes those accounts praised Uruguayan women as heroines who bravely stood up in defense of their country. One chronicler observed that the "daughters of the Rio de la Plata" assumed an important role in the region's social struggles, a fact that he credited to their "natural sentiment of bravery."[3] Another mentioned the exploits of Dolores Berbesé, "an Oriental heroine" who followed her (Portuguese) husband "riding a lively steed, exposing her breast to all the risks of battle." When her husband was wounded, Berbesé reportedly took up her husband's sword and defeated the enemy.[4]

But, for the most part, women who traveled with partisan armies were not granted such laurels. Either by choice or necessity, poor women sometimes accompanied these armed groups, acting as camp followers and occasionally as combatants. Lucía Sala de Tourón and Rosa Alonso have asserted that, during the partisan wars of the nineteenth century, "there were many women of the popular classes who accompanied and fought alongside their men," and remarked that observers particularly took note of the "ferocity of the *chinas* [indigenous women or *mestizas*]" in battle.[5] Such rural women were the female counterparts of the archetypal gaucho, whose mixed blood was often pointed to as further evidence of their irremediable barbarity. An early nineteenth-century traveler described the few women he came across in rural areas as unfeminine, unhygienic, and indolent. "Their vacant hours are numerous, and are passed in listless idleness, or in smoking cigars, of which a large consumption takes place among this fair, or rather whitey-brown part of the creation."[6] In general, poor women tended to be portrayed as passive, dependent camp followers or, if they took a more active role, as masculinized perversions. Tomás de Iriarte's extensive memoirs of the independence wars provide a good example of both images. Describing a ragtag rebel army, he wrote: "The number of armed men did not exceed seven hundred; the rest was made up of women and children: these wretches have yet to receive the ration they were promised at the inception of the journey."[7] At a later point, Iriarte noted women's presence in the early armies in highly unfavorable terms. He referred to the women traveling in the Republican army as "mannish" [*marimachos*] and "repulsive amazons" who "looked like real men" and were nothing more, in his words, than "women who robbed and killed."[8] One such combatant was Catalina Quintana—*La China Catalina*—who fought with the Colorados in the 1860s, and who was described in terms of her bravery and her mannishness.[9] The presence of women in these armies was viewed with such ambivalence that partisan newspapers tended to highlight the female presence in the rival army, and deemphasize women in their own ranks. According to Chasteen, *El Día*—a Colorado paper sympathetic with government forces—noted the numbers of women in the rival Saravista armies of the late nineteenth century, whereas other sources claimed that more women accompanied government troops than the Blanco followers of Saravia.[10] The presence of these "amazons," it seems, was taken as an emasculating mark of shame, and highlighting the female presence in rival armies apparently served as a way to depict one's adversary as less than honorable. While the use of women combatants as a rhetorical barb means that we must take all of these accounts with a grain of salt, it seems clear that, as elsewhere in the region, Uruguayan women were not merely on the sidelines of the postindependence civil wars.

Although poor women's participation in partisan conflict stretched across the nineteenth century, it is in the activities of more elite women that we see the most direct connections to later patterns of women's political involvement. Like the camp followers of the popular classes, elite women often played auxiliary roles, but in forms more in keeping with the standards of decorum and honor associated with respectable white womanhood. More affluent women tended to participate as propagandists and agitators, and as providers of charity and medical assistance. Their work often complemented or supported the activity of male family members in partisan political struggles, giving rise to a parallel sphere of female competition and combat which mirrored that of the battlefield and the ballot box. Appropriately, the most important female political figures in Montevideo during these years were Bernardina Fragoso de Rivera and Ana Monterroso de Lavalleja, wives of Colorado leader Fructuoso Rivera and Blanco leader Juan Antonio Lavalleja, respectively. These two women became their husbands' (and by extension, their parties') most important representatives in the capital and "competed in the social and cultural life of Montevideo, just as their husbands did in battle."[11] Both were frequently the main conduits of information between the party leader and his followers. When, in 1832, Lavalleja rose up against Rivera and was forced into exile in Buenos Aires, "it was one of the moments where we see politics bubble up in the salons of the patrician ladies."[12] During that time, Ana Monterroso became one of her husband's principal mouthpieces in Montevideo. She is credited with leading an uprising and with penning a broadsheet calling it the "sacred duty" of the people to rise up and overthrow the Rivera government, declaring:

"the country requires us to conspire against the monsters who shackle our happiness."[13] Similarly, Bernardina Fragoso organized meetings and acted as a principal artery of communication between her husband in the field and Colorado supporters elsewhere.

But just as camp followers occasionally took up the sword of their fallen husbands or companions, elite women's participation sometimes transgressed accepted roles. While Bernardina Fragoso's support for her husband's party largely conformed to traditional support functions, her sister Carmen took on a more direct role in advocating the Colorado cause. After the mid-1830s, Blanco forces had something of an upper hand in the civil war; Oribe himself held the presidency, and Rivera and many followers had been driven into exile in Brazil. Rivera's main stronghold was the central Uruguayan town of Durazno, where many women from leading Colorado families played an active role in a number of pro-Colorado conspiracies and agitations. Early in 1837, Carmen Fragoso was arrested and taken to the capital on charges of supporting the Colorados. She was placed under house arrest in Montevideo, and expressly forbidden to return to Durazno. The following year she petitioned President Oribe, requesting that the travel restrictions be lifted. In denying her request, Oribe added: "If Doña Carmen Fragoso had dedicated herself to her household duties, rather than to disturbing the tranquility of the State by her service to the anarchist caudillo [Rivera], the local authorities would have treated her like others in her family." But the absence of Doña Carmen from Durazno, it seems, did not prevent other Coloradas from agitating in favor of Rivera. In what became known as the "feminine conspiracy of 1837," Durazno women acted as couriers and informants, wrote and distributed broadsheets in support of Rivera, and generally propagandized against the Oribe government. As a result, four women from prominent Durazno families who had been identified as leaders of the conspiracy were arrested and transported to Montevideo. In the absence of male family members and political leaders, it appears, women were willing and able to take up a more direct role. The response of the Blanco government suggests they took these women's actions seriously.[14]

Rivera's return to power in 1839 set the stage for the most dramatic conflagration of this era, the *Guerra Grande* (Great War). With support from Buenos Aires and ensconced in the Cerro region overlooking the capital, Oribe forces laid siege to Montevideo for over eight years (1843–1851), earning the city its designation as the "New Troy."

During these years, partisan affiliations were deepened, touching entire families and even recent immigrants. "During the Great Siege of Montevideo," wrote Milton Vanger, "an Uruguayan was a Colorado or a Blanco, and neither he nor his children ever forgot it. There was little tolerance for the other side."[15] Writing from Montevideo in 1842, Argentine exile Mariquita Sánchez wrote: "All day there are gunshots, wounded people, guerrilla bands, and we lack many staples.... It's not even my country.... I don't even want to hear the name of politics."[16] But not all women felt the same way, or even had the option of remaining neutral during this conflict.

During the Guerra Grande, women were mostly active in caring for the sick and wounded, but that assistance was rarely politically neutral. Herman Kruse emphasized the partisan aspect of women's beneficence during the mid-nineteenth century, noting, for example, that in the leadership of the Women's Section of the Brotherhood of San José, founded initially in the late eighteenth century, "the majority of the participants were wives, sisters or daughters of men who in a few years would form the National [Blanco] Party." During the postindependence era, Ana Monterroso was one of the group's more prominent members. Largely because of its affiliation with the forces laying siege to Montevideo during the Guerra Grande, the city's Colorado "Government of the Defense" dissolved the San José Women's Section in 1843, replacing it with the *Sociedad Filantrópica de Damas Orientales* (Philanthropic Society of Oriental Ladies), founded under the leadership of none other than Bernardina Fragoso de Rivera.[17] Among other things, the Sociedad Filantrópica opened a hospital in the city, which operated from 1843 to 1846. At that point, the hospital closed, but the Sociedad remained an important beneficent institution, shifting its focus to other priorities. "They now propose," wrote Iriarte in 1846, "to dedicate themselves to children's education."[18] And in 1855, after the long and devastating war came to an end, officially with "neither victors nor defeated" (*ni vencidos ni vencedores*), the recently widowed Bernardina Fragoso was invited to head up the new (government-sponsored) *Comisión de Beneficencia*, which was charged with overseeing all institutions–education, hospitals, orphanages, etc.–"pertaining to the fair sex."[19] In this we can see beginnings of state-sponsored social assistance, headed up by a leading Colorada. In the meantime, women from prominent Blanco families continued their charitable activity, which was more strongly affiliated with the Catholic Church. Thus, as (male) party loyalties were congealing, traditions of female charity and beneficence were configuring and aligning themselves accordingly. While both traditions were elite, one was clearly more secular and the other more Catholic, one more associated with the Colorados and the other with the Blancos.

The 1870s marks the beginning of what Caetano and Rilla refer to as the "second foundation" of the Uruguayan state. Political violence and instability were impeding Uruguay's economic modernization, and elites sought ways to settle partisan conflicts in arenas other than the battlefield. Thus while armed uprisings would continue sporadically into the twentieth century, from this point one sees the beginning of national consolidation and the establishment of a liberal state, largely under Colorado control. At the same time, emerging global capitalism and technological change facilitated and encouraged both European immigration and the integration of the Rio de la Plata into the expanding Atlantic economy. Both the size and composition of the Uruguayan population were changing in important ways. While an African and *mestizo* presence persisted, the overall trend was toward a whitening of the population via European immigration. Although postindependence conflicts made Uruguay a less than ideal destination for immigrants, Europeans continued to arrive and stay in the Banda Oriental. By 1860, nearly 35 percent of the Uruguayan population, and nearly half the population of Montevideo, was foreign-born. Competition with Argentina for immigrants was a serious matter, and initially Uruguay had little to offer, as immigrants were likely to find more work, higher wages, and greater political stability across the Río de la Plata. But immigration increased as the political situation in the country improved, and during the 1870s alone, approximately 100,000 immigrants settled in Uruguay.[20] These immigrants would have a profound impact on the economic, cultural, political, and demographic landscape of the Banda Oriental, but that influence was always in negotiation with preexisting institutions, economic conditions, and political legacies they encountered upon their arrival.

Conclusion

In evaluating the impact of colonial and postindependence history on gender relations and especially women's political involvement, three factors stand out. First, we must consider the impact of Uruguay's weak colonial legacy. Uruguay's marginal status during the colonial period meant, among other factors, that the Catholic Church was always relatively weak. As a result, Uruguay was a much more secular place than its neighbors, a characteristic that persists to this day. Uruguayan secularism facilitated the rise of Batllismo which, as we will see, had an important impact on women's position in society. But the vulnerability of the Uruguayan church would also inspire the formation of an especially militant and conservative Catholic feminist movement early in the century, a topic we will turn to in the next chapter. Secondly, what impact did Uruguay's prolonged postindependence civil wars and corresponding "late institutionalization" have on constructions of gender and citizenship? What did this extended period of instability and warfare mean for women, families, and gender roles generally, in the city and in the countryside? An important premise of the following chapters is that the state of prolonged internal conflict and civil war and the primacy of extra-electoral political engagement during the nineteenth century laid an important foundation for women's subsequent political involvement in Uruguay. As others have argued, the unofficial and extra-political nature of civil war opened up spaces for women that were not always available during times of political peace and stability. During this time, activist women gained experience and visibility, generating a female track of partisan competition and conflict. Uruguay remained a deeply partisan place in the twentieth century, and, in a figurative sense, the divisa would make its presence felt in the feminist associations of the twentieth century.

Lastly, what impact did mass European immigration have on gender and women's politics in Uruguay? The desire to make Uruguay more attractive to both European immigrants and European capital was an important factor underlying the modernizing reforms of the late nineteenth and early twentieth centuries. In turn, European immigration itself brought an infusion of new political ideas and identities to Uruguay. These new arrivals reformulated, but did not displace, old partisan affiliations. As has frequently been noted, many Italian immigrants gravitated toward the Colorado Party, while many Spaniards became Blancos.[21] The presence of these newcomers did not leave these parties unchanged, but the fact that immigrants were plugged in to the existing party structure underscores the negotiation between immigration and local legacies and institutions. European immigration, of course, was overwhelmingly male, but this does not mean that immigrant women were nonexistent, or that their influence on Uruguayan politics was negligible. Spanish-born women like Laura

Prologue

Carreras de Bastos and Belén Sárraga, for example, became political leaders in early twentieth-century Uruguay. That the former joined up with a conservative Catholic women's organization and the latter headed up the most important anticlerical women's group in the early years of the century speaks to the diversity of immigration's political impact. But, by and large, it was not European immigrants, but their locally born daughters who raised the banner of feminism in early twentieth-century Uruguay. The arrival of men like Angel Luisi, an Italian who fought with Garibaldi and had Masonic ties, exemplifies this. He and his wife Josefa arrived in the Uruguayan/Argentine littoral in the early 1870s and proceeded to raise four children, including their oldest Paulina, who became a schoolteacher and in 1908 the first woman to earn a medical degree in Uruguay. These first-generation Uruguayans, certainly influenced by their parents' views, were born and raised in South America and learned to negotiate this borderland, hybrid society. In sum, while the international diffusion of ideas, via immigrants and other factors, was quite important to the development of feminism in Uruguay, it would be a mistake to ignore the region's early postcolonial history, or to assume that in an environment of civil war, women would somehow have remained above or outside politics. This legacy of partisan women's organizing carried over into the twentieth century, and exerted an important influence on feminism in Uruguay.

Chapter One
The First Feminisms: State Building and Women's Organizing, 1880s–1915

Women and men's social equality is prostitution forever destroyed; it is free love established...in a word, it is justice for the great human community. No more masters! Humanity cannot be redeemed without the full liberty of all.
— *Derecho a la Vida* (Anarchist newspaper, Montevideo), *July 1896*

Support, *señores*, Christian feminism, so that...[woman's] moral and political influence will shine in favor of the healthy principles of social equilibrium; while thousands of working class women will be pulled out of misery, dishonor, and desperation—For them I ask you....We are not a threat but a promise....We will not form a dangerous or destabilizing element but a solid base on which the social order of civilized peoples will rest.
— *Laura Carreras de Bastos*, Feminismo Cristiano, *1906*

The Association of Liberal Ladies...has as its objectives: to undertake the strongest and most effective propaganda in favor of freedom of conscience, especially for women; to work to improve the condition of the working classes without distinction; to support the development of secular education; [and] to use all of its resources to demand that woman assume her rightful place in civilized life, elevating her moral and intellectual level as much as possible.
— *Asociación de Damas Liberales*, Statutes, *1906*

Chapter One

Among the nineteenth-century factors that gave rise and shape to Uruguayan feminism in the twentieth century, three stand out: partisan politics, the "religion question," and the rise of an urban (anarchist-dominated) labor movement. This chapter examines protofeminist and feminist organizing in Uruguay from the 1880s to the end of Batlle's second presidential term in 1915. During this era, three distinct trajectories of women's activism became quite defined and visible. The quotations above are representative of those trajectories, as well as the order in which they appeared on the Uruguayan scene. It is noteworthy that both Christian and liberal strains—associated to varying degrees with more affluent women—claim to speak for or to be operating in the best interests of working-class women, a tutelary approach that will persist throughout the period under examination. Of course, the mostly male leadership of the anarchist and other left tendencies also often claimed to be speaking on behalf of their working class-sisters. At the same time, the worker feminism espoused in the anarchist press of this era struggled to survive and make itself heard, as a minority voice in an (increasingly) masculinized labor movement. All of these feminisms developed in relation to (and in some cases, competition with) each other, and thus we cannot understand one strain of feminist thought and action in isolation. This chapter intertwines and juxtaposes these early feminisms, in order to demonstrate the plural and relational nature of feminist discourse, as well as its connection to partisan political tradition and the growth of the secular modern state. Feminism in fin de siècle Uruguay was a broad, generalized phenomenon, which crossed political, ideological, and class boundaries, motivating very different groups of women to take unprecedented stands in favor of women's citizenship and increased access to the political system.

Gender, Secularization, and the Uruguayan State, 1870s–1890s

Rising European immigration occurred simultaneously with an era of state building, secularization, and modernization in Uruguay, setting off battles between Catholics and liberals that would provide a new framework for women's activism. Attempts to centralize power and create a true nation-state were undertaken largely from the city and by the Colorado Party, which from midcentury forward was able to consistently consolidate its control. The most important step in the process of economic liberalization and political consolidation took place during the presidency of Colonel Lorenzo Latorre (1876–1880), who undertook an aggressive plan to modernize the economy and stabilize the countryside. A '"civilizer" in the liberal tradition, Latorre imposed central state authority and regularized property rights in the countryside for the first time. The transformations of this era made the Banda Oriental a far more appealing destination for European immigrants, which in turn contributed to the period's political dynamism.

The Latorre government also created an extensive public education system, which dramatically increased literacy levels and provided a crucial springboard for women's entry into the professions and, ultimately, organized feminist activity. In 1877, the Law of Common Education created a free, obligatory, secular, and coeducational system of education in the republic, under the direction of Minister of Education José Pedro Varela, a disciple of Domingo Sarmiento and Horace Mann. The Varelian reforms had a dramatic impact. Between the late 1870s and 1915, as the population of the country tripled (from 440,00 to over 1.3 million), the number of children enrolled in school increased sixfold, and hundreds of new public schools were opened. Literacy rates increased notably. In the 1870s only about one in five Uruguayans were literate; by 1908 the reported literacy rate had grown to 60 percent.[1] Varela and others in the Latorre government saw education reform as the key to modernizing Uruguayan society and to the forging of a true nation state. Within this, women's education, which had been limited and largely confined to the more affluent, was seen as particularly crucial. The new modern capitalist era, Varela argued, required a new type of education for women that went beyond the traditional curriculum of speaking French and playing the piano. "When the supreme law of modern society is work," Varela wrote, "depriving woman of the necessary education makes her a useless instrument, a being incapable of work." Educated women, in other words, were a crucial element in creating a civilized nation-state and a modern economy in Uruguay. As mothers and as schoolteachers, educated women could help educate new generations of "civilized" Uruguayans. Uneducated women, on the other hand, made poor wives and mothers and were vulnerable to Catholic manipulations, making them a threat to family, society, and the nation. In addition to their role as

35

primary school teachers, Varela even suggested that women might have a logical place in other areas of the expanding Uruguayan state, writing "don't you think that a majority of the public employees, of those at the lower ranks at least, could have skirts?"[2] Varela's desire to elevate women's status only went so far. Women's prescribed role in the modern state was that of low-level functionaries, charged with carrying out, but not formulating, state policy. Similarly, Varela spoke of the need to make woman a useful "auxiliary" of man within the family, a helpmate rather than a mere dependent: an elevation of her status, but not so much as to disturb existing gendered hierarchies.[3]

But in encouraging women's education, and in providing a place for women within the expanding Uruguayan state, Varela's reforms laid a crucial foundation for (especially liberal) feminism in Uruguay. As the least likely to have received a formal education in the earlier era, women and girls benefited disproportionately from the increased availability of public schooling. These reforms also required hundreds of new teachers, and in Uruguay as elsewhere, mostly young women filled the ranks of this civilizing army. To fulfill this new demand, in 1882 the *Internato Normal para Señoritas* (Normal School for Young Ladies) was opened, the first women's teacher-training institution in the country.[4] Viewed as an extension of woman's natural maternal role, elementary school teaching was perfectly compatible with traditional gender norms, and many viewed it as a sort of apprenticeship and temporary career until women married and had children themselves. Not all young women followed this road however. New standards for an "enlightened" motherhood and the pressing need for young women to fill the ranks of schoolteachers in the newly expanding public education system meant that women were gaining unprecedented access to that very material that formed a cornerstone of modern citizenship. In Uruguay, as elsewhere, this was true not only in theoretical terms; many of the women who formed the first core of the liberal feminist movement were *normalistas* (normal school graduates), direct disciples of Varela, and students of María Stagnero de Munar, who headed the Internato Normal for many years. The teacher and mentor of many of the founding liberal feminists, Stagnero de Munar joined her students in the foundation of the National Women's Council in 1916 and probably remained a member until her death in 1922.

The Latorre/Varela reforms provoked resistance from those who saw in the increasingly secular and powerful state a threat to such disparate aspects of the old order as the autonomy of the gaucho and the dominion of the Catholic Church. Catholics, needless to say, rejected the formulation that Catholicism equaled antimodernization, countering that it was in fact secular liberalism which threatened women's sanctified place in the family and in society.[5] Archbishop Mariano Soler, for one, questioned the morality and honor of women educated in public schools, writing that "the disastrous results of educating a woman without religion are well known."[6] Soler also saw a Masonic hand behind these reforms. "The dangers of Masonry," he wrote "include the perdition of woman in coeducational schools...where they cultivate a learned impiety."[7] As the conflict between clerical and anticlerical factions increased, both sides sought to enlist women in the defense of their cause.

Women's Organizing and the Religion Question

The dual trajectories of elite women's organizing—one Colorado, the other Blanco—continue past the era of greatest civil unrest into the late nineteenth century. But, by this point, those traditions had become more state- and policy-oriented, and had picked up the flavor of Masonic and anti-Masonic struggles that had infused (male) partisan politics as well. These two processes—the Catholic and subsequently liberal mobilization of women—developed as interconnected precursors to the emergence of organized feminisms in the twentieth century. Catholic women, it seems, were the first to respond to the challenges of the era, founding the *Asociación de Señoras Cristianas* (Christian Women's Association) in 1885. An 1897 report provides information on the types of projects undertaken by the Señoras Cristianas. Most of their endeavors, such as job-training workshops and campaigns to encourage working-class couples to marry, reflected a desire to inculcate religious orthodoxy and social discipline among the poor. A list of association members in 1897 contains the last names of many conservative elite Catholic families, including Margarita Uriarte de Heber, who would be an important Catholic leader in later years.[8]

While evidence of early freethinking/liberal women's activity during the late nineteenth century is scarce, Catholic efforts in this area were met with attempts to organize liberal women, especially via Masonic and para-Masonic organizations. Liberal Freemasons supported secularization campaigns in Uruguay, forming the nucleus of

Chapter One

anticlerical politics by the latter decades of the nineteenth century. Not surprisingly, Masonic affiliations were most common among the more liberal Colorados than among the Blancos.[9] During the 1880s, according to Caetano and Geymonat, liberalism in Uruguay became more openly "anti-clerical," and Freemasons contributed to that shift. Thus, as the century wore on, battles between Colorados and Blancos were also being fought out on the plain of Catholics vs. Freethinkers/Masons, and conservative Catholic leaders increasingly identified their opponents as Masons, invoking anti-Masonic conspiracy theories to frighten their followers. In the 1880s, Masonic leaders began encouraging the formation of women's groups to help combat religious influence over both their own families and society as a whole. While this was a time of increased Masonic women's organizing in Europe and elsewhere in the Americas, in Uruguay these campaigns seem to have emerged in response to the growing activism of Catholic women.[10] In Colorado strongholds like Durazno, for example, Freemasonry began to enjoy "a great deal of influence within Duraznense society."[11] One such member was Alfredo Parodi, member of a local Masonic Order and editor of the Durazno paper *El Argos*. In 1896, *El Argos* announced the formation of a new group, *Las Damas de Durazno* (Durazno Ladies). The newspaper praised the organization for its work to "mitigate the suffering and sadness of the large number of poor that populate the streets and outskirts of our town."[12] The article also included a list of the founding members of the group, who, according to Durazno historian Oscar Padrón, were almost all "wives of Masons," Colorado partisans, and veterans' wives.[13]

With its emphasis on parapolitical groupings oriented around the provision of charity and/or support for a particular political faction, this phase of women's organizing differed little in substance from partisan women's activity earlier in the century. What had changed, however, is that, rather than "partisan loyalty for its own sake," women in the late nineteenth century increasingly organized around the religion question and the campaign to secularize the Uruguayan state and society. Within this new rhetorical frame, more specific discourse about women and modernization begins to emerge; namely whether secularizing trends held the key to women's emancipation or to her further subordination. In this lie the roots of both Christian and liberal feminist politics that develop later in the twentieth century.

Radical Liberalism, Working Class Women's Organizing, and Anarchist Feminism

Anticlericals counted more radical elements within their ranks as well. At the same time that Catholic and freethinking women began organizing around the religion question, working-class women began to organize themselves, not to ask for assistance from their more affluent sisters, but in favor of more profound, revolutionary changes in Uruguayan society. This new worker feminism was not uniformly welcomed in working-class politics, however, and by the end of the period in question a serious backlash against both women's activism and feminist discourses was evident. Immigrant workers formed the backbone of a newly vocal and militant labor movement that was largely anarchist in orientation. Radical anticlericals like their more moderate freethinking counterparts, the anarchists sought revolutionary change and an end to the capitalist order via its direct overthrow. Anarchist domination of the labor movement before 1910 was vitally important for working women's organization and activism. Women constituted a minority of immigrants and a minority of industrial workers in Uruguay, but they nevertheless played a role in early anarchist organizing efforts. The anarchist press was peppered with articles on woman's oppression and the need to overthrow the bourgeois family structure. Although not devoid of paternalistic overtones, many of these articles reflect a broad intersectional analysis of power and liberation, allowing for a discourse about sexuality and gender oppression that would not be possible even ten years later. This was a fascinating historical moment, a fleeting era in which a radical critique of gender inequality was incorporated into a larger general attack on exploitation and oppression.[14]

One important aspect of anarchist analysis were the connections made between capitalist property relations and the bourgeois family structure, in which male power in the family was seen as a manifestation of capitalist class power in civil society. An article published in 1899 in the anarchist paper *La Aurora* entitled "To the Women" clearly articulates this position:

> I address my words to you, *compañeras* of labor and misfortune; to those like me who suffer the double slavery of capital and of man.... All men, proletarians and bourgeois and those of the dominant classes, have always kept women ignorant to be able to dominate her more easily.[15]

Working-class women, in other words, lived under the double yoke of capitalism and patriarchy, which were seen as interdependent but separate systems of domination. Women's oppression and subordination crossed class lines, forcing many to offer their bodies in exchange for societal approval and/or economic security: marriage and prostitution were qualitatively indistinguishable institutions. In January 1895, for example, the anarchist newspaper *Derecho a la Vida* published an article entitled "Marriage and Prostitution," which concluded that there was "no appreciable difference between these two stupid terms.... The only question is whether [people] will love each other with the permission of Mr. Judge or Mr. Chief of Police."[16] Rejecting both clerical and state authority to sanction relationships, they proposed "free love" or "free union" in place of traditional marriage. Far from being a call for unrestrained libertinage, free love in this context was a defense of serial monogamy: the right for men and women to form couples based on love and mutual attraction, and to separate when those features had diminished or disappeared. In September 1897, *La Verdad* published an article entitled "Woman: her Life and Enslavement." Directed toward a female readership, this article declared:

> You are half of the human race and, just like the other half which is man, you have the right to be free, to think, to hear and to have pleasure [*gozar*].... Isn't a free union of two beings who love each other preferable to selling oneself the way female slaves were sold in markets of the middle ages?[17]

This "anarchist feminist" discourse did not go uncontested. There is a visible tension in the anarchist press between the voices calling for women's emancipation and those seeking to preserve certain patriarchal privileges. Some used the pages of the anarchist press to denounce the resistance of male colleagues to women's emancipation.[18] In the July 1896 edition of *Derecho a la Vida*, in an article entitled "The Cry of the Rebel Woman," the author questions the commitment of certain male comrades to ending women's oppression:

> On the woman question, it is not only the reactionary bourgeoisie who have stupid ideas. Certain revolutionaries, rebels but not innovators, only see one side, the smallest side, of the social question. Power torments them, they

> fight it, but more as competitors than enemies; if they rise
> up it is more to take power than to destroy it. These false
> lovers of liberty... they want the subordination of woman
> to man, and to completely dominate her.[19]

In this rather sophisticated analysis, the author is making a wholesale critique of power and exploitation, essentially questioning whether men may have a conflict of interest with regard to the anarchist project: they, like the "reactionary bourgeoisie," have more of a stake in the status quo than they are willing to admit. While anxious to free themselves from oppression and domination at the hands of capital, they are unwilling to release their wives and lovers from the same bonds. These kinds of public critiques of male privilege were rare, but testify to the persistent efforts of anarchist feminists to secure the place of women's emancipation in the revolutionary program.

We must always question the relationship between discourse and lived experience. Others have argued that anarchist feminist rhetoric was largely disconnected from "women's consciousness or mobilization." Elizabeth Hutchison's study of Chilean anarchism during this era, for example, concludes: "anarchist discourse on the woman question contributes, at least in those three decades, primarily to the history of the ideological and activist evolution of Chilean anarchism, and not to the history of women's consciousness or mobilization in Chile."[20] In the Uruguayan case, however, there does seem to be some correlation between discourse and mobilization: here the high-water mark for anarchist feminist discourse largely coincided with an apex of working-class women's activism in Montevideo.

Although undoubtedly small in numbers, working women did organize themselves during this era. Yamandú González Sierra cites an 1884 article in the anarchist publication *La Lucha Obrera,* where "Mercedes," identified by the editor as "a [female] citizen 13–14 years old" called on working women to organize in defense of their rights. "It is time that we organize ourselves," she wrote, "to struggle with unbreakable strength to face up to the arbitrariness with which we women are treated."[21] In an 1899 issue of the anarchist paper *La Aurora,* the editors posted their congratulations for creation of a woman's group, where "a good number of *compañeras* met and developed several proposals, all referring to women's emancipation."[22] Women were quite active in labor organizing during this era as well. By 1901 many women workers—including laundresses, ironers, match and cigarette workers—had organized into Resistance Societies, and in October of that year the militant cigarette workers went on strike. Forming the *Unión de Obreros en Cigarillos* (Union of Cigarette Workers), these women and men commenced cooperative production of "Boycott" brand cigarettes, which they sold in working-class communities.[23] This was a particularly common and popular tactic among women workers, who abounded in factories producing consumer goods such as cigarettes, beer, and matches.[24] Because the boycott and cooperative production relied on community support for its success, these strategies served to break down divisions between home and work, and involved women as both producers and consumers of primary goods. Here, gaining the support of working-class housewives was far from incidental or symbolic. In a summary of the labor activities of the previous year, the January 1902 issue of the anarchist paper *Tribuna Libertaria* acknowledged the important role played by women workers in 1901. The article particularly singles out the mostly female match workers:

> The strike of the matchmakers, that heroic strike, in which a handful of valiant women took a proud, haughty and defiant stand before the immense power of a capitalist company, was the climactic moment of this movement. The women receive our salute and our enthusiastic applause for having set an example for the men. *The weaker sex*—if there is such a thing—in this case, it was the men.[25]

No matter how patronizing, even this image of working-class women as conscious revolutionaries would undergo dramatic change as the Batllista era progressed.

Returning to the relationship between anarchist feminist discourse and women's mobilization, the most pertinent question here is the connection between an apparent decline in women's activities and the antifeminist backlash visible on the pages of the anarchist press. Important economic and political changes in the early years of the twentieth century brought about changes in the ideologies and tactics of the anarchist-oriented labor movement, which in turn had repercussions for women's place within that movement. Industrialization meant that the emphasis of the movement shifted away from smaller workshops and factories, where most of the female proletariat was employed, and toward larger enterprises like meatpacking plants, railroads, and ports, whose workforce was mostly male. The corresponding decline in tactics like the general strike and the boycott, which relied on women's participation as both workers and consumers, further reduced female participation in the movement. From this point forward, struggles between labor and capital took place on the docks or on the factory floor more than in the streets of working-class *barrios*. In 1905, anarchists created the *Federación Obrera Regional Uruguaya* (Uruguayan Regional Workers' Federation, or FORU), the first major labor confederation in the country, and an indication of the growing organization and centralization of the labor movement in Uruguay. The "family wage"—the demand that working men be paid sufficiently to support a wife and children—quickly became a central part of FORU labor demands, as did calls for restrictions on women's factory work, ostensibly because it "endanger[ed] maternity."[26] Such strategies, which sought to improve the conditions of (male) industrial workers, were also motivated by a desire to firmly reestablish the patriarchal family within working-class communities. Women with consistent access to male wages may have benefited economically from these changes, but they did not necessarily benefit politically, and women who did work met with an increasingly hostile reception on the pages of the anarchist labor press.

Evidence of increased insecurities over women's role in the paid labor force can be seen in a short-lived Montevideo newspaper called *La Voz de la Mujer*.[27] First appearing in 1905 (the same year of FORU's foundation), *La Voz* was a malicious and misogynistic tabloid publication that sought to enforce "honorable" behavior among working women by publicizing their alleged sexual indiscretions. The paper's main focus was on rumored liaisons between female workers and their male bosses, clearly a source of tremendous anxiety for working-class men. It is telling that the paper's attacks are aimed at working-class women and not the bourgeois men with whom they were alleged to be having relations. Claiming to stand "in defense of the fair sex," *La Voz* attacked individual women, printing their names and addresses along with the dishonorable act they were said to have committed. But beyond alleged individual indiscretions, the paper denigrated entire categories of working women en masse, a further indication of the hostilities working women provoked in some circles. An article on corset makers illustrates the paper's commitment to be "severe with the indecent woman":

Chapter One

> We have heard repeatedly that exactly the same thing that goes on with the *fosforeras* (matchmakers) of R. is going on between the corset-makers and their bosses.... If this is true...it would be yet another degenerate affront to society. We must shamefully accept the fact that our women do not know how to defend their reputations.[28]

It seems no coincidence that the primary targets of this publication—needle workers and matchmakers—were precisely those groups of women workers who had been most engaged in militant labor activity since the turn of the century. Here was one area, perhaps, where factory owners and some parts of the male proletariat could agree: militant working women, outside of the traditional bounds of male control, posed a threat to the paternalistic order in both the factory and the home. In sum, although one cannot discount the possibility that women's activism was simply less publicized than before, this shift in anarchist discourse appears to have coincided with declining activity on the part of working-class women. Surely we can conclude that anarchist feminists faced a more unfriendly environment than in earlier years.

The Early Years of the Liga de Damas Católicas, 1906–1910

With the prominent exception of the anarchists, when Batlle took office in 1903, women in Uruguay were rarely making demands for their own emancipation or speaking about the specific need to modify gender relations or change the roles of women in society. And while one may identify aspects of their analysis as feminist, anarchist women diligently avoided using "feminist" or "feminism" to identify themselves or their program. Batlle presented himself as a champion of women's rights, but in Uruguay as elsewhere, feminism emerged as an opposition movement. In this case, feminist self-identification began with conservative Catholic women opposed to the anticlerical Batllista state. During the years between Batlle's first presidency (1903–1907) and the 1916 elections, which brought an official "halt" to reform, many social sectors, both popular and elite, scrambled to influence and to make demands upon a newly responsive state. In this context, the identity of the "new woman" had yet to be defined, and her image did not yet carry the visage of the middle-class professional women whose numbers and influence were still small. During these years the first women professionals completed their studies and went into professional practice; Paulina Luisi, for example, became the nation's first female physician in 1908, and her sister Clotilde became the first woman lawyer in 1911. Others would follow, but it took a few years for this cohort to become both numerically significant and politically energized enough to define the parameters and paradigm of Uruguayan feminism. In the meantime, as an outgrowth of nineteenth-century patterns observed earlier, conservative Catholic women fought to interrupt the process of secularization that resumed after 1903, while anticlerical women's groups sought to encourage and support this same process. The word *feminism* itself entered into organizational vocabulary during these years, first with the Catholics and later with the anticlericals. Women's political activity had an optimism and effervescence during these years, but also a good deal of conflict and fragmentation. This was especially the case for the anticlerical feminists who, in the face of Batllismo's promise, coalesced into liberal, anarchist, and Socialist factions based on personal politics and animosities, but also on fundamental disagreements about the tactics, goals, and the very definitions of women's emancipation.

Batlle's first presidential term was aimed partly at reducing the influence and authority of the Catholic Church in Uruguayan society. As we have seen, anticlerical legislation and tensions between liberals and Catholics date back to the nineteenth century, but in the early 1900s a new campaign heated this simmering debate over the religion question to a rolling boil. One of the high points was the conflict over legislation proposing the legalization of divorce. Initially presented in 1902, a law allowing for "absolute dissolution" of marriage finally passed in 1907, making Uruguay the first Southern Cone nation to legalize divorce.[29] The 1907 law allowed for divorce by mutual consent after two years of marriage, and listed several conditions under which one spouse could sue for divorce without the consent of the other, including voluntary abandonment of the home and extreme cases of domestic violence. This bill also listed adultery as a cause for divorce, but reflected the prevailing (double) standards of the day. While the law provided for divorce based on "adultery of the woman in any case," it only allowed for a woman to obtain a divorce based on her husband's infidelity "when it is committed in the conjugal house or when it causes a public scandal or if the husband has a concubine."[30] These and other anticlerical, secularizing moves of the first Batlle presidency provided a catalyst for the first important feminist organization of twentieth-century Uruguay: The Catholic Ladies' League. Due to the historic weakness of the church and the related intensity of attacks on church privilege launched by the first Batlle presidency, Catholics in Montevideo perhaps felt themselves under attack to a greater degree than in other Latin American countries at this time.[31] This provides a simple explanation for the precocious organization of Catholic women in Uruguay.

The history of the *Liga de Damas Católicas del Uruguay* (Catholic Ladies' League of Uruguay, or Liga), which combined conservative Catholic politics with "Christian feminist" militancy, allows us to examine the responses and activities of Catholic laywomen in Uruguay during an era that both opened up women's roles and attacked church privileges. Although the Uruguayan Liga was founded in direct response to the removal of crucifixes and other religious images from public hospitals in 1906, the most catalyzing event in the formation of the organization was the two-year long debate surrounding the eventual 1907 legalization of divorce. This proposed legislation generated a long campaign by church leaders, who sought to mobilize public opinion against the law. On the pages of the Catholic newspaper *El Bien Público*, editor and conservative Catholic leader Joaquín de Secco Illa railed against this legislation as an attack on the church, the family, and civilization itself, and as an indicator of social decadence. "The experience of history has taught us," he wrote, "that the dissolution of the conjugal link by absolute divorce, has only appeared in legislation and practice when the perversion of its customs or its moral decline has begun to manifest itself."[32] Secco Illa argued that, with the exception of France, divorce was an unknown phenomenon in Latin countries of the world. By associating divorce with the Anglo-Saxon Protestants and, more subtly, with Jews, Secco Illa sought to mobilize nationalist sentiment in favor of the church and its antidivorce campaign.

Responding to these calls to defend the marriage sacrament and Christian principles, many Catholic women threw themselves into the antidivorce cause, creating channels for women's activity that would persist well beyond the initial campaign. Under the direction of men like Secco Illa, starting in 1905 a nationwide campaign began to gather the signatures of Uruguayan women opposed to the proposed divorce law.[33] Within a few months, the petition campaign succeeded in collecting tens of thousands of signatures, the biggest action of its type undertaken by Uruguayan women up to this point. The particular threat that divorce legislation represented to Uruguayan society, and women in particular, was said to justify this otherwise unacceptable or inappropriate entry of women into the political realm. Arguing that divorce "would be an irreparable punishment for the woman, more irreparable than death for a criminal," Catholic women felt compelled to speak out in defense of the Christian family and their own honor.[34] They modeled their petition after earlier female protests in Argentina and Brazil opposing the legalization of divorce. But unlike these cases, where conservative and church-led opposition defeated proposed divorce legislation, in Uruguay the law was approved, leaving many Catholic women enraged that their opinions were not taken into account. This, coupled with other anticlerical legislation aimed at transferring responsibility for charity and education from the church to the state caused "the feminine soul to rise up" and organize the Liga in August 1906.[35] When Archbishop Mariano Soler authored the introduction to a pamphlet entitled *Feminismo Cristiano*, calling on all Catholics to "defend the true and healthy feminism ... to save the current society, so threatened by the dissolving theories of socialism and anti-Christianity with its libertarian and anarchic ideas of the free woman," he gave the organization an official seal of approval.[36]

The model for this new organization was the *Ligue des Dames Françaises* (League of French Ladies), founded in 1902 to combat anticlerical policies in France.[37] As the first branch in Latin America, the Uruguayan Liga served as a model for Catholic women in other countries; exercising, for example, a direct influence on the foundation of the Chilean Catholic Ladies' League in 1912.[38] That Uruguay was home to the first Liga branch in Latin America is directly attributable to the unusual political context provided by Batllismo, which, in turn, reflects the historic weakness of the Catholic Church in Uruguayan society. The politics of Batllismo shaped the politics of the Liga in two, seemingly contradictory ways. First, anticlerical moves such as the divorce bill provided Uruguayan Catholic women with a strong mobilizer, justifying their entry into the political realm. Secondly, Batllismo and the internal debate over the Catholic response to it provoked a split in the Catholic political community in which rightist Catholics took over. According to Zubillaga and Coyota, Archbishop Soler's death in 1908 paved the way for a "conservative Catholic" takeover, the culmination of a schism between progressive and rightist Catholics that had been going on for several years.[39] The Uruguayan Liga, too, reflects this pattern; the group was far more conservative in its politics—and militant in its tactics—than its Chilean counterpart, for example.

Chapter One

Much of the Liga leadership reflected that elite conservative orientation. On the rosters were the wives of several important capitalists, bankers, and industrialists, as well as members of prominent Blanco families.[40] Faustina García Gómez de Secco Illa, for example, was the granddaughter of General Leandro Gómez (Blanco hero of the siege of Montevideo during the Guerra Grande) and the wife of Joaquín de Secco Illa, the Catholic leader mentioned above. Petrona Cibils de Jackson, the group's honorary president until her death in 1907, was the daughter of Jaime Cibils, a wealthy Spanish-born industrialist, and the wife of Juan D. Jackson, heir to substantial landed holdings in the country and the founder of one of the nation's largest banks. That many of these women were in some way related to each other speaks both to the family nature of partisan politics and to the degree of intermarriage within the Uruguayan elite.[41] Given the political and economic power wielded by the Liga leadership, and the strong support of the Catholic hierarchy, it is no surprise that within a few years this was a national organization which had organized hundreds of women and gained the support of thousands. By 1907, the Liga claimed to have twenty-seven committees in every department of the republic, and while there are no precise membership figures, it was surely the largest politically oriented women's organization in the country during the early years of the century.

The early rhetoric of the Liga was surprisingly militant, as the founders tried to shake women out of their complacency and out of their traditional roles and enlist them in their campaign to defend the "good cause." In the first issue of *El Eco*, the Uruguayan Liga's official publication, dated January 1907, the editors explain that their organization was

> Born of a general indignation, from the unwarranted outrages to Christ and to the Church, the Catholic Ladies' League of Uruguay wants to *protest* against injustice, *react* against indifference, *protect* the soul of the people and of the child and *work* with all of the means within the reach of women, in defense of the Faith and of liberty.[42]

In a series of conferences sponsored by the Liga in 1907, speakers tried to motivate women to join what was painted as a holy army of Catholic women that would fight to defend the church against its enemies. In a November 1907 conference entitled *La Mujer Cristiana*

(The Christian Woman), Father Bettembourg (an advisor to the Liga and important promoter of Catholic women's activism) stated that

> It would be foolish now to deny the greatness and strength that the women's movement brings to social action. This new emergence of feminist power should not frighten us...a pope called for the Catholic works of an elite army, the vanguard of the Church. Your League, above all, deserves this title; observe, then, the military spirit and you will assure your victory.[43]

Much Liga work was dedicated to the promotion of the conservative Catholic position among the more affluent sectors of society via conferences, campaigns, and support for the Catholic press. In the proceedings from a 1908 Liga conference, it was emphasized that "the press and conferences are the only way to dominate public opinion these days.... The Catholic religion has lost ground by not knowing how to [effectively] use these media."[44] The Liga thus prioritized the support of the so-called *buena prensa* (good press) as a way to help diffuse the Catholic mission. The group's most important and eloquent propagandist was Laura Carreras de Bastos, a member of the Liga from its inception. Born in 1870 in Barcelona to a Spanish father and an Uruguayan mother, she and her family later returned to Uruguay, where Laura married Juan José Bastos in 1896. She was widowed some time after 1907, but even before then Carreras was an outspoken supporter of Catholic women's activism. One of the Liga's first publications, a 1907 pamphlet entitled *Feminismo Cristiano* (Christian Feminism), reproduced an essay that Carreras de Bastos had presented at a religious conference in Buenos Aires the year before. In this essay, Carreras de Bastos was quick to distinguish herself from the "warrior feminist" whom she attacked as an "unbalanced" woman "not worthy of belonging to our sex."[45] She then differentiated her brand of "Christian feminism" from that normally associated with the term:

> I believe, *señores*, that I have demonstrated with my words, that despite being a woman and expressing my thoughts in a Congress, I am completely anti-feminist, in terms of this harmful feminism; this does not deter me from dedicating myself entirely to the defense of our

> cause, helping to establish the true feminism—the ideal feminism—Christian feminism.[46]

Rather than residing within liberal traditions, Carreras and others argued that the true feminism was to be found within the teachings of Christianity, which, they claimed, first lifted women out of slavery and degradation. Carreras thus turned the notion that the liberals were defenders of women's equality on its head, using the issue of the ongoing legislative debate over the legalization of divorce as the prime example. Weakening the sanctity of marriage with divorce legislation was a step backward for women, she argued, leading them into a state of greater moral compromise and insecurity. In one sense, Carreras saw Catholic paternalism as women's best defense. But she also criticized both society and the church for not going further in promoting women's moral and intellectual advancement. She was especially critical of wealthy women, whose "frivolity" she blamed for what she saw as women's declining status and for the misery in which most working-class women existed. Carreras did extensively discuss the fate of working-class women and, unlike many conservatives at the time, she did not oppose women's wage labor. Instead she emphasized that efforts should be made to improve conditions for the working woman, stating that "work should be the glory of the poor—her shame never."[47] Yet she remained largely silent on the issue of capitalist exploitation of the working class, advocating education as a means of uplift as opposed to any broader structural changes in the economic system.

Carreras closed her essay with a call for women's "social action," and for women to speak out in their own self-defense on issues such as the legalization of divorce. In the Catholic vocabulary of the time, "social action" aimed at reaching out beyond the elites to "restore Christian principles" to those of lower social standing.[48] Yet this last section must have gone beyond what was acceptable to the Liga and the church hierarchy, since the published version of her essay was accompanied by a disclaimer, stating that the Liga "support[s] all of the themes it develops, except that of women's political activity... because the Catholic Ladies' League is not authorized to include it in their program of action."[49] But Carreras de Bastos did in fact advocate women's political activity as the best hope for restoring a society degenerating due to its lack of faith. This is the essence of Christian feminist ideology, which used militant rhetoric to defend conservative causes. This rhetoric could

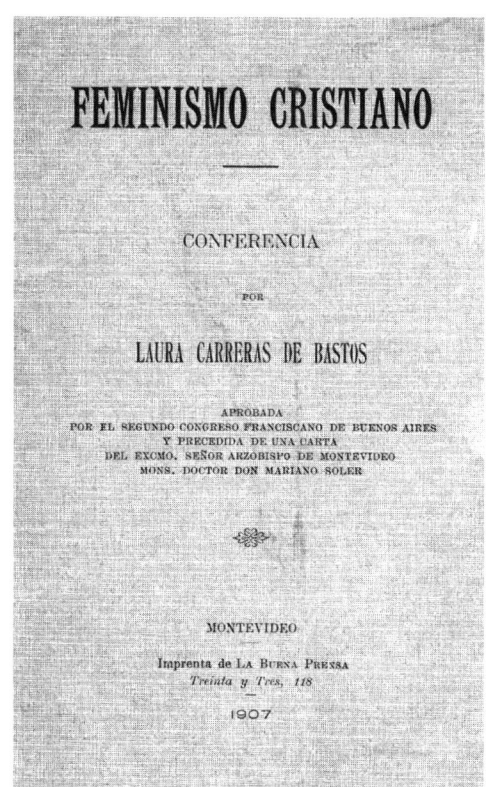

Figure 1:
Feminismo Cristiano (Christian Feminism), 1907. Pamphlet published in Montevideo with an introduction by Archbishop Mariano Soler. Author's collection.

even go so far as to criticize the traditional roles of women in society. In a 1909 pamphlet entitled *Acción social de la mujer ante el divorcio absoluto* ("Social Action of Women in the Face of Divorce"), Carreras de Bastos's chafing against traditional gender roles comes through:

> They have disdainfully relegated us to rule only in the salons, as if we were animated dolls, little glass curiosities, incapable of anything substantial. Don't be surprised that we defend our dominions.... It's the only thing we have left, and in this area we must show that we are worthy of defending a beautiful ideal; something that mechanical dolls would never get involved in.[50]

Here Carreras acknowledged the pressures on women to stay home and uninvolved in politics, but she argued that the changing times demanded that women become more engaged in the serious issues facing modern society.

It was not only the actions of the Batllista state that were menacing "Christian" values and the position of the Catholic Church in Uruguayan society. Liga women were also threatened by the activities of anarchists and Socialists, who had made significant inroads in working-class communities. Catholics attributed these groups' success to the skillful use of written and oral propaganda within target communities. Because these doctrines were seen as entering the working-class family by way of the men (generally through labor unions), the Liga targeted women as a means of defending the *"buena causa"* in working-class communities. Because the pattern of immigrant men forming households with native-born women was not uncommon, this added another dimension to the Liga's campaign to target women as defenders of the national culture. The Liga maintained a paternalistic vision, which did not question social inequality but rather sought to restore the traditional relations between elites and popular classes through charity and concepts of noblesse oblige. In one of its early conferences, the Liga called on its members, through their work with proletarian women, to "destroy in their spirits class warfare, making them understand that social differences do not exclude harmony, mutual respect and consideration among truly Christian people."[51]

In this spirit, the Liga created a number of committees targeting working-class women and families. Based on the precept that "the number of illegitimate unions and births that take place among our poor is ever more alarming," one of the group's first projects was to encourage poor and working-class couples to marry.[52] The Association of Marriages organized in late 1908 worked to "regularize" working-class unions. The committee urged upper-class brides to donate money on their wedding day so that their working-class "sisters" could have a wedding ceremony as well. In 1913, after nearly five years in existence, the Association of Marriages claimed to have overseen 470 marriages and as many "legitimations."[53] Other committees worked to feed poor schoolchildren and to provide occupational training and health care to working-class women, all of course on the condition that they undergo religious training and comply with certain moral requirements set out by the Liga.[54] Liga committee work often brought elite and poor women together and reinforced paternalistic relations between the two groups. Starting in

1909, the *Comités Populares* (Popular Committees) sought to "bring together a good number of female factory workers to provide them with healthy entertainment and good advice and to establish a union of warmth and sympathy between the different social classes."[55] Women who attended were entertained with music and poetry, and received lessons in hygiene and morality, reading, and sewing. A Mutual Aid Society was also established, where affluent women attended to the moral and medical needs of its working-class members. Liga members visited and cared for the sick, and also provided literacy and religion classes to members.[56] Beyond the immediate provision of material support, affiliation with Liga groups could be economically beneficial in other ways, since *El Eco* occasionally published the names and qualifications of "recommended" and "honorable" people looking for work as maids, cooks, and dressmakers. Yet while religious instruction and some material assistance were provided, the Liga never publicly criticized industrial working conditions or the inadequate housing and sanitation that often characterized life in the tenements of Montevideo. They viewed poverty as a fundamentally moral problem. And, of course, the Liga sought to compete with radical and other anticlerical groups, while establishing some sort of Catholic sisterhood between elite and proletarian women. Christian feminism, in sum, timidly challenged certain aspects of paternalism while it vigorously defended others.

The Freethinkers Respond: The Damas Liberales

The anticlericals, of course, did not stand idly by and watch the Catholics organize women, working class or otherwise. The Association of Liberal Propaganda, founded in 1900, revealed both its rather low opinion of women and its political opportunism in its response to the mobilization of Catholic women. Publicly, the group attacked the Catholics for encouraging women to abandon their traditional roles and neglect their duties, exhorting Catholic women to "concern yourselves with domestic tasks which are the only things a woman of high virtue should emphasize."[57] But in internal documents the association was also asking itself: "If woman ... is basically a lump of clay that the friar molds to his liking, why don't we shape her ourselves to conform with our ideas, and with our way of thinking and being?"[58] They had a base to work with. In the 1908 census, 15 percent of Uruguayan women identified themselves as "liberals" (37 percent of men put themselves in this category).[59] The challenge was to mobilize that minority to try and win other women over to the liberal side.

It is within this context that the *Asociación de Damas Liberales* (Association of Liberal Ladies) was founded in October 1906, only a matter of months after the Damas Católicas. We should understand the emergence of this group as a response to the prior mobilization of Catholic women, which was in turn a response to actions of the Batllista state. The group was headed up by a Spanish freethinker by the name of Belén Sárraga (after 1909, Belén de Sárraga).[60] Sárraga was a liberal activist of some renown who had only recently arrived in Montevideo; indeed, the overall political climate in Uruguay may well have influenced her decision to establish herself in this city.[61] A leader in the Liberal Party, Sárraga was also the editor of *El Liberal*—which published more or less daily from April 1908 to October of 1910—making her the first woman whose name sat atop the masthead of a daily paper in the history of the country. For a brief period between 1908 and 1910, Belén Sárraga was one of the leading female political figures in the Rio de la Plata, and her role as a precursor to liberal feminist organizing was an important one. Yet the *Damas Liberales* never had the financial support, official endorsement, or long life that the Catholic Liga enjoyed, and its history is consequently more difficult to trace. Other than what is preserved on the pages of *El Liberal*, we know very little about Sárraga's time in Uruguay, and even less about the Montevideo branch of the *Damas Liberales*, which curiously is barely mentioned in the group's newspaper.[62]

If the Damas Católicas sought to defend the Catholic Church's domain in Uruguayan society, the Damas Liberales sought to reduce religious influence. In fact the Damas Liberales' 1908 statutes read almost like the mirror opposite of their rival organization. The Damas Liberales opposed religious education and marriage and the baptism of children, called for an end to any funeral ceremony whatsoever, and saw the cessation of religious domination as key to the advancement of civilization. In its first issue in April 1908, *El Liberal* listed among its goals that of "annulling religious power in the State, society and the family."[63] Not surprisingly, *El Liberal* supported the new divorce legislation, arguing: "Is not a divorced woman a hundred times more honorable and less harmful to society than one obligated, by an indissoluble bond, to betray her vows?"[64] They saw religion as the principal perverting force in society, and particularly so in the case of women, where oppression and domination by the church and its teachings had left her a "physically and morally deformed being." These medicalized metaphors of sickness and health pervade the rhetoric of the Damas Liberales (and especially of Sárraga herself). In later conferences, for example, Sárraga described women as beings "sickened by religious mysticism [and] excessive sentimentality."[65] Although woman was a deformed and/or sick creature in the liberal view, her redemption was possible through education and liberation from damaging clerical influence. "Mental health produces a virtuous and valiant rebelliousness" in woman, they argued, leading her to "break the molds of tradition."[66] Just like the Catholics, the liberals saw women as central to church/state struggles, because of their perceived influence in the private sphere. "They [women] are the only ones capable of secularizing the home," they wrote.[67] The Damas Liberales shared with the Catholic Liga a particular concern for the state of bourgeois women, whom they routinely characterized as "decadent," "vain," and "ignorant." The group also worked to better the position of working-class women and to practice charity, but this received less attention than it did among their Catholic opponents. This lack of emphasis may in part be explained by the fact that the Damas Liberales saw legislation and public policy as the answer to gender and class exploitation. Unlike the Catholic women, the Damas Liberales viewed the state as an appropriate forum within which to remedy working women's situation. "The legislator," Sárraga wrote, "striving for the common good, is obligated to propose laws which will minimize, as much as possible, the martyrdom of the working woman."[68] Whereas the Damas Católicas saw the solution to the problem of the working woman as lying in the revival of older paternalistic traditions and ties of mutual obligation between elite and nonelite women, the Damas Liberales advocated an active and reform-minded state as the best solution to the "social question." Surely the progressive environment of Batllismo inspired this reliance on, and connection to, the state, an important characteristic of liberal feminism that will become more pronounced in later years.

In identifying religion as the main obstacle to women's (and, by extension, societal) advancement, Sárraga's rhetoric echoes that expressed by Varela several decades earlier. But Sárraga took the argument a step further, deploying the language of citizenship and invoking women as agents in their own liberation to a much greater degree than liberal anticlericals of the earlier generation. "We cure the sick woman [*enferma*] and we will have the woman citizen [*ciudadana*]," she proclaimed.[69] *El Liberal* emphasized the importance of women's agency,

Chapter One

Figure 2:
Reprinted from Belén Sárraga, *Conferencias sociológicas y de crítica religiosa* (Santiago de Chile: La Razon, 1913).

and the need for women to liberate themselves from pernicious influences. And like some anarchists, the newspaper cited men's role in women's subordination and deformation, and expressed its doubts about the willingness of even liberal men to relinquish their privileges. "Man (with a few notable exceptions), of whatever social class, even calling himself liberal and having progressive ideas, does not think his own woman has the right to educate herself or to have her own ideas, much less propagate them."[70] Thus the discourse of the Damas Liberales, while still harnessed to traditional ideology—especially the notion that women needed to catch up with men intellectually, culturally, and morally—was opening the door to new modalities where, like the Damas Católicas, women were called upon to play an active role, not only in societal reform, but in their own emancipation.

While the Damas Liberales spoke of the need to elevate woman's condition, they initially avoided the use of the word *feminism*, perhaps because of Catholic women's use of the term, or because of their association of the word with politics more radical than their own. A February 1909 article from the Department of Canelones accused women of "aiding the regime of prejudice and submission to *feminism*" (emphasis added), implying an association of feminism with the Catholics.[71] But by later that year, a new process of appropriation of the term by the Damas Liberales seems to be under way. A two-part article, entitled "Woman before the Church," spoke about "hope... for the triumph of feminism properly understood and interpreted" and the promotion of "feminism in its proper conception."[72] The new message asserted that the true feminism was anticlerical and strongly opposed by the leadership of the Catholic Church. Thus by 1909–1910 we see the beginning of struggles over the definition of "feminism" in Uruguayan society, as a term introduced by the Catholic Ladies' League was slowly and timidly being adopted and reinterpreted by their liberal counterparts.

Anticlerical forces found strong support outside Montevideo, especially in regions dominated by the Colorado Party. Almost from the moment of the Damas Liberales' foundation, Belén Sárraga spent a great deal of time touring the interior of the republic, making speeches and helping to organize liberal women in a number of departmental capitals. "[T]he constitution of women's associations [in the countryside] is a fundamental issue for us," the group declared.[73] Organizing women anywhere at this stage was surely a daunting task, and church pressure on Sárraga and her group appears to have begun early. In 1909, *El Liberal* reported that religious elements in the interior, "following in the footsteps of their colleagues in Montevideo," were conducting aggressive campaigns "against 'that newspaper' and 'that woman.'"[74] Nevertheless, by late 1909, the Damas Liberales had branches in a number of departments of the republic. The earliest and most important departmental committee was found in Durazno, the old Colorado and military stronghold in the center of the country. Founded in 1908, this was by far the largest and most vital of the organization's branches in the interior; although the evidence here is far from complete or clear, it is possible that the Damas Liberales had a stronger presence here than in the capital city.

The Durazno branch of the Damas Liberales was headed by Otilia Schultze, a woman described as representing "an entire era in the city of Durazno."[75] In 1908, when the *Damas Liberales de Durazno* was first formed, Otilia Schultze de Bournasell was still married to her first husband. Two years later, a now widowed Otilia Schultze made local headlines (and raised local eyebrows) when she married the eminent General Pablo Galarza, who had recently divorced his first wife. A close associate of Otilia's father, Pablo Galarza was the consummate military man: a veteran of the civil wars of the previous century, and said to be one of the few mestizos to have reached an important rank in the Uruguayan armed forces.[76] Any scandal surrounding the marriage (and Pablo's divorce) was likely muffled given the political influence of the two families. Many years his junior, Otilia Schultze was nonetheless known for her strong character and influence over the general, and is said to have polished up some of his rough battlefield edges. For her part, Schultze soon became known in Durazno as "the 'General of the Women's Army,'" in contraposition with the rank of her husband."[77] The Durazno branch of the Damas Liberales was active for several years, but Belén Sárraga's departure from Uruguay and the apparent pressure of clerical attacks appear to have weakened the organization. In a 1917 letter to Otilia Schultze, Paulina Luisi referred to the troubled history of the Damas Liberales in Durazno, writing: "I read your stories about the *Asociación Liberal*...and fear that my dear [National Women's] Council has the same threats poised over its head."[78] Many of these clerical attacks were provoked once again because of alleged connections of Liberal organizations to Freemasonry.[79] In sum, there existed two rival women's political tendencies, based in the old partisan and clerical/anticlerical struggles of the late nineteenth century, one Catholic, one liberal. They both became more mobilized and more openly feminist in the twentieth century, as they began to advocate, not just women's activism to defend a cause or political color, but changes in family structure and gender relations themselves.

Perhaps because of her transitory stay in Uruguay, or perhaps because of her Spanish citizenship, histories of Uruguayan liberal feminism barely mention Belén Sárraga. Most identify María Abella de Ramírez as the founding mother of Uruguayan liberal feminism.[80] María Abella was Uruguayan, and there is no doubt that her politics were more convincingly feminist than Sárraga's, but most of her adult life and political career was spent in Argentina, and her influence over the development of Uruguayan liberal feminism was indirect and sporadic. In 1906, at the same time as the formation of the Damas Liberales in Uruguay, María Abella presented her famous Seventeen Points at an International Freethinkers' Conference in Buenos Aires and published *En pos de la justicia* (In Pursuit of Justice), an important early feminist tract.[81] In 1909 she founded the *Liga Nacional de Mujeres Librepensadores* (National League of Freethinking Women) in Buenos Aires. Although it is not clear what relationship may have existed between Belén Sárraga and María Abella, the two women seemed to

Figure 3:
Otilia Schultze de Galarza and her husband Pablo Galarza. Reprinted with permission from the Archivo Nacional de la Imagen, Montevideo.

have alternated as head of the liberal women's movement in the Río de la Plata in the years 1909–1910. In 1909 *El Liberal* announced the foundation of the Argentine Association of Freethinking Women with María Abella as president. The following year, however, the same organization named Belén Sárraga "honorary president," and replaced Abella with Argentine feminist Julieta Lanteri Renshaw. In sum, even though she was not Uruguayan and spent relatively few active years in Uruguay, Belén Sárraga was clearly just as, if not more, important to the history of early liberal feminism in Uruguay as María Abella.

Much of this jockeying in the leadership of anticlerical feminism may have been in anticipation of the upcoming *Congreso Femenino Internacional* held in Buenos Aires in April-May 1910. At that conference, Sárraga was named the official delegate of the Freethinking Women, as well as one of the honorary vice presidents of the event, where she intervened in favor of absolute divorce and expanded state

59

welfare for the poor and greater state protection for mothers and children.[82] The 1910 Congress marked a watershed for women's history in the Southern Cone. As the first significant meeting where Latin American women organized and met on their own (rather than as a part of a larger scientific conference, for example), it marks an important early step in the Pan-American women's movement. More specifically, in the Río de la Plata, it delineates the transition from the freethinking phase of women's organizing, and the beginning of a new, liberal feminist phase, one that was less concerned about the religion question and issues of clerical influence, and more focused on the acquisition of women's equal civil and political rights. "The feminist freethinkers," Lavrin observed, "attended the 1910 First International Feminine Congress but they left few traces thereafter."[83] Fittingly perhaps, the Congress appears to have been Sárraga's last formal participation in feminist politics in the Río de la Plata. Sárraga reportedly resigned her position in Uruguay in April 1910 "for health reasons," and not much more was heard from her in Uruguay after that.[84] *El Liberal* discontinued publication shortly thereafter. The last official word of Sárraga's presence in Uruguay is in March 1911, when *El Día* reported on an anticlerical conference that she had supposedly helped organize in Montevideo.[85] Later that year, Sárraga left on a long South American tour. She resurfaced in Chile sometime around 1913, and went on to have an important impact on early feminist organizing there as well.[86] In Uruguay, meanwhile, Sárraga's legacy, and the organizations she helped found, played a formative role in the liberal feminist movement that was now starting to take shape

Divisions among the Anticlericals: Liberals, Anarchists, and Socialists

Belén Sárraga's departure from the Uruguayan political scene coincided with the beginning of a new phase in anticlerical women's political activism. The Uruguayan Socialist Party was founded in 1910, on the eve of Batlle's second presidential term. Made up largely of disaffected Batllistas and labor activists frustrated with the abstentionist politics and radical tactics of the anarchists, the Socialists advocated participation in the political system, and sought to insert themselves into the very bourgeois institutions the anarchists wanted to destroy. Both the Socialist Party and Batlle's imminent return to power formed the backdrop for a new stage in feminist activism, one characterized by the emergence of a well-defined split in anticlerical feminist ranks.

During Batlle's second term (1911–1915), the traditions of Belén Sárraga and María Abella developed a largely elite/middle-class focus on obtaining equal civil and political rights for women, coalescing eventually into something one can call liberal feminism proper. At the same time, the anarchist tradition was evolving into a more Marxist-based and Socialist Party-dominated movement. In its identification of the formal proletariat (rather than the working-class community) as the revolutionary vanguard, women were increasingly marginalized. After 1905, as we have seen, feminist discourse within anarchism met with an increasingly hostile reaction. This does not mean that worker feminism simply vanished, or that women stopped organizing, but it was now visibly on the defensive. The short-lived newspaper *La Nueva Senda* (the New Path), for example, published in 1909–1910 by veteran anarchist feminists Virginia Bolten, María Collazo, and Juana Rouco Buela, reflected the rather grim state of working-class women's activism in Montevideo during this era. In an April 1910 article entitled "To Women: The Need to Organize," Juana Buela lamented the "little conviction woman has of her rights." So disillusioned by what she saw as women's passivity in the face of exploitation, she even proposed that women abandon the paid labor force, stating that "it would be best if woman left the contest... in order to put a stop to the abuses that are committed with her."[87] Buela nevertheless maintained hope that organizing women was possible, and believed that, in a better time, women could be shown the path toward their own emancipation. Worker feminism was indeed revived, mostly as a reformulated socialist feminism, but it will struggle under the weight of orthodox Marxism and the difficulties involved in weaving gender into the ideology of class struggle.

In the meantime, liberal feminism was on a more upward trajectory. In May 1910, at the Women's Congress in Buenos Aires, a Chilean delegate proposed the creation of a Pan-American Federation dedicated to "work for women's happiness, the prosperity of the home, the morality of tradition, and universal peace, all as a means of improving the American nationalities."[88] As the official delegate for Uruguay, María Abella was charged with setting up an Uruguayan branch of the Federation. Despite the short travel distance, Abella did not make the trip right away.[89] There is speculation that the formation of an Uruguayan Section of the Federation was stalled due to Abella's close ties to the Batlle administration and her belief that necessary reforms would be undertaken from above. Whatever the reasons for the delay,

Figure 4:
María Collazo, Buenos Aires, 1907. The Uruguayan-born Collazo was a leader in the tenants' strike in Buenos Aires in that year. She was expelled from Argentina and returned to Montevideo shortly thereafter. Reprinted from *Caras y Caretas* (Buenos Aires), 2 November 1907.

several months later a group of women in Montevideo appear to have taken matters into their own hands, creating a new organization dedicated to secular education and the "liberation of women from religious prejudice and social convention...[which is] damaging to her physical and intellectual independence."[90] The *Asociación Femenina "Emancipación"* ("Emancipation" Women's Association) was constituted in early April 1911, only a matter of weeks after Batlle had assumed the presidency for the second time. Emancipación appears to have been an effort to unify anticlerical women in a single organization. Yet this unity was destined to be fleeting: the founding meeting of the organization was a tumultuous one, where a "big debate over the program developed," a harbinger of conflicts to come.[91]

Almost immediately, an unnamed delegate from the Pan-American Federation was dispatched to Montevideo to meet with the women of Emancipación seeking their affiliation with the Federation. Representing a largely middle-class liberal feminist tendency, the Federation program favored rational and scientific education, temperance, divorce, protection of motherhood, free access to professions, and women's economic independence.[92] The program also contained a vague endorsement of women's suffrage, arguing that: "where woman cooperates in the development of nations and improvement of the race she should take part in the business of the State, and it is thus necessary to take steps towards this type of social reform."[93] Not all Emancipación members embraced this platform, it seems, since the discussion of the regulations was reportedly "animated."[94] In fact, it is clear that, from its inception, Emancipación was controlled by more radical elements than those affiliated with the Pan-American project.

Apparently unable to control this new upstart, María Abella and others decided to create their own organization. Shortly after the foundation of Emancipación, Abella finally arrived in Montevideo, where she oversaw the foundation of the *Sección Uruguaya de la Federación Pan Americana* (Uruguayan Section of the Pan-American Federation). The Pan-American Federation then once again attempted to solicit the affiliation of Emancipación. But the radicals controlling the latter group, among them anarchists María Collazo and Virginia Bolten, rejected the offer:

> Sra. Bolten read...an anti-suffragist discourse, opposed to the Pan-American Federation, maintaining the necessity of not affiliating with this organization. Other speakers took the same position, declaring themselves against suffrage as well....The Assembly...voted not to affiliate with the Pan-American Federation.[95]

That a group opposed to women's suffrage would be considered "radical" perhaps bears some explanation. In keeping with its anarchist roots, the leadership of Emancipación stated that it "opposed orienting the struggle towards the conquest of political rights."[96] The statutes of Emancipación—issued immediately after rejecting the Federation's overtures—speak to the more anarchist and worker feminism that dominated the organization. While there is some agreement on the need to support women's education and combat clerical influence, the language is much more militant and in keeping with older anarchist traditions. Although stating a preference for nonviolent struggle and "licit" means of combating social prejudice, the statutes imply a willingness to use violence in self-defense and other unlawful means of attacking social convention if necessary. The program also states that "this association does not desire to separate itself from the male progressive movement; on the contrary, its purpose is to join forces in order to make up for a deficient female presence."[97] The decision whether to work within or outside male political structures, and to organize primarily along class lines or gender lines, will continue to be a differentiating feature between anticlerical feminisms. Liberal feminists generally sought to work independently from (male) political parties, while anarchist and socialist feminists usually insisted on inclusion and integration.

Women's suffrage was another area dividing feminist groups. For the anarchists, the ballot box was the tool of the bourgeois exploiters, and not the primary arena of political and class struggle. The vote was a diversion, a distraction, and an attempt by the bourgeoisie to co-opt working women and divide them from their male comrades. Thus while it did define itself as a feminist organization, struggling for women's rights, Emancipación continued to also define itself as an "antisuffragist" association acting in favor of working-class women. While the Federation held its meetings in the Ateneo de Montevideo, a local gathering spot for intellectuals, Emancipación held its meetings at the headquarters of the Electrical Workers' Union. The latter group emphasized the need to struggle alongside working-class women, particularly the organizing drive of seamstresses which was ongoing at that time. Emancipación also started organizing telephone operators, a relatively new profession that employed mostly young native-born women. The group even taunted the more middle-class supporters of the Federation, at one point inviting "all women, especially those who suffer under the weight of economic privilege, to participate in feminist struggles."[98] These slings and arrows went in both directions, as partisans of both groups traded veiled insults and sarcastic praise on the pages of *El Día* for several months after the split. It appears, in general, that the Uruguayan branch of the Federation was relatively dormant, while Emancipación continued its activity under anarchist (and Socialist) leadership.

Socialist Party women initially worked with anarchist women and participated in Emancipación, but subsequent divisions further splintered the radical anticlerical feminist camp. María Casal y Canda, for example, was a member of Emancipación and an organizer of feminist conferences for the Socialist Party. But as early as August 1911, *El Día* announced separate women's meetings, organized by Casal y Canda and held in the Socialist Center. Socialists and anarchists continued to work together through 1912, but Socialist Party calls for the creation of a separate Socialist women's organization were growing. By 1913 relations between anarchists and Socialists had become more strained, both within women's groups and in general. Early in the year, the Socialist Party paper *El Socialista* quit promoting Emancipación or listing it among its sponsored organizations. In July 1913, *El Socialista* published an attack on anarchist Virginia Bolten, accusing her and other anarchists of being dupes of the Batllistas, reproducing an alleged statement of Bolten's in which she praised the Batlle government as "progressive" and "unlike anything we have ever had in this country."[99] By the end of the year, the rift between Socialists and anarchists was wide open, with *El Socialista* publishing in large letters an attack on the anarchists for betraying the workers' movement, and calling on workers to reorganize their unions, sending the anarchists "to the devil."[100] From this point onward, we hear very little about anarchist women's organizations. Although it began under the anarchist umbrella, worker feminism had now passed almost entirely into the Marxist camp.

It seems that Emancipación did not survive the anarchist/Socialist split. The Socialists did carry out their plans to form their own organization, and in April of 1914 the *Agrupación Socialista Femenina* (Socialist Women's Group) was created. Among the new group's members was a young Julia Arévalo, who would go on to be a lifelong leader in the Socialist and later Communist parties. Born in the Uruguayan Department of Lavalleja in 1898, Arévalo's family came to Montevideo around 1906. She began working at the age of ten, mostly in a cigarette factory where she and her sister Hortensia were employed for many years. Arévalo's father was already a member of the Socialist Party when she joined in 1913, at the age of fifteen. By the time she helped found the Socialist Women's Group in 1914, she was already writing regularly for *El Socialista*. Her early columns betray her age and inexperience, but also her passion for the cause (at one point she refers to Parliamentarians as "rabid and deranged vampires").[101] Many of these early works contain crude, but eloquent, defenses of women's suffrage, corresponding with the presentation of the first women's suffrage bill by Héctor Miranda in July 1914. Arévalo systematically took on all of the objections raised: that women would have to serve in the military; that women's suffrage will serve the interests of the Catholic Church; that it will cause division in the family and between husbands and wives, etc. Thus the Socialists, while rejecting the reformism and charity-oriented focus of the "bourgeois" (i.e., liberal) feminists, did share the liberals' endorsement of women's suffrage, something that clearly distinguished them from their anarchist foremothers.

Chapter One

Conclusion

By the end of Batlle's second term in 1915, the three main poles of Uruguayan feminism—Christian, socialist, and liberal—were clearly identifiable. While we can distinguish these three separate strands, the lines of demarcation between these groups were never very clear. Catholic "Christian" feminists maintained a united organizational front during these years, and espoused a distinct version of feminism that saw religion (specifically Roman Catholicism) as the source of women's salvation and emancipation. The history of anticlerical feminist organizing, on the other hand, is complex, messy even, and no similar unity was maintained. Some of the issues separating different types of anticlerical feminism were real and undoubtedly substantial. The divisions between Emancipación and the Pan-American Federation, for example, centered on the desirability of women's suffrage and whether and how to work politically with men. As of 1915, women's suffrage was still a controversial topic among feminists, and would remain so in later years. Anarchist feminists disagreed with electoral strategies in principle and saw women's suffrage as potentially disruptive of the labor movement. Wounded by accusations that women's cheap labor had weakened and undermined the labor movement, many were keenly sensitive about any hint that they were not in full solidarity with their male comrades. While liberal feminists generally sought to create their own autonomous organizations, ostensibly separate from any (male) political forces, anarchist and socialist feminists generally insisted that women's emancipation was part of the larger project of social emancipation, and that women should work within the larger party or movement. Thus the suffrage question was intimately connected to the issue of working-class solidarity and thus to the rejection of any kind of separatist strategy on the part of radical women. Historian Universindo Rodríguez Díaz, for one, has lamented the lost opportunities resulting from this split in anticlerical feminist ranks. Uruguayan women missed a golden opportunity, he argued, to take advantage of the possibilities offered by Batllismo. Speaking of the tensions between Emancipación and the Pan-American Federation, he wrote:

> The programmatic differences between the two feminist organizations prevented the development of a joint action that would have effectively unified their efforts, during a time when conditions existed—a popular movement in a clear state of reorganization, the existence of feminist

organizing, the presence of Batllismo in the government—that could have allowed for significant progress... and improvements in the situation.[102]

Catholic women, on the other hand, took a slightly different approach. In keeping with older traditions of female participation in the church (i.e., convents, etc.), the Liga maintained an all-female organization, generally under the direction of a male leadership (both clergy and lay Catholics), preserving paternalistic structures even while (timidly) critical of them. Because of their class and family status, elite women derived certain privileges and authority from traditional paternalistic relations. In a new order based on the autonomous male citizen and state-sponsored social assistance, these women may well have experienced a decline in their prestige and position.

The state played an important role in this history. If Catholic women became active in part because of Batllismo, some anticlerical women (such as María Abella) may have remained inactive because of it. In the anticlerical camp, it appears to have been the radicals (anarchists and later Socialists) who drove things forward, compelling the more moderate Batllista liberals to jump on board or miss the boat altogether. The relatively low level of activity of those most loyal to Batllismo highlights the contradictions of the Uruguayan state, where reformers sought to forge a paternalistic feminism that handed out reforms from above, and may have understood that any awakening of civil society could be its undoing. Finally, this history underscores how much Uruguayan feminism was the hybridized product of international ideas and movements, and local historical, political, and social conditions. It also underscores the blurred boundaries between local and foreign. Who was more relevant to Uruguayan women's history? The Spanish freethinker who organized women in the Uruguayan interior, or the Uruguayan who worked mostly in Argentina? The Spanish-born wealthy conservative who defended Catholicism as part of national culture, or the Uruguayan working-class radical who advocated socialism and anticlericalism as the best solution for her country? We will return to these questions of birthplace, identity, and feminist genealogies in Uruguay in subsequent chapters, but it is already clear that these issues resist simple conceptualizations.

Chapter Two
Batllista Ideology and Policy: Gender, Class, and the Politics of Compensation, 1910–1933

> TEACHER [Maestra]: "Johnny, let's see if you can solve this math problem: if four men worked eleven hours a day..."
> JOHNNY: "I would report it immediately to the Labor Office."
> — *Mundo Uruguayo*, *5 February 1919*

> MATTERS OF DIVORCE:
> At a table at the Parque Hotel:
> — "There goes my first husband with his new wife."
> — "And who is she?"
> — "Don't you remember? She's the first wife of my second husband."
> — *Mundo Uruguayo*, *26 February 1920*

Culled from reader submissions and other sources, the jokes published regularly in the weekly magazine *Mundo Uruguayo* suggest some of the perceptions and concerns of the middle and upper classes that made up its principal readership. The first selection above speaks to the newly important place of the state in Uruguayan society. Both the schoolteacher and the Labor Office reflect this new public presence, and the joke itself indirectly addresses some of the anxieties provoked by shifting class and gender relations in this new society. The schoolteacher represents an increasingly feminized middle-class public employee, while the male student arguably symbolizes a newly conscious citizenry, informed as to its rights and viewing the state as a defender against abuse. The second selection deals with divorce and apprehensions concerning shifting gender relations and the family. Still heavily restricted in most Latin American countries, the availability of divorce in Uruguay was a unique regional feature at this time. While there were still strong taboos against it, divorce was becoming more acceptable and commonplace by 1920. In this joke a woman, seated at a well-known casino and nightspot, speaks in a cavalier way about her revolving-door marriages, probably to another woman. Much had changed in Uruguay during the first two decades of the twentieth century, and those changes were alternately and simultaneously invigorating, inspiring, frightening, and offensive to diverse members of Uruguayan society.

The previous chapter concluded with a discussion of feminist organizing during Batlle's second presidential term (1911–1915), when the truly significant changes associated with Batllismo took place. During this era, women's activism and especially liberal feminism acquired a complex relationship with the state, and we can clearly see the links between Uruguay's precocious welfare state and feminist discourses and activities. But in order to understand women's political organizing and the history of feminism in Uruguay, it is important to explore the specific class/gender politics of Batllismo and the ways it helped to shape women's activism and engagement with the political process. This chapter provides an overview of the gender ideology and key policies of the Batllista era affecting women and gender relations. This material demonstrates why Uruguay earned a reputation for being a "model country" and Latin America's first welfare state, and the unique context this provided for those seeking to challenge the boundaries of citizenship and create a more inclusive, democratic polity. This era saw unprecedented spaces open up for women and new rights and protections for working people, but Batllismo remained fundamentally top-down and hierarchical in its approach. In this paradigm, rooted in older paternalistic traditions, class inequality and gender inequality were viewed largely through the same lens, and the woman question and the social question were two sides of the same coin.

Batllismo, Paternalism, and Citizenship

Reforms associated with the *estado batllista* began during Batlle's first presidential term, but it was during the last years of the interim Williman administration (1907–1911) and especially during Batlle's second presidency (1911–1915) that the most progressive legislation associated with Batllismo was implemented. A laundry list of reforms introduced and passed during the years 1910–1915 alone is impressive, testimony to the utopian flavor of this era: the eight-hour day and old-age pensions for many workers; the establishment of free secondary education and the extension of rural education; and the creation of a National Public Assistance that sought to bring universal care to the poor and infirm were among the more important social and labor reforms. The state came to play a larger role in the economy as well, creating a public electrical and insurance monopoly and a national railroad, and placing (limited) restrictions on foreign capital and large landholdings. Lastly, there were also a series of laws addressing women's place in the family, the workplace, and women's political rights, which this chapter will discuss in more detail.

Following Batlle's first term, the presidency of Claudio Williman (1907–1911) was a mostly conservative interlude, more known for its repression of the labor movement than for any progressive social legislation. The National Public Assistance Law of 1910 was a notable exception, however, furthering the secular state-building project that began in Batlle's first presidential term, and laying important ideological and discursive groundwork for the reforms that would take place in his second. The Uruguayan Public Assistance Law established the notion of the right to universal care, declaring that "anyone... indigent or lacking resources has the right to free assistance at the expense of the state."[1] The law created a government body, the *Asistencia Pública Nacional* (National Public Assistance or APN), charged with overseeing the implementation of the provisions of the 1910 law. The guarantee of the right to free assistance at the expense of the state set Uruguay apart from its neighbors in the Americas in the 1910s and 1920s.[2] In fact, as late as 1922 APN Director Miguel Becerro de Bengoa claimed that Uruguay was "the only country in the world with an organism with characteristics such as our own Public Assistance, [with both] the legal right of the poor to free assistance, and the centralization of a Directorship of Assistance for the entire country."[3]

The Public Assistance Law is a clear example of Batllista political ideology and its vision for state/society relations. The estado batllista was conceived of and positioned as a mediator between conflicting groups, one where the state had an obligation to favor those least able to defend themselves. Batlle once defined his project and his party as the *"escudo de los débiles"* or the "shield of the weak," where "weak" had age, class, and gender components.⁴ This was, in other words, a modernized (state-centered, secular) paternalism with Batlle as its figurehead. The keyword for all of Batllista social policy was *compensation*: the state was to compensate for social and economic inequalities so as to promote social harmony and order. This conceptualization is in evidence as early as the 1910 Public Assistance Law. While characterizing its project as "contrary to the principles of Christian charity and also contrary to the teachings of the individualistic schools," the APN defined the right to assistance guaranteed in the 1910 law as *"compensation for social injustices and a consequence of the solidarity that exists between men"*(emphasis added).⁵

There was a clear connection between the class project of Batllismo and its particular brand of feminism. Nowhere was this ideology of compensation made more explicit than in the theories of "compensation feminism" explicated in the writings of Carlos Vaz Ferreira, Batllismo's most important philosopher. Vaz Ferreira's theories were based on the principle of sexual difference, and on the premise that human beings "belong to a species organized physiologically to the detriment of the female." Gender inequality, in other words, was biologically determined, and thus immutable and permanent. Vaz Ferreira criticized those who sought women's total legal equality with men because, in his view, this ill-informed approach would only exacerbate the situation. In denying the reality of women's biological disadvantage, he wrote, these "feminists of equality" do women a disservice by underestimating their need for legal protection from the state, leaving them vulnerable to abuse and society subject to a state of potentially dangerous disequilibrium. This did not mean that women's oppression was inevitable, or even desirable, however. Vaz Ferreira was equally critical of those he called "anti-feminists" who, for religious or other reasons, defended the status quo and saw women's oppression and exploitation as part of the natural order of things. Besides being unjust, he argued, this position too leaves women unprotected and undermines societal harmony. In contraposition to these two poles, Vaz Ferreira lauded the so-called good feminists: those who recognized and acknowledged women's biological disadvantage and sought to "do whatever they can to correct or compensate for it." Vaz Ferreira argued that the ideals of "compensation feminism," where the state acts to "correct or compensate" for women's natural disadvantages, would improve the lot of women and of society as a whole.⁶

Figure 5:
José Batlle y Ordóñez, c.1920. Reprinted from William B. Parker, *Uruguayans of Today* (London/ New York: The Hispanic Society of America, 1921).

Vaz Ferreira's theories of "compensation feminism" underlay much of Batllista legislation dealing with women and gender issues. In many ways, the form in which Vaz Ferreira envisioned intervention to protect women from men served to reconfirm women's dependency, just as labor policies reinforced the dependency of labor on capital.[7] Here the woman question became qualitatively inseparable from the social question.[8] One need only replace "women" with "working class" and "men" with "capital" to arrive at the basic paradigm of the Batllista welfare state, where the state sought not to challenge the capitalist system itself, but to "compensate" for labor's vulnerability to abuse at the hands of capital through proactive intervention. The goal was a reordered secular paternalism, in which inequalities would exist but not be exploited, and in which the state (rather than the church) would act as arbiter and judge of unequal social relations.

Batllista policy focused on two groups among the "weak": urban workers and women, although these categories were hardly regarded in the same way. By the time of Batlle's return to power in 1911, the labor movement had become a more substantial force in Uruguayan society. Batllistas saw greater worker protection as a way to bring about social harmony and engage moderate organized labor as an ally of the state while marginalizing its more radical elements. Just as Batllistas believed in greater worker protections, so they believed that society would benefit from a modification and expansion of women's traditional roles. Thus while Batlle defended the rights of workers to organize and strike on the pages of *El Día*, he also defended women's right to an education and to participate in the political system. As the editor of *El Día*, he often wrote columns using the pseudonym "Laura"; as early as 1912, Laura was calling for women's political rights. But while Batlle believed in the principle of women's suffrage and equal rights, he felt that the Uruguayan woman was not yet ready to exercise full citizenship, that she required further preparation in the form of education, experience, and liberation from clerical influence before she would be ready to participate in the political sphere on an equal footing with men. Thus while adult male workers were approached as autonomous agents vis-à-vis the state, most women were viewed as passive recipients of assistance, not quite mature enough to be entrusted with the rights and responsibilities of citizenship. This passive/active dichotomy will cut across class lines as well, granting middle-class women more entitlements than her poor and working-class counterparts. In sum, Batllismo was profoundly ambivalent about power and inequality, speaking both the language of social justice and equality and the language of paternalistic protection of the "weak" by the "strong."

The "Shield" Applied: Compensation Feminism and Social Policy, 1911–1915

Silvia Rodríguez Villamíl and Graciela Sapriza have observed that Batllista gender ideology contained "two seemingly antagonistic tendencies": protective "gentlemanly paternalism" on the one hand, and a championing of women's rights on the other.[9] Indeed, Batllista legislation on the woman question fit largely into two categories: laws aimed at shielding women from excessive exploitation and abuse at the hands of husbands, lovers, and employers, and those aimed at the expansion of women's opportunities and at the achievement of equal rights. Both in theory and in practice, Batllismo made clear distinctions between wealthy and/or professional women on the one hand, and poor and working-class women on the other, and it was much more likely to be the protector of the former and the champion of the latter. Educated and/or well-off women were more capacitated and further along the road to full citizenship than their less-educated and more working-class sisters, who were still too servile and oppressed to act as full members of the public sphere.

Batlle did understand the obstacles that traditional gender relations and notions of female honor represented for women seeking educational and professional advancement. These individual obstacles were also barriers that the state had to overcome if it wished to incorporate middle-class women into the Batllista project. Building upon earlier models that envisioned a key role for women in the expanding secular state, Batllismo sought to use the power of the state to counteract some of these restrictions on women's advancement, a position solidly within the framework of compensation feminism. Shortly after he assumed the presidency in March 1911, Batlle proposed a kind of affirmative action for women in the public sector. The legislation proposed that "managers should exercise a preference for members of the female sex when filling vacancies for appropriate positions.... The intention of this project is to give women, as much as possible, a role in the general activities of the administration."[10] The law was never approved, but it set the tone for the Batllista state's preferential option for women, especially middle-class educated women. Perhaps as an example of its commitment to women's public employment, Clotilde Luisi, Paulina's sister and the first woman lawyer in Uruguay, was named diplomatic attaché to Belgium later in 1911. The *London Times* noted: "Uruguay is probably the only country in the world that may boast of having a lady in its diplomatic service."[11] These early actions were an inspiration to some and an ominous sign to others, but many years would pass before women began to make any significant inroads into the state bureaucracies.

The educational infrastructure posed a serious obstacle to Batlle's plan to incorporate women into the state project. Women's education had expanded a great deal in the late nineteenth century, but there were still powerful impediments to women's access to higher education. While the teacher-training institutions created in the late nineteenth century gave women important new opportunities to seek economic independence as schoolteachers, a normal school education was mostly a dead end.[12] Furthermore, many families hesitated to send their daughters to traditional institutions of secondary education, where they would intermingle with a mostly male student body. As a result, women were largely relegated to a separate educational track, one coded as inferior and channeling them into careers as public schoolteachers. While some, such as the Luisi sisters, overcame these institutional obstacles, moving from the normal school to the university and professional degrees, the existing structure meant that in the short run only a brave, unconventional few were likely to follow in their footsteps. In 1912, for example, there were several thousand female schoolteachers (nearly 90 percent of all schoolteachers in public schools by this time), yet there were only about one hundred women enrolled in traditional secondary schools, and only fifty of the eight hundred students attending the National University at this time were women.[13]

Batlle responded by overseeing the creation of the *Sección de Enseñanza Secundaria y Preparatoria*, better known as the *Universidad de Mujeres* or Women's University. In June 1911 Batlle spoke before Congress in favor of the university project. Here he reiterated a common theme in his policy toward women—that women's position in a society was the best barometer of the level of civilization that society has attained. Uruguay, with all its high aspirations in this regard, still lagged behind the "civilized" world, especially in terms of women's education. Continuing prejudice existing within society was the main reason very few women studied at the secondary level:

> The meagerness of female attendance must be attributed principally to the fact that the majority of families resist sending girls...to pursue secondary studies in the University, where however much attention is paid by the respective authorities, strict vigilance or the effective protection of parents and teachers is not possible.[14]

Creating a Women's University, he concluded, would allow women to obtain a higher education without placing their honor at risk. The legislative debate over the creation of the Women's University went on for many months, and provoked a good deal of debate in the public arena over the question of women's education and, more broadly, women's intellectual capacities. Critics argued that it was a waste of money and effort to try to educate and elevate beings who were inherently intellectually inferior. In response to this charge, "Laura" (Batlle) wrote in *El Día* in April 1912:

> The debate between man and woman over who is more intelligent cannot be justly resolved, until such time as both find themselves in the same conditions, that is, when both are educated in the same manner, encouraged with the same determination, and surrounded by the same liberty.[15]

Batlle did not really take a strong stand here on the question of women's intellectual capabilities vis-à-vis men; he merely asserted that the conditions have not been created to be able to answer the question of women's abilities aptly and fully. Compensation feminism never asserted women's full equality, just her need for elevation from her current state.

The university did represent a departure from the limited educational opportunities previously available to Uruguayan women, however, and in that sense challenged traditional gender roles and domains. While the institution did offer courses on sewing, childcare, and the like, it also provided a general preparatory and secondary curriculum in fields such as mathematics, natural history, and chemistry. Precisely what was at stake here is best read in the words of one congressional opponent to the project. Luis Melián Lafinur, a liberal of the old guard, agreed that the Women's University would promote women's citizenship and her presence in the public sphere, but saw this as a running counter to the economic and political needs of society. "Although having educated women citizens [*ciudadanas ilustradas*] would be nice, what we really need are male citizens [*ciudadanos*]." And this, in his reasoning, was something of a zero-sum game. "The entry of women into scientific careers and public employment," Melián Lafinur argued, "displaces the male citizen who, finding no work, emigrates." Not only did educated women "become haughty" and "neglect labors appropriate to their sex," they effectively emasculated the nation by making Uruguay inhospitable terrain for male workers, both immigrant and creole.[16] Despite this and other opposition, however, the proposal was approved, and the Women's University opened its doors in April 1913. "Gentlemanly paternalism" and "champion of women's rights," it seems, could coexist in the same legislation, especially that which was aimed at middle- and upper-class women.

Chapter Two

Figure 6:
Women's education had become more widespread and accessible by the 1910s: the *Escuela de Aplicación de Señoritas* (Young Women's Applied School), Montevideo, 1914. Reprinted from *Enciclopédia Uruguzya* no. 38 (1969) with permission from Editorial Arca.

As Melián Lafinur predicted, women took advantage of new educational opportunities provided by the state.[17] Uruguayan women used the university to prove their intellectual abilities, and the Women's University itself became an important incubator of liberal feminist ideas. Women who stood as models of feminine achievement in their professional fields were the institution's leaders. The first dean of the university was Clotilde Luisi, sister to Paulina and the Uruguayan diplomat mentioned above. Another Luisi sister, Inés—a physician like her older sister—served as dean from 1922 to 1928. Both subsequently joined their sister's liberal feminist movement. The women who attended and ran this institution had become citizens (ciudadanas ilustradas) in important ways, but were still blocked from full political participation. It must certainly have appeared absurd and unjust that a lawyer was deemed unfit to witness a legal document, or that the dean of a public university was unable to vote in national elections. Not surprisingly, many of the early calls for women's suffrage were based implicitly or explicitly on this fact: that educational achievement and service to the nation had proven women worthy of full citizenship rights.

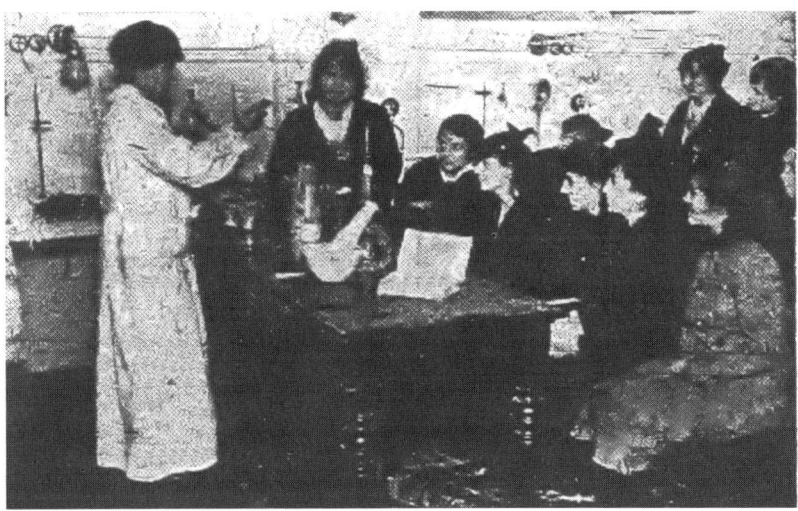

Figure 7:
Experimental Chemistry Class, Women's University, c.1915. Reprinted from *El Día*, 21 September 1915.

Batllista projects addressing the woman question were not limited to expanding women's educational opportunities and political rights. Some of the most important—and controversial—legal changes in this arena dealt with the question of women and the family. One of the most unique pieces of legislation—and one of the best examples of compensation feminism in practice—was the divorce law of 1913. This law was an amendment to the 1907 legalization of absolute divorce that had prompted the formation of the Liga de Damas Católicas several years earlier. This new divorce legislation faithfully reflected the new compensation paradigm. It began as a 1912 proposal to allow divorce on the "simple will" of either spouse, eliminating equally for men and women the need to prove grounds for divorce if the other party were opposed. But it soon became obvious that the proposed legislation was destined for defeat on the Senate floor, due in large part to the perception that the law would "leave women powerless in the face of male libertinism."[18] Men already had de facto possession of the right to divorce at will, it was argued, and the state should not be in the business of making it even easier for husbands to abandon their wives. The law was thus modified, and the language changed to allow for divorce "on the simple will of the woman."[19] Husbands were still required to prove grounds under a unilateral divorce petition, while the

Figure 8:
Professors at the Women's University, c.1918. Pictured, front row center, Clotilde Luisi, the first dean of the university. To her left is Francisca Beretervide, dean, c. 1917–1922. Reprinted from *Nuestra Causa* (Buenos Aires), 18 July 1918.

courts would grant a divorce to a wife based simply on her stated desire to end her marriage. The result was a legal first: legal scholar Ricardo Gallardo called the Uruguayan law a "form of divorce unique in its genre, not only among legislation in Latin America, but also in the world."[20] Vaz Ferreira called this "his law"; believing the original proposal would have harmful consequences for women, he was instrumental in brokering the compromise bill. This legislation reflects the ideals of compensation feminism in that it was premised upon the unequal status of husband and wife within society and sought to compensate for that inequality to protect the woman. It also illustrates the way that the state was willing to intervene in the family on behalf of women at the same time and in the same way as it was intervening in the factory and the workshop on behalf of labor.

The Uruguayan state also sought to protect those victimized by long-standing traditions of concubinage and illegitimacy. In 1914, legislation was passed granting illegitimate children (and by extension their mothers) expanded rights to their father's wealth. Under the old (pre-1914) version of the law, illegitimate children could only sue for recognition under the conditions of kidnapping and rape (i.e., when impregnation occurred during the commission of a crime).[21] The 1914 amendment greatly expanded the conditions under which such a legal procedure could occur. Under this "investigation of paternity" legislation, a woman could ask the court to declare a man the father of her child, and require him to provide for that child's financial support. The new law also applied to inheritance, but only the child, not the mother, had access to the father's estate. Lacking means of scientific proof, evidence of paternity focused on the alleged father's behavior toward the child and known circumstances surrounding his relationship with the mother. Thus the state could make a finding of paternity when the father had provided for the support and education of the child in a public way and for at least a year; when the father was living openly with the mother at the time of conception; when conception coincided with a promise of marriage; or when the father had recognized paternity in writing.[22] While this legislation was aimed more directly at children than at women, it nonetheless fits within the larger gender project of Batllismo. Because these situations often involved fathers of higher social class than the mothers of their illegitimate children, this law had both class and gender dimensions, and thus spoke to both the social question and the woman question simultaneously. More specifically, it aimed at reinforcing paternalistic responsibilities, and at curbing the ability of those with power in society from abusing their privileges.

Not unexpectedly, the new paternity law struck deep at the anxieties of the affluent classes. Many wealthy families had likely reason to be concerned about the possible past indiscretions of male figureheads, and now faced the possibility that those indiscretions could result in sharing the family estate with "illegitimate" heirs. Others feared false charges from unscrupulous pretenders to their fortune, and legal proceedings that could irreparably damage their honor and public standing. In September 1918 such a case made headlines for a week in *El Día*, when apparently false claims were made against the estate of "millionaire" Francisco Pérez. This complicated case captivated Montevideo. In the course of the investigation, allegations of fraudulent testimony and coerced witnesses began to surface, with the result that many of the actors in the plaintiff's case were arrested. This incident provoked renewed calls for the revocation of the investigation of paternity law, based on claims that it threatened the sanctity of the family and encouraged blackmailers and other unsavory types to make false claims on the inheritance of "honorable" families. The editors of *El Día* and others rigorously defended the law, reminding readers that the law "repairs a flagrant social injustice."[23] That such a case made headlines during a time of deep economic crisis and heightened class and social conflict is telling. It served as an indication that the "national family," if it ever existed, was closing ranks along class lines.

The "Alto de Viera" and the End of Reform

Until 1915, one of the most effective and mobilized segments of Uruguayan society was organized labor, which overcame the repression of the Williman years and enjoyed a resurgence in activity and militancy after 1911. Although Batllista reforms were certainly very top-down, one should not discount the role of labor militancy in the acquisition of key labor reforms of this era. But these conditions were only temporary, and by the end of Batlle's second term conservative opponents of reform were making their influence felt in the political arena. Although one could make the case that the Catholic Ladies' League was one of the earliest examples of anti-Batllista elite organizing, the creation in 1915 of the *Federación Rural* (Rural Federation), a landowners' association, best exemplifies this political awakening of the conservative and elite sectors.[24] The leadership of the Federación Rural, many of the wealthiest and most powerful landowners in the country, entered directly into government and the political parties during this decade as well.

The main issue that galvanized the anti-Batllista opposition, and provoked a split in the Colorado Party, was Batlle's proposal to include the creation of a plural executive (or *Colegiado*) in the new Constitution. Initially proposed in 1913, the Colegiado would have replaced the individual president with a nine-member executive committee. This was a proposal that would have divested power from any single individual and all but assured Colorado Party dominance over the Uruguayan state for years to come. Opposition to the proposal was swift and fierce, and the Colegiado soon became the issue around which Batllista and anti-Batllista forces rallied their supporters. Joining the Blanco opposition was a more conservative, anti-Colegialist Colorado faction (known as the Riveristas), created in 1916. Only the Socialist Party joined the Batllistas in supporting the plan for a plural executive.

In September 1915, universal male suffrage was approved for the first time in the election of members of the Constitutional Convention of 1916–1917. What transpired surprised everyone involved: the anti-Colegiado forces—made up of the Blanco (National) Party, the Catholic Civic Union Party, and the dissident Riverista Colorados—won a majority of votes against the proreform Batllistas and Socialists. This vote, which mobilized and politicized Uruguayans in unprecedented ways, was considered a plebiscite on Batllismo generally, and the results interpreted as a public consensus that the process of reform had gone far enough (although a modified version of the plural executive did exist between 1919 and 1934). The immediate consequence of this historic election was the famous *"alto de Viera"* delivered by then President Feliciano Viera at a Colorado Party Convention in August 1916:

> The advanced economic and social laws of the last legislative sessions, have alarmed many *correligionarios* [coreligionaries: members of the same party] and it was they who denied us their support in the elections of the thirtieth. Fine, sirs: we will not advance any more in matters of economic and social legislation; we will reconcile capital with the worker. We have moved rather quickly; we will take a pause in the journey.[25]

Largely unsuccessful attempts at further conservative unification meant that the "alto" would remain largely that: a halt in the expansion of the reform process rather than a rolling back of existing legislation.

It was in this era of preparations for the 1917 Constitutional Convention, growing conservative opposition to Batllista reforms, and the emergence of "modern pressure groups" that the National Women's Council, the first liberal feminist organization in Uruguay, was founded. Although passed over in more traditional histories, the emergence of feminist organizations was part of the same process of the modernization of Uruguayan politics traditionally associated with the Federación Rural and working-class mobilization. During this reform era, women, too, entered the fray, struggling over the place that women's rights would have in this process of redefining the role of the state in society. The Constitution of 1917 (which went into effect in 1919) provided for universal male suffrage and the separation of church and state, among other provisions. It also specifically provided for the recognition of women's suffrage, pending ratification by two-thirds of both legislative houses. Francesca Miller notes that the 1917 Constitution made Uruguay, "in theory, the first of all Western Hemisphere nations to recognize female suffrage."[26] But while historians have correctly identified this as evidence of Uruguayan progressivism, it also effectively meant that suffrage could not be enacted by the Colorado Party alone, and had to await some consensus among more conservative factions. Although it would be another fifteen years before this ratification occurred, this constitutional language made women's suffrage, in Lavrin's words, a "mesmerizing near reality," raising expectations and facilitating the mobilization of women across the political spectrum.[27] During those intervening years, feminist organizations and others debated the relative importance of women's vote within a variety of distinct and sometimes conflicting feminist agendas, and speculated about how much and in what ways women's suffrage would affect the broader political panorama in Uruguay.

Uruguay under the New Constitution: Ideology and Policy, 1919–32

The postwar crisis of 1918–1919 created deep social polarizations that helped pave the way for a brief return to the reformist ideas and politics of the Batllista era. While the anti-Batllista Riveristas continued to make important gains, the economic crisis of the postwar years saw a new upsurge in labor militancy. The candidacy of thirty-five-year-old Baltasar Brum represented an attempt by some Colorados to swing the pendulum back in the direction of reform rather than retrenchment. Brum had long been an open defender of women's equality in the political and legal sphere, and many feminists were hopeful that a Brum presidency would bring important gains. In July 1919, *Nuestra Causa*, a Socialist-affiliated Argentine magazine, published a special issue on the women's movement in Uruguay. One of the articles, entitled simply "A Feminist President," profiled the newly elected Brum. In this article, Brum spoke of women's elevation and expanded political and civil rights as part of the historical process of modernization and civilization, thus underscoring his ideological continuity with his predecessors on the "woman question." An admirer of the United States, Brum wrote that one of the things he esteemed most about this "model country" was the level of education of its women, something that "has made that democracy one of the most active, powerful and well organized propelling forces in the world." He also clearly connected the woman question to the social question, linking—as did Varela before him—the historical emancipation of woman with that of the class emancipation brought about through Enlightenment-era notions of the universal rights of man:

> One can thus affirm that if the French Revolution produced the recognition of the rights of man, the great war [World War One] that just ended with the complete

triumph of justice, democracy and honor will lead to the universal recognition of the rights of women, that is to say, in the equal rights of all human beings.[28]

One of the big projects of Brum's presidency was a massive study of the Uruguayan Civil, Penal, and Commercial codes, a main goal of which was to remove all double standards and language that put women on an unequal legal status with men. The proposal comprehensively took on existing legal language in areas such as marriage, divorce, adultery, property rights, and even military service. "As a blueprint for change," Lavrin has noted, "the report was brilliant and had no rival anywhere in South America." One of Brum's goals in the reform of the civil codes was to create legal symmetry, giving husbands and wives equal responsibilities and obligations within marriage. As an example, Lavrin cites Article 128, in which men were obliged to provide "protection" to their wives, and wives in turn owed "obedience" to their husbands. The committee proposed to change this language to read instead "spouses owe each other reciprocal respect and protection."[29] Brum also sought to revise the 1913 divorce law, returning it to its original language allowing for divorce on the simple will of either spouse. While the proposed reforms were ambitious and sought to put Uruguay back on track as a South American utopia, this was not to be the case. Brum's proposals were formally brought before the legislature toward the end of his term in 1923, but met with a cool reception and basically went nowhere. The only feminist policy change dating to the Brum years was the 1926 law (passed after Brum had left office), which allowed women to legally hold the position of notary and to act as legal witnesses in most cases, something for which liberal feminists had lobbied heavily. It was an important step in a strategy of incrementally increasing women's citizenship status.

Brum's ideological stance moved noticeably away from the ideals of compensation feminism espoused by Vaz Ferreira and Batlle toward one based more on gender equality. But this was still reform from above, focused on anticipating (and preempting) rather than responding to social mobilization. After his presidency, Brum continued to develop his ideas concerning liberal feminism, and in 1925 published a book outlining his thoughts on the topic in great detail. *Los derechos de la mujer* (Women's Rights) laid out the history of past women's rights legislation in Uruguay, and presented Brum's specific program for continuing along that road to women's emancipation. It also underscores the way that Brum, like Batlle, used the woman question to endorse the paternalistic and partisan traditions of the Colorado Party. After listing several initiatives by Colorado politicians in favor of women's rights, Brum came to two interrelated conclusions: one, that "the initiative of recognizing women's civil and political rights, integrally corresponds to the Colorado Party," and two, in Uruguay "public men have taken it upon themselves to repair the situation, without waiting on feminine solutions." Brum still placed the issue of women's rights clearly within the paternalistic rubric of Batllismo, claiming that Uruguay was one of the few nations where change had come from above (i.e., made by men) without a "difficult and painful struggle" of women (i.e., from below). It was better, he claimed, to grant women's suffrage before a real movement got started: under such circumstances, where women were less mobilized, they would be less likely to vote, and thus implementation would have a less disruptive effect.

While Brum's feminism remained rather circumscribed, he did make an articulate defense of women's suffrage. Brum rejected the notion that as voters women would be puppets of the Catholic Church, arguing that women were much more likely to vote in the interests of "the husband, father, brother, fiancé or lover" rather than to follow their priest. The notion that women might vote autonomously, independent of male direction and persuasion, seemed unlikely. Moreover, while Brum defended women's right to vote, at no time did he entertain the possibility that a woman might hold office. In sum, while his approach was more symmetrical and more equality based than Vaz Ferreira's, Brum clearly did not see women as equal to men, and saw women's full participation in politics as an undesirable outcome of feminist mobilization, which the timely enactment of prudent reforms could minimize or avoid altogether. The parallels with class politics could hardly be clearer: preemptive feminist legislation, like preemptive labor reform, would undercut the growth of any oppositional social movement and leave the state (and the party leadership) a freer hand with which to act.[30]

Polarization of the Late 1920s and the "Second Reformist Impulse," 1928–1933

Despite the pacifying efforts of the Batllistas, by the late 1920s the moderating forces within the state were disappearing. The foundation of the *Comité de Vigilancia Económica* (Committee of Economic Vigilance) in 1929, like the emergence of the Federación Rural fourteen years prior, represented the further consolidation of the economic elite and the emergence of a newly radicalized right in Uruguay. As in other neighboring countries, many conservatives and nationalists were inspired by the rise of fascism in Europe, and embraced its models as the best solution to Uruguay's domestic crisis.[31] At the same time the progressive wings of both parties joined forces to take advantage of the global economic crisis to further the statist project. Gabriel Terra's assumption of the presidency in early 1931 encouraged a further unification of conservative and reformist forces across party lines. The conservative classes saw Terra as a potential "second Viera," who could be persuaded to act as a buttress against reemerging reformist forces. Attempts by reformists to counter this move with their own political unification yielded temporary results, and the period 1928–1932 is known as the era of the so-called second reformist impulse. During this time a national *frigorífico* (meatpacking plant) and a state oil and alcohol monopoly were created. One of the last pieces of legislation of this era was women's suffrage, passed in December 1932.

But it would be another six years before Uruguayan women would actually get to exercise the vote. On the morning of March 31, 1933, members of the Assembly were denied entry into the Legislative Palace by troops loyal to the president and other top government officials were arrested. Newspapers were heavily censored, and many opposition leaders were imprisoned. The only death immediately linked to the coup was that of Baltasar Brum who, reportedly distraught by the lack of a popular uprising to resist Terra's coup d'état, committed suicide shortly thereafter. Luce Fabbri, the Italian-born anarchist activist during this time, described the events of 1933 in the following terms:

> [With the coup d'état] the situation changed radically, from one day to the next. Uruguay was a very, very free country.... In the early years, everybody lived their lives without the harassment of continuous surveillance.... But after [the coup], yes, one felt it a lot.[32]

Despite the coup, Uruguay retained its reputation as one of the few Latin American nations with a deeply rooted liberal democratic tradition, and one of the exceptions in a continent identified with economic inequality and authoritarian political structures. For many years, the 1933 coup was generally viewed as an anomaly.[33] After the military dictatorship of the 1970s and 1980s, however, historians have seen more continuity than aberration in these events. Gerardo Caetano and Raúl Jacob, for example, introduce their study of the Terra era with the assertion that "the events of March 31, 1933 demonstrated that, despite our peculiar formation and our uniqueness as a country, we could not escape our Latin American destiny."[34]

Conclusion

In *From Motherhood to Citizenship*, Nitza Berkovitch wrote: "it is clear that official rights cannot abolish patriarchy. But at the same time, official rights, state policy, and state action do participate in helping to shape the meaning of gender."[35] The extent to which Uruguay was ahead of many of its neighbors in areas of divorce, labor legislation, and women's suffrage is important for understanding the unique and specific context within which Uruguayan liberal feminism (and other women's movements) operated. Yet while the legislation passed during these years would have provided more options to at least some women in Uruguayan society, these laws were, in essence, compensation for the vulnerable and exploited in a society unwilling or unable to contemplate more fundamental changes. This chapter has demonstrated that the way reform-minded elites (Batllistas and Socialists) talked about class inequality and gender inequality was nearly interchangeable. Policy was designed and implemented based on this understanding, and women in general, just like workers of both sexes, both gained and lost ground under this model that granted them protection based both on the premise of their weakness and the promise of their docility.

In seeking to be a balm on social inequality, rather than challenging the foundations of that hierarchy and stratification, the Batllista state placed limits on women's advancement. Many feminists were in the middle of this paternalistic equation, encouraged by an environment that was challenging old restrictions and hierarchies, but also constrained by its hierarchical, compensatory approach to social policy. Liberal feminists in particular sought to take full advantage of this historical moment, challenging traditional restrictions on women's advancement, and, therefore, the boundaries of citizenship in this new era. As we will see in the next chapter, however, liberal feminists were nevertheless strongly connected to the Batllista state, and shared many of its ideological premises, limiting their own ability to challenge class/gender hierarchies and forge cross-class women's coalitions.

Chapter Three
Women and the "National Family": Education, Social Assistance, and the State

> We women are familiar with the ulcers of our societies, because it is almost always our hands which apply the balm. Social assistance and beneficence are our patrimony, and this work, like nothing else, has opened our eyes to the horrors that entrap our current civilization.... And we female physicians have seen even more.
> — *Paulina Luisi, speaking at a Scientific Conference in Buenos Aires, 1919*

> The general interest and sympathy provoked by the inauguration of the Casa de la Maternidad and the Maternal Protection Service of the National Public Assistance, awakened Montevidean society to the large number of mothers, married and unmarried, that, deprived of material and moral support, endure a precarious existence...[In response], a group of damas met in the Casa de la Maternidad on June 14, 1915 and...agreed to found an Association whose goal would be to bring together the means to alleviate such misery.
> — *Asociación Pro-Matre, Memoria 1916*

The quotes above speak to the links between state formation, social reform, and women's politics in Batllista Uruguay. In the first selection, Paulina Luisi identifies two groups of

Chapter Three

women—physicians like herself and women involved in social assistance—as the vanguard of both social reform and feminism. Their work brought these women out from behind the sheltering jalousies of bourgeois womanhood, exposing them to the social realities facing the poor and disenfranchised and to the inequalities and injustices of their society. For some, this new sanctioned public role sharpened their feminist consciousness and emboldened them to speak out on behalf of women's rights. As the second selection makes clear, the Uruguayan state also had a role to play in encouraging women's associational activity. Here, the women of the *Asociación Pro-Matre*, an organization founded in 1915 to assist poor unwed adult mothers, cited state projects and institutions as inspiring their decision to take a more active stand in social assistance. The state did not simply encourage by example; it provided significant financial resources subsidizing the work of Pro-Matre and other women's beneficent associations. In return, these associations were entrusted with carrying out social assistance, effectively making these women agents of the Batllista welfare state.

The previous chapter illustrated that the Batllista state was sympathetic to feminist ideals and sought to expand women's rights and societal roles, albeit in a rather top-down and paternalistic way. But, in addition to legal measures aimed at compensating for women's disadvantage in both public and private spheres, changes in state structure and policy also meant that more women were incorporated, directly or indirectly, into the infrastructure of the state itself. As schoolteachers and students, lawyers and physicians, and as the staff and leadership of state-supported social-assistance agencies, women were participating in the day-to-day functioning of the state in unprecedented ways. For some women, these new spaces were a platform and a passageway into (mostly liberal) feminist organizing. Social historical data allows us to trace the connections between state formation and feminism in more than theoretical ways, by looking at who exactly held membership in liberal feminist organizations. What the data reveals is that female professionals and women involved in social-assistance activity formed the backbone of liberal feminism in Uruguay. In the first group were women of the educated professional classes, from schoolteachers to lawyers and physicians: products of the Varelian schools and subsequent Batllista expansion in women's higher education. This included women, like Paulina Luisi, who were also strong proponents of state intervention as a means of protecting women and children from patriarchal domination. In the second group were mostly elite women, whose social-assistance work came under increased state sponsorship and control starting in the 1910s. Although they often had significantly divergent class backgrounds and political ideologies, both groups shared a new relationship with the state and a status as direct beneficiaries of Batllista-era policy.

This chapter shows how a combination of state policy and women's agency brought about important changes in the gendered definitions of citizenship and the public sphere, creating new relationships between certain groups of women and the Batllista state, which ultimately helped mobilize them under the liberal feminist banner. This chapter first explores the history of education, professionalism, and the state during the first third of the twentieth century. In the late nineteenth century, Varelian education reforms created new educational and professional opportunities for women, particularly as schoolteachers. During the Batllista era especially, many of these young female educators sought to push these boundaries even further, demanding access to higher learning and professional degrees and careers. And many of these pioneering professionals were also leading figures in Uruguayan liberal feminism. None better exemplifies this than Paulina Luisi, Uruguay's most important feminist leader and the subject of the first half of this chapter. This section serves both to introduce Luisi to the reader and to illustrate the ways in which her educational and professional background informed her feminism (and vice versa).

At the same time that Luisi and others were challenging the gendered barriers to higher education and professional careers, other women were becoming important players in the development of a broad-based, publicly subsidized social-assistance infrastructure. The previous chapter discussed the 1910 Public Assistance Law that created the Uruguayan National Public Assistance, or APN, an important first step in the professionalization of social assistance in Uruguay. A circle of elite women, many of whom had a good deal of prior experience in beneficence, were incorporated into the Batllista project in an attempt to bring coverage into line with the universal language of the Public Assistance Law. This largely transitional phase in the development of social assistance had an important transformational impact both on the Uruguayan welfare state and, I argue, on the political consciousness of many of the women involved. To these women and their organizations we will turn in the chapter's second half.

Chapter Three

Scholarly Women:
Paulina Luisi and the Clase Médica

One is struck, although perhaps not surprised, by the number of female professionals who appear on the rosters of the two main liberal feminist organizations active in Uruguay during this era (the National Women's Council and the Women's Suffrage Alliance). Among the women involved in these groups over the years 1916–1929, there were at least nine physicians, seven lawyers, six dentists, and three pharmacists. Most of these women received training at the University of the Republic or other public institutions of higher learning. While by the 1920s these numbers represented only a portion of the female lawyers, dentists, and pharmacists licensed and practicing in Uruguay, a high percentage (if not a majority) of female physicians were members at one time or another of one of the two main liberal feminist groups. This was a profession that was still heavily male dominated in the 1920s, with only a handful of women in practice.[1] As we learned previously, the liberal feminist movement was in fact headed up by the country's first female medical school graduate, Dr. Paulina Luisi. This section will focus on the personal, professional, and political persona of Luisi, and use her individual story to gain some insight into the ideology of the female professional as it was congealing in these years.[2]

Asunción Lavrin has written: "[Paulina] Luisi's professional career is almost a stereotype of the intense and passionate activity that developed within the first professional generation in Latin America."[3] She exemplifies like no other Uruguayan woman the complex relationships between education and professionalism, party politics, the state, and feminism in the Batllista era. As the symbolic mother of Uruguayan feminism, Luisi's life and politics remain the source of conjecture and controversy. Feminists and other scholars still debate her political affiliation, her autonomy from the Batllista state, and her impact on the lives of Uruguayan women. There is no question, however, about the extent of her accomplishments. The first female physician in Uruguay, Dr. Luisi was also the founder and leader of both the Uruguayan National Woman's Council and the Uruguayan Women's Suffrage Alliance, as well as a leader in international and Pan-American feminism during the 1920s. What is important for our purposes here is the degree to which Luisi reflects and embodies the process of state formation in Uruguay, and particularly its gendered meanings.

Paulina Clelia Leonia Luisi was born in 1875 in Entre Rios, Argentina, the first child of Angel Luisi and Josefa Janicki, recent immigrants from Europe. Angel was an Italian citizen and Josefa was of Polish descent, although Paulina would lay claim to more prestigious French blood in her maternal line.[4] Angel was politically active while in Europe, mostly via his Masonic affiliations, while Josefa was a teacher and the daughter of Polish exiles living in France. After they met and married in France, Angel and Josefa immigrated to Argentina, where Angel ran a Masonic bookstore for a time (he remained an active Mason for the rest of his life).[5] Shortly after Paulina was born, the family settled across the river in Paysandú, Uruguay, where she spent most of her childhood. In comparing her family and childhood to that of Durazno activist Otilia Schultze de Galarza, Paulina Luisi once wrote: "Like you, no baptism or religious marriage, [not for myself] nor for my dear parents, who have suffered pain and misery because of it."[6] This family environment surely had a strong influence on Paulina's life. The eldest of eight children, seven of them girls, Paulina was not the only Luisi sister to break new ground for Uruguayan women: her sister Clotilde became the first female lawyer in the country in 1911, while Inés became a physician and Luisa a well-known poet.

Not only were the Luisi daughters born to progressive and unconventional parents; they were born just as new possibilities for women's education were starting to open up in Uruguay. Over and above her parents' influence, Paulina was first and foremost a product of the academy, representative of a new generation of university-trained professional women with a strong commitment to feminist ideals. In 1879, when Paulina was four, Luisa Domínguez became the first woman to request an entrance exam for the University of the Republic; when she passed the exam with flying colors, she provoked praise and ridicule from the expected political quarters.[7] Paulina was seven years old when José Pedro Varela's Normal School for Girls opened in 1882. Five years later, the family moved to Montevideo, where Paulina earned her teaching degree in 1890. She completed a bachelor's degree in 1899, the first Uruguayan woman to earn such a title. Shortly thereafter, she entered medical school where she was the only woman.

Paulina Luisi's experiences in medical school surely helped shape her feminist consciousness and her stance toward male aggression and hostility. In a 1924 interview, she spoke of her experiences as the first woman in the medical school. She insisted that most professors and students were supportive, but that others tried to drive her out. "I remember one exam which was like a real duel," she reminisced. "But I knew I was prepared, and I defended myself tooth and nail.

They had to give me a high pass, even against the professor's recommendation."[8] It is reported she was harassed by her fellow students who, for example, reportedly left a human penis, severed from a cadaver, in the pocket of her lab coat. As the story goes, Luisi was completely nonplussed by this, and instead of the expected reaction of shame and horror, she waited until the end of class and—holding up the offending body part—asked her classmates "did one of you lose this?"[9] Not surprisingly, Luisi did not speak publicly about this incident. In 1924, when she was asked about hostility or harassment that she might have encountered in medical school, Luisi was circumspect: "Best not to say any more about that...boys games [*cosas de muchachos*]."[10] But upon completion of her studies, Luisi's gender was not always to her disadvantage. With a specialization in gynecology and obstetrics, she quickly built a successful practice, particularly since many women (and sometimes their husbands) were uncomfortable with the idea of a male gynecologist.[11]

Feminists in neighboring Argentina took notice of Luisi after she entered medical school, seeing in her a promising leader who could help get the feminist movement off the ground in Uruguay. While Luisi was still a student, Argentine liberal feminist Petrona Eyle wrote her in her capacity as president of the *Universitarias Argentinas*—the Argentine affiliate of the American Association of University Women (AAUW)—recruiting her to join their organization. Founded in 1902, the Universitarias was an important organization around which the ideology of the female professional as natural feminist leader coalesced in these years; it appears that Luisi and others in Uruguay joined with their Argentine counterparts in 1907.[12] Important also to Luisi's insertion into Pan-American liberal feminist networks and in her propulsion to the leadership of still germinating Uruguayan liberal feminism was her participation in the *Primer Congreso Femenino* (First Women's Congress), held in Buenos Aires in 1910. Organized by the Universitarias, the conference brought together more than two hundred women, representing Argentina, Uruguay, Peru, Paraguay, and Chile. It was probably at this conference that Luisi first came into contact with many of the leaders (or soon-to-be leaders) of liberal feminism in South America, and where she would establish contacts and friendships that would endure for decades afterward.[13]

Luisi shared this distinction as *"primera médica"* with many other leaders of South American liberal feminism. Physicians during this era were seen as the embodiment of rationality and scientific

Figure 9: Paulina Luisi and the first-year medical school class of 1901, Universidad de la República, Uruguay. Reprinted from *Enciclopédia Uruguaya* no. 38 (1969), with permission from Editorial Arca.

method, the new priesthood of the modern age.[14] Women physicians carried an even greater obligation: many saw themselves as the natural leaders of the woman's movement in their countries and with a particular duty to assume this role.[15] In 1900, Argentine physician Cecilia Grierson helped found the Argentine National Women's Council, the first branch of the International Women's Council in Latin America. Grierson and Luisi maintained a correspondence, and Grierson offered advice and assistance to Luisi when she founded the Uruguayan branch in 1916. When a Chilean branch of the International Women's Council was founded in 1918, its president was Dra. Eloísa Díaz, who had become Chile's first woman physician thirty years earlier. A letter of congratulations from Luisi to Díaz underscores the particular ideology and self-identity of this exclusive group:

> It personally gives me great satisfaction to know that for the third time in South America a National [Women's] Council has been formed, and that the responsibility of organizing these three voices [Argentina, Uruguay, Chile] has fallen on us, the women medical doctors, who more than anyone feel daily the painful social condition of woman.[16]

Here, the ideology of the physician as vanguard and social engineer is presented in a gendered form. These women understood themselves to be the harbingers of "male" rationality within the female world, a masculine mind combined with feminine heart that was the embodiment of what was needed to guide this new modern society. The correspondence between Luisi and her counterparts in other South American countries, moreover, reveals that there was a secondary component of this ideology among female physicians, one that included a notion of themselves as the natural leaders—and the "mothers"—of liberal feminism in their respective countries.

"Eugenic Feminism," Socialism, and the State

Luisi's distinction as "primera médica," therefore, made her not only a natural leader of the liberal feminist movement, but one who was best equipped to define the direction and priorities of that movement. Other aspects of Luisi's educational and professional background combined to shape her political outlook in fundamental ways. Specifically, Luisi's anticlerical upbringing and her medical training informed her sympathies for eugenic thought, and her sympathies for eugenics in turn informed both her feminism and her later affiliation with the Socialist Party. While it is significant that Luisi was not a Batllista, her position as a moderate socialist positioned her as among the loyal opposition to Batllista policies.[17] All of these views help underscore Luisi's connections to Uruguayan state formation: a product of the liberal secular state, who in turn saw that state as a principal force for the improvement of women's lives and society in general.

Especially in the early years, Luisi's understanding of sexual difference was profoundly medicalized, fundamentally anatomical, and essentially genital. In a 1911 article on women's education, for example, Luisi wrote: "I am a strong supporter of co-education always and at all ages...given that man and woman are nothing but two forms of the same being, equipped only with the differences that the preservation of the species requires."[18] She did not believe that physiological differences in any way affected intellectual capacity. "There are intelligent men and stupid men," she later wrote, "women of talent and women who are complete fools: on a balance, measuring the respective utility [of men and women] to the species, the scale remains level."[19] Because she believed that men and women were not substantially or fundamentally different from one another, Luisi generally resisted protective labor legislation and campaigns that placed women in a separate legal category. She did feel, however, that societal advancement was predicated on both men and women learning to be more responsible toward their progeny, and responsibility went beyond biology. Continuing with her medicalized imagery, Luisi wrote in 1917 that "if woman's mission is the perpetuation of the species, she must fulfill it with more than her breasts and her internal organs."[20] Women's intervention was also needed to help contain male sexuality, which Luisi saw as aggressive, dangerous, and disruptive to society as a whole.[21]

This conception of male sexuality as disruptive and dangerous is most clear in Luisi's writings on eugenics. Both in Luisi's particular case and in Latin America generally, connections between eugenics and feminist thought have generally been downplayed. Some scholarship emphasizes the separation between these two schools of thought and their respective adherents, depicting feminism's connections to eugenics as tenuous at best.[22] Others, while acknowledging the overlap of feminist and eugenics circles, argue against the compatibility of eugenic thought with early twentieth-century feminist politics, seeing eugenics as a patriarchal body of thought with little to offer to the project of women's emancipation.[23] More recent work on European as well as Latin American eugenics has implicitly and explicitly questioned these paradigms, however, pointing to the existence of a "feminist eugenics" and underscoring the points of compatibility between eugenic thought and early twentieth-century liberal feminist politics.[24] Studies of Luisi specifically have tended to ignore or minimize her eugenic affiliations.[25] Yet Luisi was both a eugenicist and a feminist, and she reconciled these two ideologies in an internally coherent way. While she moved away from more radical eugenic views early on, a eugenics-inspired framework remains clearly identifiable in her writings and priorities. Lastly, taking Luisi's views on eugenics into account helps us to understand her politics in its proper historical context, rather than trying to make her views conform to contemporary feminist sensibilities.

While French style "positive" eugenics, which sought to affect heredity through improvement of the social environment, dominated eugenics thought in Latin America at this time, Luisi was initially sympathetic with "negative" eugenics, which endorsed controls and limits on the reproduction of those identified as "unfit" via birth control, sterilization, and other restrictive measures.[26] In 1916, Luisi presented a paper, *"Algunas ideas sobre eugenía"* (Some Ideas about Eugenics) at the First American Congress of the Child, held in Buenos Aires in 1916. In a talk that generated no small amount of controversy, Luisi spoke frankly about the need to limit procreation of the physically and mentally unfit, endorsing vasectomy and even abortion (at the discretion of the physician; i.e., potentially involuntary sterilization and pregnancy termination) as a way to limit degenerate or "uncivilized" reproduction.[27] Among the other eugenic policies she endorsed in 1916, Luisi argued for laws that would criminalize the transmission of venereal disease and endorsed the wider availability of contraception (such as it was at that time). She also supported, in theory, health certificates for marriage, although she acknowledged that such legislation was improbable in Latin America. Stepan has argued that where negative eugenics existed in Latin America, it was directed largely at women. Luisi's negative eugenics, however, were directed mostly at men, in keeping with her understanding of sexual difference mentioned above. In endorsing sterilization for "unfit" individuals, for example, Luisi argued that male sterilization was preferable to female sterilization, both because the procedure was simpler and safer for men and because "man is much more dangerous to the race than woman, because of the greater number of children he can bear."[28] In fact, Luisi saw male sexuality as "dangerous to the race" in more ways than this. In keeping with others of her cohort, Luisi viewed male sexuality as uncivilized and unconcerned with the greater good of the community.

By 1919, while she still endorsed negative eugenics in theory, Luisi's views had softened somewhat. She still felt that procreation by alcoholics, syphilitics, and other "unfit" types was harmful to society and should be discouraged, but she no longer endorsed surgical intervention (via sterilization and/or abortion). Instead Luisi encouraged education and improved public health as the best way to improve living conditions in working-class communities and to educate people about their "responsibility" to their progeny. She called for sexual education in the public schools, for example, as a way to provide young men and women with "an understanding of their sexual responsibility" and help combat the spread of venereal disease.[29] In particular, she urged aggressive campaigns against what she saw as the "trinity" of threats to humanity: alcoholism, syphilis, and tuberculosis.[30] It is important to note that within this "trinity" the first two, alcoholism and syphilis, were generally associated with working-class males; therefore even this positive or soft eugenics was gendered and, in Luisi's mind undoubtedly, compatible with her feminist views.

Like most eugenicists, Luisi saw the state as a necessary ally. New state regulations, education, and assistance programs were a way to displace the church as the principal arbiter of morality, sexuality, and reproduction, while enforcing and encouraging new "scientific" codes of behavior and social responsibility. This helps us to illuminate a further connection between liberal feminism and the state. Eugenicists, by and large, called for greater state intervention in the family, marriage, and reproduction in order to secure the greater social good of "improving the race." This intervention was quite gendered in the minds of many eugenicist feminists. For many "privacy was a male conspiracy," and state intervention was seen as a way to "reformulate the meaning of paternal authority."[31] The interventionist state was, in this formulation, woman's protector from arbitrary male authority in the home. Since the idea of the state as the "shield of the weak" was already being articulated by Batlle and others, this view found a good deal of traction in Uruguay, further cementing the relationships between Batllista state formation, eugenics, and liberal feminism.

Luisi's eugenics also shaped her position on prostitution. Like many feminist eugenicists, but contrary to many of her male physician colleagues in Uruguay, Luisi took an abolitionist position on prostitution.[32] As a physician and eugenicist, Luisi was quite concerned about the spread of venereal disease, which the regulation of prostitution was meant to control. Yet as a feminist she could not acquiesce to treating this problem by means that would in effect institutionalize double standards of morality and sexual conduct, criminalizing the prostitute and casting her customer as the innocent victim. An avid admirer of Josephine Butler, in a 1919 talk Luisi described in rather grisly detail both the medical exams that registered prostitutes underwent, and their fate if they were found to be infected with a venereal disease. She reminded her listeners that male clients bore equal responsibility for the spread of such diseases, and argued that the role of the state should be to "reduce immorality, not justify it."[33] Most importantly, she also argued that regulation did not serve its primary purpose, and that the rates of infection of venereal diseases had actually increased, in part because regulation sanctioned male infidelity. Once again, the role and responsibility of the state in Luisi's view was to intervene to control the irresponsible male sexual impulse for the greater social good. Feminism and Civilization, in other words, went hand in hand.

While many aspects of eugenics thought have been (rightly) criticized as disempowering to women, Luisi saw eugenics as a means for women to assert more control over their reproductive lives. In her campaign against regulated prostitution, for example, Luisi took an activist stand, urging women to speak out on this issue. For Luisi, the counterpart to male animalistic egotism was willful female ignorance and false prudery, which rendered women unable to defend themselves (and by extension, society as a whole) from the dangers posed by an undisciplined male sexuality. She saw rebellion against traditional notions of female gentility and naiveté as necessary to overcoming women's oppression and subjugation, and as part of her responsibility to the race.[34] In a 1918 essay. "White Slavery: A Social Crime," Luisi argued that women's priggishness and false sense of shame was a contributing factor to the ongoing sexual enslavement of women. Women ignored such issues, she argued, for fear that it would damage their honor and purity. She urged women that for the good of society and the good of her sisters (and she tries to emphasize this point), she needed to open her eyes to what was going on around her:

> It is necessary, therefore, that we detach our spirit from the heavy chains that weigh on our wings and, free of worries and prejudices, seek out, combat, and destroy whatever customs, concepts, regulations, and laws make the female being eternally disinherited from life.... Woman, this is about your sister!!... Be strong enough to overcome cowardly prejudices... and descend with me into the abyss, to scrutinize the causes of this painful situation that has transformed women—like you!— into a repugnant tatter of life.[35]

Luisi practiced what she preached in this regard, and did not shy away from scandalous issues or topics seen as inappropriate for women. Amalia Polleri described Paulina's style: "she practiced "terrorism," she said, "no holding back, no diplomacy, none of that. If she had to yell at men she yelled at them, if she had to insult them, she insulted them. She didn't have the 'feminine hang-ups' that other women had."[36] An unpublished satirical poem, attributable to Luisi, which also echoes Luisi's medicalized understanding of sexual difference, illustrates this "terroristic" style. The poem is addressed to Blanco politician Aureliano Rodríguez Larreta, who had participated in the Constitutional Congress of 1917 and opposed votes for women.[37]

SOBRE EL VOTO FEMENINO
Al doctor Aureliano Rodríguez Larreta, Constituyente en 1917

    Señor:
    Si mi memoria no yerra
    Declaró el Doctor Larreta
    Que la mujer no podía
    Dejar su voto en las urnas
    Porque el sexo carecía
    "De la...capacidad completa"
    Y entonces, don Aureliano
    Cuando los años, pasando,
    Como no pasan en vano
    Van poco a poco gastando
    La capacidad para...el voto,
    No le parece, paisano,
    Que le ha llegado la hora
    De poner violín en bolsa
    Porque a sus años, amigo
    Querido amigo Aureliano
    "Llora, llora urutaú,"
    Cantaba un canto paisano.
              ANANKÉ

ON THE FEMALE VOTE
To Dr. Aureliano Rodríguez Larreta, Delegate to the Constitutional Convention of 1917

    Sir:
    If I remember correctly
    Doctor Larreta declared
    That woman could not
    Leave her vote in the ballot box
    Because her sex was lacking
    "The complete...capacity"
    And so, Don Aureliano
    With the passing years
    (And they do not pass in vain)
    The capacity to...vote
    Is diminished bit by bit.

Chapter Three

> Doesn't it seem, paisano
> That the time has come
> To throw in the towel
> Because at your age, friend
> Dear friend Aureliano
> "Weep, weep urutaú"
> Goes the *paisano* song.[38]
>   ANANKÉ

Although the poem remained unpublished, it is remarkable for what it reveals about Luisi's personality and politics. As does most satire, it makes one's opponent and the opponent's position look ridiculous; it is also the response of the rational, scientific physician who sees the only difference between men and women as residing in anatomy. Here Luisi has chosen to interpret "capacity" in biological, reproductive terms. If, in other words, the ability to penetrate/procreate is the distinguishing feature of masculinity, what happens when the male, due to advanced age or other reasons, is no longer able to perform that function? By essentially equating elderly (and impotent) males with women, she is underlining the absurdities of making such distinctions when discussing voting rights, while at the same time taking the opportunity to make a devastating and pointed assault on the masculinity of one of liberal feminism's more outspoken opponents. It has high shock value, and is scandalous coming from the pen of a woman. In short, it is Paulina.

Luisi's shift toward a positive eugenics, more French than North American or British in inspiration, and more focused on environmental improvement than limitations on reproduction, seems to have gone hand in hand with her growing sympathy for socialist politics. The issue of Luisi's affiliation with the Socialist Party remains a matter of some controversy and debate.[39] There is little question that Paulina Luisi was deeply sympathetic with socialist views and with the politics of the Uruguayan Socialist Party, although she was not officially (or openly) affiliated with the party. Luisi's eugenics informed her socialist orientation, especially her support for greater worker protections. In a 1918 talk on alcoholism and women's suffrage, Luisi focused on the "social illness" of alcoholism, which she explicitly associated with working-class and poor men. "All laws that tend to improve the conditions of the working class, represent further barriers to the spread of alcoholism," she wrote.[40] Worker protections, in other words, and even the redistribution of wealth were in essence eugenic measures aimed at improving the environment in working-class communities, where, in her inference, alcoholism, criminality, and other degenerative ills were most widespread. Luisi's support for socialist ideas, in other words, was not simply motivated by the party's consistent support for women's political rights. Luisi's clearest endorsement of Socialist politics comes at the end of her 1919 pamphlet *Para una mejor descendencia* (For a Better Lineage). Following a summary of her main views, conclusions, and recommendations regarding eugenics and reproduction, Luisi wrote the following:

> The electoral platform presented by the Socialist Party in the recent elections has bravely taken up many of these problems... aimed at attaining the broadest well-being and happiness of our species.
> They should be broadly supported by the people who, for their own betterment, have a duty to support them with all their strength and energy.[41]

Yet despite her ideological affinity, and occasional public endorsements, Luisi maintained a curiously arm's-length relationship with the Uruguayan Socialist Party for much of the years under examination. In 1929, for example, the party announced that a Socialist library was being named for Luisi, who had donated many volumes for the library's collection. Luisi was described as "someone who has so much ideological affinity" with the party. At the same time, it was acknowledged that there was some question about naming a library for someone who was not "affiliated" with the party.[42] Exactly why Luisi maintained this stance toward the Socialists is not known: possibly she felt that remaining politically nonaligned was key to maintaining her leadership role in Uruguayan feminism. Indeed, as we will see in the next chapter, Luisi's more definitive moves toward the Socialists in the late 1910s contributed to a split in liberal feminist ranks. She also may have kept her distance from the Socialists because of her increasingly important diplomatic activities, which also brought her into even closer and more direct contact with the Uruguayan state. In 1913, she was sent to Europe by President Batlle y Ordóñez to represent Uruguay at a conference on sexual education. For the next two decades, she spent a great deal of time out of the country, attending conferences of both a feminist and a medical nature, often with the full or partial sponsorship of the Uruguayan government. In the early 1920s, Luisi became one of the first women representatives in the newly created League of Nations. In 1922, she was named Uruguayan Delegate to the League's International Labor Conference, and during that same year she reportedly served on a commission to oversee the Sino-Japanese conflict.[43] Finally, Luisi served on the League's Commission for the Suppression of White Slavery, a post that was particularly close to her heart. Luisi's diplomatic position served to further confirm her as something of a political insider in Uruguay, and as someone who was able to project Uruguay's image as a "model country" abroad. Luisi was a prominent player in international feminism as well, playing important leading roles in the International Council of Women, the International Women's Suffrage Alliance, and other Pan-American and Pan-Hispanic women's organizations. As with the League of Nations, her international work was concentrated on organizing against international trafficking in women. In addition to providing her with the opportunity to travel and make contacts with others of a like mind, Luisi's diplomatic work may have influenced her decision to remain unclaimed by any particular political party.

All of these factors—anticlericalism, eugenics, and socialism—converge in Luisi's support for women's suffrage. Male domination and its handmaiden, religion, in Luisi's view, had joined together to keep women isolated, uneducated, and in a state of perpetual dependence and immaturity. The average woman in contemporary society, she wrote, has no "personality," meaning she has not transcended childhood/thinghood into personhood.[44] Demanding the vote was therefore demanding women's right to personhood. Women's suffrage, in Luisi's view, was also crucial to the success of eugenic projects. Key to improving the race was the development of a sense of reproductive responsibility; and an ignorant, childlike woman could not be expected to be responsible. Only woman as person could take charge of her destiny and oversee the improvement of the population. As the primary victims of vice and sickness, women had the strongest interest in implementing hygienic reforms (such as laws against alcoholism and the abolition of prostitution):

> There are now an infinity of voices which from every corner of the world have proclaimed the importance of woman's influence in the battle against alcoholism, and the corresponding necessity of providing her with all the

tools necessary to continue this work, the most important among those undoubtedly being the right to vote.⁴⁵

And as the party which had most strongly and consistently favored women's votes, the Socialist Party, in Luisi's eyes, was the political party most committed to securing woman's personhood and improving the race, two goals which, in her view, necessarily marched hand in hand. At this point it is clear that Luisi's professional training, her views on eugenics, her feminism, and her affinity for socialist views were part of a coherent whole. Lastly, it is clear that for Luisi the reformist, interventionist state was at the center of her social-reform analysis. She shared this state-centered view with many of her liberal feminist colleagues, and as a result Batllismo was a central factor in the structure and orientation of liberal feminism in Uruguay.

In sum, the personage of Paulina Luisi can perhaps be summed up in a few words, words that hopefully now contain more significance than they would have at the beginning of this chapter. Describing her as a physician (*médica*), a eugenicist, a feminist, and a socialist (but not necessarily a Socialist) properly conveys the nature of this woman. Cerebral and rational, she was also passionate and deeply moved to correct injustice and eliminate suffering, but always within the boundaries of scientific method and controlled passions. Luisi was also very much a product of Batllista state formation, well positioned to take advantage of every new opening being presented to women in the areas of educational and professional achievement. In general, she embodied and internalized the ideological framework of the Batllista state, acting completely from within the constitutive agenda of the Batllista system. Luisi clearly believed the state had a vital role to play in civilizing society, and an obligation to assist those most in need. But, just like Batllismo itself, her commitment to equality was not total. Indeed, the language contained in her early writings reveals an elitism common to much of her professional cohort: that the educated, scientific community was best suited to define and articulate the needs of society as a whole.

While we can hardly say that Paulina Luisi's story is representative of the experiences of all early professional women in Uruguay, her biography nonetheless gives some insight into the relationship that existed between secular middle-class professional women and the Batllista state (and, in most instances, the Colorado Party). These were women who were clear beneficiaries of the Uruguayan welfare state, and many (although by no means all) may have seen themselves connected to and invested in the state-building project. On the other hand, however, this social position would also have invested them with a sense of citizenship and entitlement to enter into the political arena and demand rights for themselves and those they claimed to represent. Professional women were not the only group of women to undergo such a transformation. Some elite women too entered into a new and closer relationship with the state, inspiring a parallel process of politicization, a topic we will turn to below.

Gender and Citizenship: Elite Women, Social Assistance, and the State

In August of 1919, police in the Uruguayan interior town of Durazno sent a letter to Juvenile Court officials in Montevideo requesting assistance with M.A., a sixteen-year-old pregnant servant in their custody. The young woman's employers, who had been her guardians since she was two years old, turned M.A. over to state officials when her pregnancy was discovered. Describing her as "bitter, quarrelsome, moody and disrespectful to those who have provided her with everything she needed," M.A.'s pregnancy was the ultimate demonstration of ingratitude and disrespect as far as her employer-guardians were concerned.[46] From the Durazno Police, jurisdiction over M.A. was transferred to the Council for the Protection of Delinquents and Minors in Montevideo, a public agency, which sent her first to a church-run orphanage, and subsequently to a state-sponsored home run by elite women.

Much of this scenario was nothing new within the history of the often tense and conflictive relationships between employers and servants, poor and affluent, in Latin America. It was not unusual for more well-to-do families to "adopt" young servant girls, nor was it unusual for conflicts to arise in these relationships, especially as that servant approached adulthood. What is different here is the fact that—by the late 1910s—the Uruguayan state had inserted itself into these conflicts and was taking custody of these young women, often at their employer-guardians' request. Elite women and the beneficent societies they oversaw were central players in this early phase in the construction of the Batllista welfare state, making it possible for reformers to implement the sweeping legislation enacted during this era. In turn, these women's experience as parastatal agents had a

Figure 10:
National Public Assistance and programs assisting women and children: the first *Gota de leche* ("Drop of Milk") office in Montevideo, c.1913. These programs encouraged breast feeding but also distributed clean, pasteurized milk to the mothers of poor children. The centers also provided basic medical assistance to children and gave poor mothers instruction in childcare. Reprinted from La asistencia pública nacional. *Publicación oficial de la dirección nacional* (Montevideo: Barreiro y Ramos, 1913).

politicizing effect, and they and their organizations became crucial players in the early phases of liberal feminism.

As in other countries, much early social-assistance legislation targeted poor women and children and relied on elite women for much of its implementation.[47] Among their many goals, the authors and supporters of this legislation sought to address a perceived demographic crisis in the country through programs aimed at reducing infant mortality, abortion, and infanticide. Poor juvenile (under the age of twenty-one) women were a particular target, both because they were viewed as being at especially high risk for the social problems identified above, and because their age and class status allowed the state to assume direct control over their bodies and those of their children in the name of "protection" and national well-being. Thus the eugenic views that inspired feminist physicians like Luisi were also in operation here.

Chapter 2 discussed the sweeping 1910 Public Assistance Law and the creation of the Asistencia Pública Nacional (APN) to oversee social-assistance programs and activity. Not surprisingly, this sweeping legislation and the centralized apparatus it created placed tremendous strains on the APN. The state never provided the kinds of funds necessary to implement such an ambitious plan or to satisfy the demands it created. Vigorous state efforts to divest the Catholic Church of its monopoly over social assistance only made things worse. As a result, by as early as 1913, the APN directorte began to call on private initiative to attend to some of the surplus demand left by an underfunded and overextended state structure. APN board member Dr. Augusto Turenne encouraged the formation of secular *comités de damas* (ladies' committees) to help with social-assistance efforts and create a bridge between public assistance and private philanthropy. In calling for elite women's participation, Turenne stated that "the National Public Assistance will never reach its fullest potential until the day that, instead of being seen as a colossal administrative machine it is considered as an affectionate mother."[48] Thus, in this model the ideal was for the state to be both father and mother to the inherently disadvantaged by providing both financial support and moral guidance. The APN and elite women's committees seemed the perfect marriage for such a project. Although there was some resistance to the policy of subsidizing these ladies' committees, economic expediency ultimately outweighed concerns for elite lifestyle, and government subsidies were granted in one form or another to a number of private women's beneficent societies by 1916.

This partnership was meant to be a temporary and transitional solution, but the creation of the hoped-for cadre of middle-class female health and social-work professionals to replace elite women was not immediately forthcoming. One of the conundrums of this combination of "late institutionalization" and "early modernization,"' mentioned in earlier chapters, was that policy formation prematurely anticipated the existence of a supporting class structure needed to create the cadre of bureaucrats and professionals that reformers had envisioned. More specifically, Uruguayan state formation was circumscribed by a class/gender structure that restricted the state's ability to incorporate middle-class female functionaries into public social assistance. In 1913, a nursing school was opened in Montevideo, initiating the process of training young women to replace the nuns who staffed many of the public hospitals. But the introduction of female auxiliary medical personnel took longer than many had hoped. No doubt the school's policy of admitting only unmarried women with no children to their program further slowed this process.[49] A program to train professional social workers took even longer to get off the ground—the systematic training of social workers did not get started until the mid-1920s. The result was that nuns and elite women remained vital to the provision of social assistance, for many a temporary, necessary evil to be tolerated until adequate replacements became available.

Whether as a result of direct encouragement from the APN or a more spontaneous outpouring of enthusiasm, the years 1910–1915 saw the emergence of a number of important secular elite women's social-assistance organizations, most dedicated to assisting poor mothers and disadvantaged children. The link primarily took the form of the *subvención*: long-standing and open-ended subsidies of ostensibly private organizations. This section focuses on one of these organizations, the Asociación *"La Bonne Garde,"* which was founded in 1911 to assist unmarried pregnant juveniles whose families or guardians could not afford (or were unwilling) to take care of them during their pregnancy and early stages of motherhood.

Before dealing with the Bonne Garde in detail, a brief overview of the history of two similar ladies' committees will serve to illustrate that the Bonne Garde's relationship with the state was not unique. The *Asociación Pro-Matre*[50] (Pro-Mother Association) was founded in June 1915 by Elena Puig de Turenne, wife of Augusto Turenne, one of the most important physicians and social reformers of the era. The organization was oriented toward assisting and educating poor mothers who, for one reason or another, found themselves without the financial support of a husband (women who were either abandoned, widowed, or had a husband who was too ill to work). The group was concerned with declining birthrates and with high rates of child abandonment, along with a general belief that "the lack of moral and material protection of mothers and children is one of the principal factors in the debasement of the people."[51] Pro-Matre provided housing to "deserving" mothers and their young children, and also worked to regularize "illegitimate unions," by providing unmarried couples with the moral persuasion and the financial resources to marry. In 1916, Pro-Matre reported that the director of the National Public Assistance had donated beds, couches, and money to the organization. By 1918 this *"contribución"* (a one-time public donation) changed to a *"subvención"* (permanent subsidy) when the association was granted an annual subsidy of thirty-six hundred pesos.⁵² From this point, Pro-Matre's work was heavily subsidized by the state.

The *Instituto de Ciegos* (Institute for the Blind) was founded in late 1913 by Teresa Santos de Bosch after she visited an analogous institution in Buenos Aires earlier that same year. The Institute was a school for blind children, which provided them with a nurturing environment and specialized education in order to prepare them to be "useful and productive citizens."⁵³ While it is true that this institution "owed its existence to private initiative," it certainly owed its expansion and possibly its survival to the Uruguayan state.⁵⁴ Only a matter of months after its foundation, in early 1914, the Executive Power (in this case Batlle y Ordóñez himself) "understanding the significance of this feminine initiative," agreed to support the Institute. In 1917, Santos de Bosch reported an annual subsidy of ninety-six hundred pesos to Carmen Cuestas de Nery, the group's new president. In this same letter, published in *Acción Femenina* in 1917, Santos de Bosch described this somewhat complicated relationship between private charity and the state. The Instituto de Ciegos, she wrote, was

> headed by a Ladies' Commission free of all political and religious influence, but that fulfils the goals of a public Institution tightly connected to the State that subsidizes it and to whom the Direction gives monthly accounts.⁵⁵

There are many common links between the women who founded or headed up these affiliated organizations. Both Santos de Bosch and Cuestas de Nery were the daughters of pre-Batlle Colorado Party presidents of Uruguay, and starting in around 1925 (and until at least 1929), Pro-Matre was headed by Celia Álvarez de Amézaga, wife of Juan José de Amézaga, a lawyer, director of the State Insurance Bank, and an important legislator during the early part of the century, who went on to become president of the republic from 1943 to 1947.⁵⁶ All of these women, therefore, fit within the older nineteenth-century pattern where the wives and daughters of important political figures involved themselves in charity work. The difference, by this point, is that these women, via their associations, were now receiving public funds and, in effect, implementing state policy. In addition, Puig de Turenne, Santos de Bosch, and Cuestas de Nery were all the wives of physicians—Augusto Turenne and Carlos Nery were especially prominent reformers.

Might these associations have served as a kind of ladies' auxiliary for these male-dominated reform circles, with husbands and wives working in gender-specific and acceptable ways to formulate and implement social policy? Lastly, all four of these women were early members of Conamu (the Uruguayan National Women's Council), listed as members on the 1918 rosters, but gone from the rolls by 1923: part of that most conservative and elite (but nonetheless important) first generation of Conamu members. These organizations, in sum, were crucial to both the implementation of Batllista policy and the development of liberal feminism, and their history underscores the role of medicalized social-reform discourse and the politics of elite patronage to both of these processes.

The Asociación La Bonne Garde: Juvenile Mothers as Foster-Servants

Like other ladies' committees, the Bonne Garde began as a private endeavor, but within a few years it was brought into the state's orbit. In 1915, the group began receiving permanent subsidies from the state; in 1916 the association received the first of many young mothers sent to them directly from Child Welfare Services (orphans, juvenile delinquents, etc). So while the association continued to work with the same target group, as time passed the young mothers and babies the Bonne Garde housed and cared for were increasingly likely to be wards of the state, supported in large part by public funds. As a result, after 1915 many pregnant juveniles became wards of the state, often spending the remaining years until reaching their majority in a variety of parastatal spaces that sought to protect them and their children and to oversee their development into productive and disciplined citizens. The Bonne Garde filled a particular niche in state policy toward female juvenile offenders by housing a ward immediately pre- and post-partum. Many of these young clients arrived at the doors of the Bonne Garde via the *Asilo Buen Pastor*, the principal (state-run) home for delinquent and orphaned girls and one of the few public-assistance institutions where the church still maintained a presence. A "religious establishment of a correctional nature" run by nuns, the Buen Pastor would not house a ward in an advanced state of pregnancy, seeing her as a "source of moral contamination" for other residents.[57] Nor would the Buen Pastor house the minor once the child was born (if the child survived and remained under its mother's care). The Bonne Garde helped fill this policy gap, taking these women in both before and

Figure 11:
Lottery ticket, 1924. Another way that private funds were brought in to support state-sponsored projects. This lottery helped support the *Asilos Maternales*, daycare institutions that cared for poor children, ages two to seven, while their mothers were at work or otherwise unable to look after them. Author's collection.

after giving birth at La Maternidad. From this point, if the woman did not have morally acceptable family willing to take her in after she had given birth, she was likely to remain in the juvenile system—in one capacity or another—until reaching legal majority.

What we see is no clear or direct supplanting of old paternalistic structures by a secular social-assistance state, but rather a complicated combination of private households, church institutions, state-subsidized ladies' committees, and state agencies themselves.[58] Many of the young women who became official clients of the Bonne Garde had previously been incorporated into the ranks of these orphan-servant dependents by a private paternalistic arrangement. A typical case would be that of a young woman born in the Uruguayan interior, generally the illegitimate child of a mother who worked as a domestic servant. While still a child, the girl was placed in the home of a more well-off family in the capital where she followed in her mother's footsteps and embarked on a career in domestic servitude. Her new patrons would likely have pledged to care for the child and raise her in a morally correct way, and in turn the girl would assume and accept her place as a permanently subordinate member of the household. But the paternalistic ideal of protection and obedience did not, of course, always match reality.[59] While surely there were cases where these children were well cared for and even loved (within the boundaries of social inequality), they were also vulnerable to abuse, neglect, and exploitation. Adolescence and the transformation of the young girl into a sexual being meant that the servant woman was now a real potential threat to the honor and reputation of her guardians' household. A pregnancy was a scandal and an economic burden, and it reflected poorly on the household's moral tutelage of the young woman and its ability to control those under its direction. In such a case the loyalty of the patron to the youth and her family would likely have been strained. Household honor was predicate upon the control of subordinate household members, yet it was also defined by the upholding of obligations and a promise to look after the youth until reaching the age of majority. In an earlier era, the guardians' options may have been more limited, but in Uruguay by the 1920s new state structures of public assistance allowed these families to (more honorably) dispose of their problem by introducing her into the juvenile legal system and transferring guardianship to the state.

These young women were not always the mere victims of the whims of their guardians or of state policy. There are cases where these women sought to take advantage of new state structures themselves, endeavoring to use the state to gain leverage or improve their circumstances. It was L.F., for example, and not her guardians, who first involved state authorities in her case. L.F. asked for state intervention herself, claiming that her guardians were treating her badly and not paying her for the work she did in the home. This bad treatment was most associated with the fact that she was not allowed to see her daughter, P., who had been born the previous year and placed in a state orphanage by her guardians. Interviews with all parties concluded both that her guardians no longer wanted her and that L.F. did not want to remain under their guardianship. It was revealed that L.F. was pregnant again, no doubt prompting the final confrontation within the family. In subsequent investigations, L.F. reported that the father of both children was her guardians' son. Although he himself denied paternity, his own parents agreed with their servant's claim that he was the biological father. But despite her best efforts, L.F. had little ability to control her destiny once the state assumed guardianship. Throughout her roughly five years under the state's custodianship, she was apparently only allowed very limited contact with her daughter, which she seemed constantly to be seeking, and she alternated her time between confinement in the Buen Pastor asylum and placements where she worked as a servant for minimal remuneration.

As L.F.'s story demonstrates, while this newly constituted network of state-supported religious and private secular organizations provided a solution for the guardian family, it did not necessarily mean much change or improvement for the young servant woman. The state simply recycled these women back into much the same situations they had been in before, only now with a promise of public oversight and protection they did not enjoy previously. Beyond safeguarding the lives of their babies, one of the goals of the state was to isolate young mothers from bad influences and shape them into productive and disciplined citizens. So in addition to providing shelter, food, and protection to these women and their babies, both child welfare services and the Bonne Garde itself placed these women (with and without their children) with families who were to provide them with both moral guidance and vocational training.[60] In an arrangement that lies somewhere in between the old colonial practice of "deposit" and newer notions of foster care, citizens could petition the state—and later the Bonne Garde directly—for a *"muchacha"* to come live in their home as a domestic, paying her a small salary, and, supposedly, providing her with the good example she needed to become an upstanding citizen-mother. This salary seems to have ranged between five and twelve pesos a month and was kept in an account for these minor females until the woman reached the age of majority, when she was allowed to withdraw her accumulated funds.[61] Guardian-employer families had to sign a long list of conditions, most emphasizing the responsibility of the guardian to provide for the "moral, physical, and intellectual education of the minor," and to teach the minor a useful trade (in this case, domestic service). But there were other obligations as well, which included the need for guardians to "exercise over them the strictest vigilance" with the goal of "slowly and gradually accommodating them to a spirit of necessary discipline, without going so far as to deform [their] character."[62]

For most of these women, this was involuntary confinement, and unless one could find a way of manipulating the system, running away likely meant an arrest warrant and incarceration. The only other way out, it seems, was if a parent or close relative successfully petitioned to have the mother released into their custody, or if an adult male made a successful marriage petition. All of these requests were subject to review, and could be (and were) turned down if the petitioner was not deemed "morally" worthy, a classification often heavily laden with class and ethnic connotations. Not even the death of one's child, it seems, was sufficient to change one's status with the state. After M. V.'s child died shortly after birth, she was sent back to the Bonne Garde and hired out as a wet nurse. After running away, she was recaptured and was held at the Bonne Garde until she reached her majority. So while it may have been their pregnancy that brought them to the state in the first place, once they were declared juvenile wards these women remained in custody until majority regardless of their parental status.

Elite Women and the National Public Assistance:

If the Bonne Garde's clients were some of the most vulnerable and marginal members of society, the women who ran the organization were the wives and daughters of the political and social elite, the model matriarchs of society, ideal for fulfilling the state's goal of being the "affectionate mother" to the poor.[63] On the membership rosters of the Bonne Garde were names long associated with elite charity and benevolence. Members of the leadership included women like Carmen Cuestas de Nery (mentioned above); Bernardina Muñoz de De María (wife of the important jurist/reformer/politician Pablo De María), and Carmen Martínez de Williman (wife of Claudio Williman, president 1907–1911). Perhaps state officials hoped that these women's administrative skills and experience could somehow be turned toward the public sector. As members of wealthy and politically influential families, there were surely other potential benefits as well.

The appearance of the publication *Página Blanca* (White Page) in mid-1915 testifies to the expansion of the state-sponsored beneficence. Described as "the first magazine of its type, the result of the strength and initiative of women," *Página Blanca* provided a bimonthly report and overview of the activities of women's social assistance.[64] It also doubled as a sort of society page, listing the names of the women involved in the various activities and organizations profiled. The magazine regularly reported on the activities of *Entre Nous*, the Anti-Alcohol League, Pro-Matre, the women's commission of the Anti-Tuberculosis League, and various training centers and schools established for working women.[65] The publication also illustrates the overlapping memberships of many of these organizations, and the fact that, in this sphere, noteworthy liberal women like Paulina Luisi often crossed paths with notable Catholic *damas* like Laura Carreras de Bastos. The years of the magazine's publication—1915 to 1922—correspond with the heyday of state-sponsored elite women's social-assistance activity. On these pages one also sees timid steps toward more moderate feminist politics, congratulating women who had achieved educational milestones, and publishing articles on what would constitute the "right kind of feminism" (*feminismo bien entendido*).

The marriage between women's committees and the National Public Assistance was seen as a way to bring private philanthropy and public assistance together, but as time passed the balance shifted markedly to the latter. In the early years, for example, it appears that the campaign to take in these young mothers as foster servants was somewhat of a short-lived cause célèbre among the Montevidean elite. The first of these women placed by the Bonne Garde were taken in by wealthy and influential Montevideo families, an indication of the connections of the Bonne Garde to Montevidean high society and of the prestige (at least initially) that accompanied taking in these young women.[66] Much of this enthusiasm seems to have worn off, however, and eventually most of these women were "taken by families who in the majority of cases are only concerned with getting a servant in an even worse situation than the rest."[67] Housing the state's wayward orphan girls, it seems, had become less an act of charity and community service and more a part of household financial management, essentially a means of supplementing the income of urban middle sectors by providing them with inexpensive (and captive) domestic help. Social reformers like Augusto Turenne constantly complained about this lack of support among the elite for the social-assistance work of the state, writing that "in our country with a very few exceptions the incomprehension and indifference of the rich has meant that the marble tablets where they inscribe the names of the benefactors of the Social Assistance have remained almost virgin."[68] The result was that during the 1920s the Bonne Garde and groups like it became increasingly dependent on government subsidies as private support for their work began to dry up.

By 1927 state subsidies amounted to fully 80 to 90 percent of the Bonne Garde's budget. This money, of course, did not come without strings, and by the early 1920s there was increasing pressure from both bureaucrats and legislators to secure greater direct government oversight of the daily operations and expenditures of these organizations. In 1922 the Bonne Garde revised its statutes, stating that if the organization were to dissolve, "all its property would revert to the state," and shortly thereafter the group began presenting monthly reports (*rendimiento de cuentas*) to the APN, accounting for funds spent and the number of mothers and children housed with them.[69] The increasing importance of public subsidies required new skills of those running these organizations. In addition to being organizers of grand galas, the damas now had to become skilled lobbyists for public funds. In 1925, outgoing Bonne Garde President Margarita de la Sierra de Sánchez detailed her achievements at the helm of a number of organizations, including the Bonne Garde:

> I was President of the Anti-Alcohol League when they had no resources to conduct the publicity necessary for their development. Before I left the city was giving us a percentage of the proceeds from the *Parque Hotel* [a state-run casino in Montevideo]... and [we were getting] another 100 pesos a month from the [APN]... At the Bonne Garde I have tried to do as much good as possible... we got [Congress] to raise the monthly subsidy they receive... to 800 pesos.[70]

It is clear, in sum, that ten years after the first official ties were created between the ladies' committees and the state, the relationship had undergone significant evolution. The Uruguayan welfare state had become more permanent and formal, and the elite women running the organizations had become savvy political actors in new and important ways.

This experience with the state, I argue, had an important politicizing effect on some of these elite volunteers. Lobbying for government funding and negotiating with the bureaucracy gave them a direct interface with the state that was new to most of them. At the same time, increased state supervision did not translate into increased input into policy formation by the women involved, and the public-health bureaucracy remained an almost exclusively male domain during the entire period under examination. From early on, it seems, many of these women's associations and their members were critical of this one-sided intervention and began demanding more input into policy-making and, eventually, into national politics.

Yet as the percentage of private funds in these organizations' budgets shrank, the raison d'être for the presence of elite women in social assistance declined accordingly. Growing tensions between elite women and the state were also fueled by changing class relations, changes in part engendered by the growth of the Batllista state itself. After 1929 especially, in a climate of deepening economic crisis and political polarization, the APN and other bodies found themselves in a situation of shrinking resources and political support as well as increasing demand. This led naturally to demands for greater efficiency in the provision of social assistance. Furthermore, by the late 1920s the middle classes had grown to sufficient size (and in the years of the Depression, of sufficient economic need) that it was now becoming possible to staff state-funded institutions with those middle-class female functionaries desired since the 1910s. By the late 1920s certain state bureaucrats openly favored replacing the comités de damas with professionally trained staff, or at least with paid public functionaries. In 1929, APN member José Arias stated, "I have seen how these Ladies' Commissions, even while they have all the good will in the world, lack the *technical expertise* and the resulting responsibility, that is fundamental for the Direction of an establishment such as this"(emphasis added).[71] This desire for "technical expertise" reflected the changing nature of social-assistance work and views of poverty and delinquency. Starting in 1928, we see a concerted effort by the APN to bolster its (until then, practically nonexistent) program to train social workers (*visitadoras sociales*).[72]

Elite women responded to these accusations of obsolescence, offering their own critique of this new "scientific" view of social assistance. Nowhere is this more clearly expressed than in the fiction of Laura Cortinas, a moderately successful author and playwright who was also in the leadership of the Bonne Garde in this later era. In August 1929, a play of Cortinas entitled *El Buen Amor* (The Good Love) premiered at the Teatro Solís, the principal theater of Montevideo. The plot of *El Buen Amor* is nothing unusual for the era: it tells the story of the poor but morally pure Rosario, competing for (and eventually winning) the love of the wealthy and handsome Roberto, despite facing competition from the beautiful and wealthy but morally decadent Beatriz.[73] What is more unusual is that Cortinas chose to set her play in an orphanage, where our heroine Rosario was raised and stayed on into adulthood to help take care of the children. The fictional orphanage, the play explains, was originally founded as a private institution but government subsidies had turned it into a semi-public entity. The play is quite critical of the consequences of this change, mostly in terms of the new staff members, who Cortinas portrays as more concerned with discipline and enriching themselves than with caring for the children. The state is, in essence, a character in this play, one that is portrayed as morally perverting society and undermining natural and maternal instincts. It is important to underline here that Cortinas's critique of the state is not that it has put men in charge of social assistance, but

Figure 12:
Laura Cortinas, late 1920s. A member of both the Alianza and the Bonne Garde, Cortinas was a playwright whose works touched on feminist themes as well as those pertaining to social assistance. Reprinted from Alianza Uruguaya y Consejo Nacional de Mujeres, *La mujer Uruguaya reclama sus derechos políticos* (Montevideo: Editorial Apolo, 1929).

middle-class female public functionaries.[74] Whereas the discussion of private vs. public charity in the 1910s was a fundamentally gendered discussion, in which men were the public administrators and women the private providers of moral guidance, the debate in the late 1920s and 1930s had also become one of volunteers versus professionals, carrying fundamentally class-based connotations. Instead of the wives and daughters of the elite providing a moral example to wayward youth, assistance was now being increasingly provided by wives and daughters of the middle and even working classes who, in Cortinas's view, were morally unqualified to do the job. It was imperative that women like Cortinas define the needs of clients, like the children in this fictional orphanage, as in need of moral guidance and motherly affection, for it was the only way for them to justify their position. They undoubtedly understood that the more the social question was defined as a scientific problem requiring "technical expertise," the more they would be marginalized from the process.

These elite women, in sum, were caught in the contradictions of a society in transition. Trying to simultaneously uphold the ideals of social solidarity and noblesse oblige, they were themselves increasingly part of a state apparatus that was effectively undermining this tenuous balance. In this we can see the tensions inherent in the modernization of social assistance, and its connection to Uruguayan state formation and changing class structures in Uruguayan society. Women's role in social assistance remained central throughout the period in question. What changed was the type of woman performing the caring work of the state and her relationship to public, private, and religious entities and administrators of care. The same forces that were supplanting traditional elite responsibilities to the poor were also giving rise to a new stratum of middle-ranking professionals, in which women figured prominently. Much of this new group was also financially dependent on the state, but with a very different relationship based on salary instead of subsidy, and an ideological outlook that reflected distinct class/gender politics from their more elite foremothers.

It is not only in social assistance where one sees this shift in the center of gravity from elite to more middle-class and professional women; it is visible within the women's movement as well. The history of elite women and the welfare state coincides chronologically with the rise of liberal feminism in Uruguay, and there were important connections between many of these comités de damas and the nascent liberal feminist movement that emerged in Uruguay in the 1910s. I suggest that the political and economic relationships that developed between these women and the Uruguayan state helped to make the Bonne Garde and other similar groups a principal point of entry for many women in the early (and more conservative) phases of Uruguayan liberal feminism.[75] In turn, the particular ideology these women brought to the feminist movement colored the class/gender politics of the feminist movement during these years.

Conclusion

The gendered process of Uruguayan state formation was a catalyst for liberal feminist organizing. Liberal feminism was distinguished by its confidence in the secular, capitalist state as a forum within which women's equality—and in many cases, these women's own personal and professional agendas—could be advanced. Many of the women who led liberal feminist organizations had prior connections to the public sector, and were professionally and/or financially connected to and invested in the liberal state. The years 1910–1915, in particular, represented an embryonic stage in both welfare-state formation and in the development of liberal feminism in Uruguay. Professional educated women and elite women involved in social assistance were key players in both. Elite women's participation in social-assistance organizations gave them political experience and the confidence to confront state structures and to fight for their autonomy. The ambitious plans for universal care in the spirit of the paternalistic politics of compensation under the auspices of the state brought elite women into a new relationship with the state structures, in effect transforming them into parastatal actors. Middle-class and professional women, on the other hand, were the direct beneficiaries of Batllismo, and were hence much more invested in the project than their more elite counterparts, who had in contrast seen an erosion of their social position and territory since 1910. That this new generation of feminists were on the whole more interested in legal equality than in moral tutelage of the poor did not mean that they made greater efforts to elicit the participation of—or support issues important to—working-class and poor women. Because of their particular place in the state (and class) structure, many of these women still viewed poor women as clients, students, and patients, but rarely as partners, colleagues, sisters, or equals. In addition to their particular brands of feminist politics, an underexplored link between these two groups are the politics of eugenics, which underlie both the ideology of the medical class and the discourse of the National Public Assistance. More research on the links between feminism, eugenics, and the female agents of the state will help us to better understand the gendered, classed, and medicalized nature of state formation in Latin America.

While professional women saw their stars rise throughout the period in question, elite beneficent women benefited only temporarily from their new relationship with the National Public Assistance. As the social-assistance infrastructure developed, elite women were gradually displaced by more middle-class professional and semiprofessional women, who ushered in the professionalization of social assistance in the 1920s. Understanding these changes, and the groups of women involved with them, helps to illuminate and contextualize the particular history of liberal feminism in Uruguay, as well as larger questions of gender, citizenship, and the state during the Batllista era. As we will see in the next chapter, these two groups of women enjoyed an uneasy alliance; but they were able to work together, it seems, whereas in many other Latin American countries this alliance was impossible.[76] I argue that the nature of Batllista state formation is the key to

Chapter Three

understanding this tenuous, short-lived, but ultimately powerful alliance of women under the liberal feminist banner.

Lastly, this history provides a different view of the development of Uruguayan civil society, whose emergence also dates to this era. Women, too, became politicized during these years, and a direct relationship with the state and state agencies was a principal conduit for this politicization. It stands to reason that both professional women and the members of ladies' committees, for different reasons and with different goals perhaps, would have seen themselves increasingly as political actors, and might have sought to increase their influence over social policy more directly through lobbying and campaigns for full citizenship. That these groups came together in the early stages of liberal feminist organizing is thus not surprising. But we should also not be surprised that there were tensions in this relationship, leading to splits in the movement along class and ideological lines. These two groups of women, after all, were politicized by ultimately antagonistic tendencies of Batllista policy. The very trends that were alienating and marginalizing elite women from the state—expanding educational access for women and a growing middle class—were benefiting and strengthening the social capital of educated professional women. The competing notions of national womanhood presented in Cortinas's fiction were also at the core of the liberal feminist politics of the same era, as women of varying classes and political ideologies debated the terms and timing of women's entry into politics and the ideal nature of women's citizenship.

Chapter Four
Liberal Feminism, 1916–1932

FEMINISMO:
A mother, bragging about her daughter to a potential suitor:
— My daughter sings, plays the piano, paints, speaks English, French, German and Italian, knows physics, chemistry, zoology; in other words, she knows a little bit about everything. And you sir, what do you know?
— Nothing *señora*...I cook a little and I know how to sew on buttons.
— Mundo Uruguayo, *5 June 1919*

Idiots! No one loves her husband, children, and home more than I do but I rebel against this order of things where, while the men have all the liberty possible, the woman, who has the reputation of not doing anything because she is a *servant without salary* twenty-four hours a day, cannot set aside one minute for spiritual distraction. With good reason they consider us inferior beings. How can we not rise up against this?
— *Letter from Fanny Carrió de Polleri to Paulina Luisi, c.1919*

*J*uxtaposed, these two selections speak to the popular reception and intimate realities of feminism in early twentieth-century Uruguay. A number of jokes published in the middle-class magazine *Mundo Uruguayo* mocked feminists as silly, frivolous beings, more concerned with fashion than emancipation. Some, like the selection above, hint at a more threatening prospect: that feminism would encourage an inversion of traditional gender roles. In this example, women's educational advancement has reduced men to a subordinate, feminized position associated with cooking and sewing, pointing to some of the anxieties that women's organizing may have provoked among *Mundo Uruguayo*'s readership. Liberal feminist Fanny Carrió de Polleri, in contrast, responded to the accusation, inferred by the joke above, that feminism is anti-male and anti-family. Carrió was not a professional woman like Paulina Luisi, but a housewife and mother of six, married to prominent Riverista politician Félix Polleri. Her letters reveal a visceral and passionate commitment to feminist ideals, and an indication as to what motivated many women to throw themselves into feminist organizing, even in the face of hostility and public disapproval.

But these selections speak only to the hostility feminists encountered with the society at large. Rivalries between or within feminist groups were rarely aired publicly. Private discourse reveals that feminist politics, by any variant, were also infused with and shaped by partisan and class conflicts and competitions. This can be seen most clearly in the case of the liberal feminism, which by the late 1910s had come to significantly monopolize "feminism" in Uruguay, as opposed to its Catholic and Socialist variants. This chapter traces the history of liberal feminism in Uruguay from the founding of the National Women's Council (Conamu) in 1916 to the final approval of women's suffrage in 1932. This was the central core of feminist organizing during this era, and its members and organizations have left behind a more comprehensive body of historical documentation than feminisms on the Right or the Left, making a more in-depth historical analysis necessary and possible, and allowing us to see patterns that are only suggested in other cases. A chronological overview examines the ideology and programs of both Conamu and the Women's Suffrage Alliance (Alianza), focusing on the interplay of centrifugal and centripetal forces that operated within and between the organizations. Like their counterparts on the Right and Left, liberal feminist associations were affiliated with international organizations and movements, but were nevertheless profoundly shaped by local events and networks, and by (often overlapping) personal friendships and rivalries.

As the previous chapter has shown, liberal feminism was distinguished from other feminist groupings by its close linkages to the state, through educational achievement, professional position, or connections to state-sponsored social-assistance activity. These relationships shaped the outlook, orientation, and agendas of liberal feminist organizations. Partisan politics also influenced internal liberal feminist politics. Debates, conflicts, and competitions within the ruling coalitions, especially increased factionalism within the Colorado Party and a complicated relationship with the Socialists, are reflected in the internal politics of liberal feminist groups. Connected to this were important shifts in class structure and class politics that took place during this era. In addition to a growing middle-class presence, both Conamu and the Alianza attempted to incorporate working-class women into the movement, but were unable to fully transcend class prejudices or abandon tutelary models of interaction. In this, liberal feminism shared Batllismo's ambivalence toward mobilizing the working classes, and, in turn, reflected the limitations of the political moment.

The Awakening of Civil Society and the Early Years of Conamu, 1916–1918:

In September 1915, universal male suffrage was approved for the first time for the election of members of the Constitutional Convention of 1916–1917. The removal of voting restrictions on adult male citizens also meant that for the first time Uruguayan women were now uniquely disenfranchised, as gender now remained one of the few insurmountable barriers to formal political participation.[1] That uneducated immigrant males who had arrived in Uruguay as recently as three years earlier were empowered to vote, while educated women whose families may have been in Uruguay for generations were disenfranchised, likely seemed a terrible injustice to many women. This was undoubtedly keenly felt by those elite and professional women who, as described in the previous chapter, had become significant political actors in their own right in preceding years. The upcoming Constitutional Convention represented an unmatched opportunity to rectify this injustice, as well as a last best chance to implement changes when most perceived that the door of Batllista reform was slamming shut. It would be another fifteen years before women's suffrage was ratified, however. During those intervening years, feminist organizations and others debated the relative importance of women's vote within a variety of distinct and sometimes conflicting agendas, and argued about how much and in what ways women's suffrage would affect the broader political panorama in Uruguay. Thus, while Batllismo was a crucial factor in catalyzing and shaping liberal feminism, liberal feminist groups exerted their own influence over the gender politics of the Uruguayan state, and should be seen as an important element in the awakening of civil society that occurs from 1915 onward.

It was during this era of preparations for the Constitutional Congress, when conservative opposition to Batllista reforms was growing and "modern pressure groups" were emerging, that the first liberal feminist organization in Uruguay was founded. In September 1916, Paulina Luisi led the creation of the *Consejo Nacional de Mujeres Uruguayas* (Uruguayan National Women's Council, or Conamu). Conamu was a national branch of the International Council of Women (ICW), originally founded in 1888. One of the first high-profile acts of Conamu was a petition presented to the Constitutional Convention in favor of women's political rights. This was not the first time a group of women had petitioned an Uruguayan government body; Catholic women opposing divorce had done so years before. But while the Catholic antidivorce petition was initially organized and orchestrated by the leadership of the conservative Catholics, the pro-suffrage petition appears to have been a more autonomous women's project. Nor was the Conamu petition the only such document in favor of women's suffrage presented before the Constitutional Convention. A second pro-suffrage petition, organized by the Socialist Party, was also submitted. While nothing in the text of the second petition openly identifies its provenance, it contains the names of well-known Socialist women like Julia Arévalo and much of the leadership of the Socialist Women's Center, founded in 1916. The fact that there was no unified petition drive in favor of women's suffrage testifies to the fact that feminism remained plural, partisan, and divided in Uruguay. This was apparently not for lack of effort on Luisi's part. According to Amalia Polleri, Luisi asked Julia Arévalo (and, by extension, other Socialist women) to join her in the foundation of Conamu, hoping to create a broad-based organization, and perhaps to gain some leverage against the more conservative elements within the organization. Arévalo refused the offer, however, reportedly based on her view of Conamu as a "petty bourgeois movement."[2]

There were also countervailing tendencies in Conamu itself, the seeds of divisions that would mature in later years. The early Conamu membership can be largely divided into two categories: wealthy women associated with charitable work and social reform, and a circle of women representative of the first wave of female professionals in Uruguay. In the early years of the movement—from roughly 1916 to 1920—there was an important component of upper-class reformers within the groups' membership. In fact, the original and complete name of the organization was the *Federación de Sociedades Femeninas Consejo Nacional de Mujeres del Uruguay* (Federation of Feminine Societies National Women's Council of Uruguay).³ In other words, the group that presented the first women's suffrage petition to the 1917 Constitutional Convention, thus launching one of the first women's suffrage campaigns in Latin America, was in fact an umbrella organization for the social-assistance organizations of elite women, testimony to the connection between women's social assistance, Batllista state formation, and liberal feminism in its early years. These women were joined by educated professional women like Luisi, who were often of more middle-class origins and whose views on politics and the state were often quite different from those of the damas of the social-assistance set. Thus, not unlike other national branches of the ICW, the internal politics of Conamu were fraught with division and conflict, both personal and political.⁴

Such conflict was perhaps not inevitable, but it was foreseeable, as Luisi herself had been warned by an Argentine counterpart of similar problems that had emerged earlier in Buenos Aires. Liberal feminism in Uruguay, in fact, owed a great deal to the encouragement and experience of the much older movement on the other side of the Río de la Plata. Following in the footsteps of the Argentine branch, Luisi had the advantage of looking across the river to learn from others' errors. Leaders of the Argentine movement, disenchanted with the outcome of liberal feminist organizing in their own country, offered Luisi advice both before and after the 1916 foundation of Conamu. In October 1913, for example, Luisi received a letter of warning from Cecilia Grierson, the feminist physician who founded the Argentine branch of the ICW in 1900, but who later found herself pushed out of the organization. In this letter, a disenchanted Grierson advised Luisi not to repeat her mistakes:

> I have had nothing to do with the Council since 1910. We had that Congress [the Women's Congress] and the group ceased to be a Council and has become a literary-musical society (very lovely) but without the direction it should have.... I advise you that when you form the center not to be so modest as I because it can happen to you. I will give you some advice, that you reserve for yourself and your *true friends* the executive posts and the councilors....
> I hope you have more luck than I in the task.⁵

Here and elsewhere, Luisi was advised as to the necessity of involving elite women in her organization—to give the group credibility, financial support, and a more solid base. But she was simultaneously urged to be wary of this sector, and to keep them from taking control over the organization. Luisi would not be entirely successful in avoiding the pitfalls that Grierson and others warned her of, although over the long term she did manage to maintain her position as the undisputed leader of Uruguayan liberal feminism. In Uruguay at this time, the relative weakness of the middle sectors and the strength of a more elite brand of paternalistic feminism (bolstered by the state-supported ladies' committees) made a more conservative, ICW-style organization a more logical and feasible choice, at least in the early years. But rapid changes in Uruguayan society, the challenges and opportunities of an unusual political moment, and Luisi's fierce determination not to share Grierson's fate meant that the era of a relatively unified liberal feminism in Uruguay was short-lived.

Although Conamu's first official political act was a pro-suffrage petition, the vote was not the principal or even preferred focus of the organization. True to its roots in elite women's social assistance, Conamu devoted much of its early efforts to assisting and centralizing the work of the ladies' committees. In July 1917, Conamu published the first issue of *Acción Femenina*, the organization's official periodical. The inaugural issue reveals quite a bit about the group's eclectic membership base. In the early years especially, Conamu was a coalition of women with very different interests and ideological positions, and of very different social and class backgrounds, held together by the threads of a common conviction that an expanded feminine presence in the public sphere would improve women's lives and have a moralizing influence over society as a whole. The organization tried to further the social assistance agenda of the more elite membership base and to promote and defend the civil and political rights of women of varying social classes. The elite social-assistance position is seen in the Children's Assistance, Women's Assistance, and Publicity committees, whose directors spoke of poor women's and children's need for "moral assistance" and "moral hygienization." The committees saw elite women as especially equipped to do this work, and affluent women were encouraged to volunteer their time to teach poor women to live better.[6] The Legislation, Education, Professions, Finance, and Suffrage committees, on the other hand, pursued a more progressive agenda of expanding women's civil and political rights: namely the right to work, to vote, and to pursue an education.

Especially noteworthy in this respect is the Finance Committee, which announced it was pursuing a study of the salaries of working-class women with an eye toward launching what was essentially a living wage campaign on behalf of working women. This campaign ultimately came to nothing, but it indicates the breadth of feminist politics that were housed under one organizational roof.

Conamu's leadership underscores the bifurcated nature of the organization. Heading up the first group of social assistance-oriented committees were women like Dolores Estrázulas de Piñeyrúa, Berta De María de Prat, and Margarita de la Sierra de Sánchez. These three women all came to Conamu with prior experience with groups like the Unión Jeanne D'Arc, Pro-Matre, and the Bonne Garde. Estrázulas and De María came from notably affluent backgrounds: Dolores Estrázulas's husband was the first president of the Jockey Club, and Berta De María was the daughter of Bernardina Muñoz and Pablo De María, both wealthy benefactors active in social assistance and Uruguayan politics, respectively. Margarita de la Sierra was the lobbyist (mentioned in the previous chapter) who headed up a number of ladies' committees and successfully channeled public funds in their direction. In the leadership of the more progressive-oriented committees, on the other hand, were representatives of the educated professional class, those much more directly tied to the Colorado Party, and women with less experience working in state-sponsored social assistance. The Luisi sisters were well represented in the group's early leadership. Clotilde headed the Library Committee, Luisa the Professions Committee, and Paulina the committee dedicated to "Unidad de la moral," which sought to attack the sexual double standard in the law and in society. Enriqueta Compte y Riqué, a distinguished educator of relatively modest origins, directed the Education Committee; and lawyer Isabel Pinto de Vidal the Labor Commission. There were some exceptions to the pattern, of course. Carmen Cuestas de Nery, daughter of a former president and wife of the physician-reformer Carlos Nery, headed up the Suffrage Committee, and Adela Rodríguez de Morató, whose husband was a wealthy banker, headed up the Finance Committee. Surely many of these women understood that holding the group together was going to be a challenge, and the leadership had to work hard to contain all of these views and tendencies within one organization.

Conamu had some early successes. Supporters in the Constitutional Convention did get the word *man* stricken from the list of qualifications for full citizenship, and a campaign to combat "white slavery," or the international-prostitution trade, yielded some results. In 1917 Paulina Luisi reported on the efforts of women's groups and sympathetic legislators, especially those of the soon-to-be president, Baltasar Brum. "Thanks to him," Luisi wrote, "we can say that Montevideo is no longer the *American free port* for the sale of white slaves."[7] But, in general, the early work of the organization focused on the social assistance-oriented and surely less controversial work of moral reform and providing assistance to the poor. The September 1917 issue of *Acción Femenina* was dedicated exclusively to the campaign against tuberculosis, and the May-June 1918 issue focused on women's work in antialcoholism efforts. Campaigns for expanded programs of social assistance and state protection served the professional and organizational interests of many Conamu members and affiliates, but it also asserted women's right to a voice in the negotiations over the nature and extent of reforms taking place during this era. In this they were successful, and Conamu quickly became the closest thing to an official women's organization in Uruguay at this time: largely loyal to the state and able to influence the terms of feminist discourse during these years.

Polarization and Divisions, 1918–1921

The ICW was a relatively conservative organization that sought to avoid taking a strong stand on the suffrage question; this and other differences led to the formation of a new and separate international, the International Women's Suffrage Alliance (IWSA), in 1904. Realignments within the liberal feminist movement in Uruguay followed a similar path, but they reflected the particularities of local politics as well. In Uruguay, the postwar era was a time of economic and political crisis that would contribute to the split in liberal feminist ranks. The years 1918–1919 saw an economic recession coupled with painful spikes in the cost of living, fueling a tremendous upsurge in labor militancy. Politics became more polarized during these years. The economic situation and the example of the Bolshevik Revolution deeply radicalized the Socialist Party, which made important electoral gains, while within the Colorado Party the conservative Riveristas continued to broaden their support. To counter this, Batllistas attempted to win the allegiance of newly enfranchised working-class and middle-class urban voters in order to gain needed leverage against the increasingly consolidated Right and Left, culminating in the election of Baltasar Brum to

Figure 13:
The Uruguayan National Women's Council during the 1920s. Paulina Luisi does not appear to be in this picture. Reprinted from *Enciclopédia Uruguaya* no. 38 (1969) with permission from Editorial Arca.

the presidency in 1919. As we saw in Chapter 2, Brum's election and subsequent proposals to create a "feminist" civil code significantly increased expectations in liberal feminist circles. In this environment, debates and power struggles between more conservative and more progressive elements within Conamu were revitalized.

It was within this context of crisis and polarization that an important split took place within the liberal feminist movement, between a more conservative and elite faction and a younger, more middle-class and progressive group that was more aggressively pro-suffragist. In August 1919, Paulina Luisi and others founded the *Alianza Uruguaya por el Sufragio Femenino* (Uruguayan Women's Suffrage Alliance, or Alianza), an affiliate of the IWSA. Both Conamu and the Alianza publicly portrayed this split as an amicable separation and/or one dictated more by international events than local politics. Based on public discourse and official documents, it does appear to be a friendly separation. But internal and private correspondence reveals that the personal and political divisions were deeper and more substantial than the public discourse suggests. The split in late 1919 certainly was about the priority of suffrage, as well as bureaucratic issues related to international affiliation, but it was also about party politics and personal power struggles specific to the local context. There is little question, for example, that serious problems emerged between Luisi and another Conamu leader, Isabel Pinto de Vidal, the second Uruguayan woman to earn a law degree, an instructor at the Women's University, and a loyal Batllista. That there was a clash of personalities between Luisi and Pinto de Vidal there is no doubt, but these conflicts were of a political nature as well, part of a power struggle between Batllistas and anti-Batllistas within the organization.[8] Socialists and Batllistas were vying for control over the progressive reformist space within Uruguayan politics, and this competition naturally made its way into Uruguayan liberal feminism.[9]

Internal tensions were exacerbated by the fact that, in 1918–1919 Paulina Luisi made some definitive steps toward the Socialists, moves that probably antagonized more loyal Batllistas, and alienated her from the group's more conservative elements. In December 1918, Luisi was a featured speaker at the first conference of the Socialist Women's Center in Montevideo. As we saw in the previous chapter, Luisi courted Socialist women while maintaining some distance from the party itself. While she clarified that she was not an active member of the Socialist Party, Luisi lauded the Socialists for being "the only party that proclaims the equality of the sexes... which [I consider] a badge of honor."[10] In April of 1919, when the First Pan-American Socialist and Labor Congress was held in Buenos Aires, Luisi authored a letter of adherence on behalf of Conamu. Here she spoke of the "debt of gratitude" Conamu had to the party, and closed the letter calling for "the triumph of the noble ideals pursued by this Congress."[11] Perhaps in response to Luisi's warm approbation, in July 1919 a special issue of *Nuestra Causa*—a magazine affiliated with the Argentine Socialist Party—was published in Buenos Aires on the subject of Uruguayan feminism. Here Luisi praised Uruguayan Socialist Julia Arévalo as "intelligent and enlightened" and called on working women to join with Conamu.[12] Luisi then claimed that "the affiliation of the Socialist Women's Center and the Telephone Operators' Union [with Conamu] is currently in process."[13] These public declarations on Luisi's part, I argue, were both cause and effect of a deepening polarization between conservatives and progressives within Conamu. While Luisi may have wanted to redefine the organization's orientation and push conservatives aside, what happened instead was a split in liberal feminist ranks. Her attempts to bring Socialist women into the Council fell largely on deaf ears, and her overtures to the Socialists may well have antagonized more moderate and conservative

Figure 14:
Paulina Luisi, 1918.
Author's collection.

elements within Conamu, fueling preexisting tensions between Luisi and Pinto de Vidal. The Alianza was founded in August 1919, two weeks after the *Nuestra Causa* issue came out.

From its foundation, the Alianza sought to define a new agenda for liberal feminism, one that moved away from an emphasis on social assistance and sought to appeal to middle-class professional women interested in the vote and in gaining access to state employment. The Alianza consistently and persistently sought to influence state officials and governing bodies, seeking to interject what were seen as women's issues into the state and, in some cases, women themselves. They were, of course, active around the issue of women's suffrage, a priority of the IWSA. Because language allowing for women's voting rights was already in the Constitution (requiring ratification to become law), the Alianza concentrated its efforts on lobbying the legislature, formally presenting their case in 1921–1922, and again in 1926–1927. They also organized around issues of antimilitarism and disarmament, another emphasis of the IWSA, invoking maternalist rhetoric to urge the administration to involve itself in peacemaking efforts: "woman cannot consent without the severest pangs in the depths of their maternal being...to woman war means the overthrowing of the destructive work of her pain and sacrifices, that creative work to which she has been dedicated by nature."[14]

The Alianza was also very active in trying to expand women's access to government posts and other restricted professions. Placing women in positions of authority within the Uruguayan welfare state was a way to assert women's citizenship and open a path toward women's suffrage. In the early 1920s, the Alianza resuscitated an earlier Conamu campaign to place women in government bodies overseeing social assistance and education such as the National Public Assistance, the Council of Delinquents and Minors, and the Council of Primary and Secondary Education. They cited woman's "natural" aptitude for such work, "which corresponds perfectly with woman's temperament and characteristics."[15] The campaign was seconded and supported in a regular feminist column in the newspaper *La Mañana* under the direction of Fanny Carrió de Polleri. Echoing Luisi's medicalized discourse, a March 1921 column employed corporeal metaphors to advocate women's greater participation in the state, arguing: "the State deprived of women is as reduced to impotence as an individual who has had an arm or a leg amputated." The lack of women in state agencies, Carrió argued, has left them inefficient and ineffective: "it has been clearly demonstrated that male eyes have suffered from a fatal myopia; [perhaps] feminine eyes that can see intelligently could restore the prestige of some institutions and extend that of others."[16] The campaign to increase the feminine presence in public posts continued, in fits and starts, for most of the decade; its goals were not realized until 1929, when Alianza leader and lawyer Sara Rey Álvarez became the first woman named to serve on the Council of Delinquents and Minors. During this same era, the Alianza lobbied hard for legislation allowing women to serve as notaries and as legal witnesses (women were barred from both because citizenship was a requirement).[17] It was not until 1926 that the law was actually passed to allow women to act as notaries and "revoking the measures which disqualify women from acting as witnesses."[18] Access to state employment—beyond the lowest rungs of schoolteachers and low-level functionaries—simultaneously served the feminist and professional interests of many Alianza members.

Liberal Feminism, 1916-1932

For a number of years after the foundation of the Alianza, relations between the two groups apparently remained friendly. But after 1921 tensions increased as relations between Luisi and the Conamu leadership (especially Pinto de Vidal) continued to worsen. In 1921, Luisi left Conamu, issuing an angry resignation in which she accused the organization of unethical and conspiratorial behavior. While most of the internal details of this confrontation are lost, the evidence suggests continued struggles between Batllistas and anti-Batllistas (Socialists and others) for control over Conamu and liberal feminism generally. Luisi had imperious (and sometimes paranoid) tendencies, but in this case her apprehension of a conspiracy against her may well have been correct. In July 1921, for example, the Batllista press published a number of articles on the subject of feminism and the Colorado Party. There seems no question that there was a concerted effort going on to discredit Luisi, although the source of or the motivation for that campaign is not entirely clear. The letter, signed Edelmira U. de Márquez, asserted the following:

> The numerous articles appearing in the newspapers about the recognition of women's political rights and the erroneous claims that some of them contain with respect to initiatives attributed to Miss Paulina Luisi... oblige me to ask the Editor to publish these lines.... It is not my intention to discredit the merits of this distinguished *compatriota*, but I am interested in... making it perfectly clear that initiative, that dates many years back, completely belongs to the First Committee of Colorado Ladies [*Damas Coloradas*] of Uruguay, to whose foundation I contributed on August 1, 1916, and over which I had the honor to preside.[19]

There is little evidence to support this author's claims, however, and the main motivation seems to be to rewrite history so as to discredit Luisi. First, there is no evidence that the Damas Coloradas existed prior to Conamu's foundation. Second, the manifesto of the Damas Coloradas never called for women's voting rights, and the group played no official role in the 1916–1917 petition campaign in favor of women's suffrage. The group's self-proclaimed reason for existence was to support a presidential candidacy of Batlle y Ordóñez, whose "strong and virile hand" they credited for bringing an end to the bloody civil wars of the previous century. The name Edelmira U. de Márquez appears nowhere in the rosters of any feminist organizations during the years in question. The group seems to have been most active in 1918–1919, precisely at the time that Batllista/Socialist splits were beginning to emerge and Luisi was moving toward the Socialists, suggesting that the organization may have been revived in an attempt to (re)assert Batllista control over liberal feminist organizing.[20] The letter which appeared in *El Día* was likely an indication of a larger campaign against Luisi going on within Conamu. It was only a few months after the *El Día* letter, in December of 1921, that Luisi resigned from the organization that she herself had founded five years earlier. Batllista Isabel Pinto de Vidal became the new president of Conamu. Luisi cited irregularities with the minutes, "disloyalty," and "insidious editing" as her reasons for her decision to resign, and it seems clear that personal and political factors had combined to push Luisi and others out of Conamu's leadership.[21]

There is, in fact, some evidence to suggest that the Alianza was (at least initially) home to some sort of anti-Batllista feminist alliance, made up of more conservative Colorados (Riveristas and Vieristas) in conjunction with Socialists and their sympathizers. At the same time that Luisi was moving toward the Socialists, her friend and ally Fanny Carrió de Polleri began publishing her regular column "Para Nosotras" in her husband's Riverista newspaper *La Mañana*.[22] Carrió wrote using the pseudonym "Fafhm," the initials of her (then) five children. "Para Nosotras" was above all a regular defense of the need to incorporate women into the political process. Over many months, "Fafhm" argued in favor of women's right to vote and to participate in state bodies overseeing children and education. Her discourse centered on two main points: women's vote as part of the process of historical evolution, and defending feminism against charges of being anti-male or anti-family. On many occasions, and in different ways, "Fafhm" maintained that the new capitalist and individualistic era had made women's suffrage necessary, and rendered traditional notions of woman's place anachronistic and unrealistic. The old paternalistic model might have been fine in the days of "gallantry," "chivalry," and "well-being," she argued, "[b]ut how different is this chimera from the current reality! The economic struggle has ripped women from the sweetness of the home and has subjected her to all its demands and uncertainties."[23] In a society based on individuals, it was no longer possible to justify denying women the vote. Carrió further asserted that women's political rights were in keeping with Uruguay's self-image as a champion of advanced social policy, and in

Figure 15: Fanny Carrió de Polleri, c. 1918. One of Luisi's closest friends and political confidantes, Carrió's eloquent and impassioned letters to Luisi reveal much about the internal workings of liberal feminism in Uruguay. Reprinted from *Nuestra Causa* (Buenos Aires), 18 July 1918.

keeping with the moral agenda of the Batllista state, which was to "facilitate the improvement of the least capacitated."[24] Lastly, Carrió and others vigorously criticized the notion that feminism undermined womanliness. "Our feminism is feminine," she wrote, using her own status as a loving wife and mother as proof that feminism did not emerge out of "hostility towards or rivalry with men."[25] This argument was seconded by another regular contributor to *La Mañana*, Carmen C. de Queirolo. Identifying herself as "the most womanly among women," she asserted: "I strongly maintain that to be a feminist is the most exquisite manifestation of femininity."[26] Lastly, the feminist columns in *La Mañana* in 1919 strongly urged women to unite to demand women's suffrage and other necessary reforms. The fact that such a strong feminist and pro-women's suffrage push was coming from a Riverista paper suggests that Batllismo was losing its grip on liberal feminism, and that a strong mobilizing impulse was now coming from outside of the Batllista camp.

Chapter Four

In December 1922, Fanny Carrió wrote a letter to Luisi describing her efforts to recruit women into the Alianza, writing that "today we came to an agreement with [Rosa Mauthone] Falco to work to attract women. They say that the Socialists are not Batllistas and I am going to see if I can bring them into the Alianza."[27] This letter is intriguing on many levels, not the least of which is the apparent aversion—at least on Carrió's part—to the presence of Batllistas in the organization. Unlike Conamu, the Alianza did have some minimal success in recruiting Socialist women. There were at least five women who held membership in both the Alianza and the Socialist Party for at least some part of the decade between 1920 and 1930. Of these members, the most prominent was María Devita, a Socialist who was very active in the leadership of the Alianza.[28] It is important to note, however, that this Alianza/Socialist link takes place after most radical Socialists had left to found the Communist Party, a subject to which we will return in a later chapter. Thus the divisions and reconfigurations of liberal feminism during these years were as much about local partisan politics and rivalries as they were about international trends and personal animosities.

Liberal feminist realignments were also the result of changes in group membership; namely, the departure of many of the older more elite conservatives and the entry of a new generation of younger, more middle-class, and more progressive professional women. Between 1917 and 1923, the membership base of Uruguayan liberal feminism changed significantly, reflecting a relative decline in elite participation and an increased middle-class presence. Within the first few years, many of the most conservative and wealthy women left Conamu, while many of the more middle-class members joined the Alianza. Amalia Polleri (the daughter of Fanny Carrió de Polleri) described the women who abandoned the liberal feminist movement during this era: "The ladies quit going because [they disagreed with] all this about turning over society and no longer being the pampered little girls, the queens of their homes.... In the end... they wanted to be queens.... Many stayed... but the most elegant and well dressed, with jewels and all of that, they left."[29] "The circle (elenco) changed in the Alianza," Polleri added. "The Alianza was extracted from more popular roots."[30]

Polleri's impressions are corroborated by the membership data for both organizations, most dramatically if one compares the early membership of Conamu (those who left before 1923) with the general membership of the Alianza. There is, as one might expect, an age difference, with the average birthdate for the first group being 1882, and the average birthdate for the Alianza group being 1892.[31] Differing residential patterns echo these generational differences, but also point to class differences between Conamu and Alianza members. Home addresses reveal both the suburbanization of the new middle sectors and the changing class affiliation of this new generation of feminists. In both groups the percentage living in the older and more aristocratic Old City is limited (5 percent of each group); within the 1918–1923 Conamu group, 64 percent lived in the Centro/Cordon (New City) section, with another 22 percent living in the Prado/Unión section of the city (another sector of the city mostly associated with old wealth), and with only 9 percent living in Pocitos, an emerging zone of the city associated with the middle class and "new" bourgeoisie. In the Alianza group, on the other hand, while the majority (52 percent) still lived in the New City, only 11 percent listed their residence as Prado/Unión, and fully 30 percent were living in the Pocitos area.[32] Thus, just as we saw in the previous chapter, the shifts that were displacing elite women from social assistance were marginalizing them within liberal feminism as well. Even after the departure of many of the "millionaires," Conamu remained an older, more conservative organization with direct ties to Batllista leadership. Yet even though the Alianza may have better fit her political orientation and style, Luisi tried to maintain her connection to Conamu. After resigning in 1921, Luisi returned temporarily to Conamu shortly thereafter, only to have a new round of conflicts within the group's leadership. "The prodigal son always has a special place in a mother's heart," she later wrote.[33]

Finally, in a country like Uruguay, where European immigration was such an important factor, it is important to take a look at the role of immigrants within feminist organizations. Lavrin has seen the preponderance of Italian, French, and English surnames as indicative of a strong immigrant presence in Uruguayan liberal feminism.[34] Yet judging by last name in a nation of immigrants can be problematic and, at times, deceiving. By this method, Spanish immigrants are indistinguishable from criollos and the grandchildren of immigrants indistinguishable from recent arrivals. More detailed personal data, in fact, reveals the opposite of what Lavrin concludes: the vast majority of liberal feminists in Uruguay were native-born. Out of more than 150 members of Conamu and the Alianza for whom data is available, no more than 5 were European-born. The percentage of immigrants may indeed have been slightly higher, given that this sample is likely skewed in favor of the native-born (for whom better documentation would certainly have been available), but the evidence points away from immigrants having a prominent place in either group. Moreover, placing "natives" into one category and "immigrants" in another creates a false dichotomy in a society whose patterns were more complex. Many of the liberal feminists were in fact the locally born children of an immigrant parent (usually a father) and a native-born parent (usually a mother). This was the case for fully half of the Alianza sample. How should we classify such women? While the preponderance of non-Spanish surnames reminds us that Uruguay was a nation largely built upon European immigration, most liberal feminists were criollas doing politics at home. Where we are most likely to find first-generation immigrants is not among the affluent and middle-class liberal feminists, but in left, labor, and working-class women's groups. We find immigrants among the signatories of the Socialist Party suffrage petition, members of the Sectional Committee of the Alianza discussed below, or members of the Communist Party discussed in the next chapter. In sum, the use of last name as data for social history in this case is at best uninformative, at worst misleading, and cannot be used in the place of more substantial data.

Downturn to Victory?
1923–1932

The end of Brum's presidency in 1923 marked the beginning of a roughly six-year downturn in liberal feminist activity and in social reform generally. In two separate 1924 letters, Fanny Carrió de Polleri complained to Paulina Luisi about the sad state of feminist organizing during these years. "Feminism among us is suffering a period of inertia," she wrote, describing the organizing environment as one of "desperate apathy."[35] Perhaps as a way to reenergize a flagging movement, in December 1923, the Uruguayan Pro-Suffrage Alliance changed its name to the *Alianza Uruguaya de Mujeres* (Uruguayan Women's Alliance). Signifying a broadening of the scope of the organization, this change also made the group a more direct competitor with Conamu. This change officially extended the field of activity of the Alianza to include civil and economic rights and the struggle for a single moral standard for men and women (specifically referring to the campaign against white slavery and regulated prostitution).[36] Conamu suffered even greater troubles during this time. Having lost many of the damas and the more progressive middle-class professionals, the group was left with a skeleton of its former self.

This era saw yet another round of serious conflicts between Luisi and Conamu (Luisi had since returned to the organization), and these conflicts again made their way onto the pages of *El Día*, this time by Luisi's initiative. Luisi was out of the country a great deal between 1923 and 1925, active in international feminist organizing and working with the League of Nations on issues such as the international trafficking in women. Angry letters and misunderstandings between Luisi and the Conamu leadership (over the alleged rewriting of her work and other irregularities) climaxed with an interview published in *El Día* in July 1924, where Luisi publicly criticized Conamu as a conservative, moribund organization, more so even than the International to which it belonged. "The International [Women's] Council supports antiquated ideas," she explained, "but I would go along with the Uruguayan Women's Council if they at least shared these ideas." Asked about the Alianza, Luisi replied: "the Alianza, in all ways, represents advanced women. There is more awareness about the current situation among the members."[37] Airing these grievances in public was an extraordinary move on Luisi's part, since both organizations tried to maintain the appearance of amicability. Shortly thereafter, Luisi was relieved of her duties as external secretary of Conamu. This move created waves, both in Uruguay and at the level of the International, and did nothing to halt Conamu's slide into obscurity. Shortly thereafter, some members sought a rapprochement, and in 1925 *Acción Femenina* dedicated an issue entirely to Paulina Luisi, an obvious attempt to mend the damage done in earlier years. But Luisi refused to return to Conamu without a change in the organization's leadership. She appears to have gotten her way when, later that year, both Isabel Pinto de Vidal and Cata Castro de Quintela, president and secretary respectively, resigned their offices, and a new board was established. As it turned out, the 1925 homage to Luisi was the last issue of *Acción Femenina* to be published.[38]

Both Conamu and the Alianza continued their activity through the doldrums of the mid-1920s, and liberal feminist activity began to pick up again during the presidency of Juan Campestiguy (1927–1931), as the political and economic polarization of the late 1920s began to make itself felt. Both Stalinism and fascism were taking shape in Europe, and once again the climate called for reformist action on the part of the state. It was during this "second reformist impulse"

(1928–1932) that liberal feminists were energized by what they saw as a new opportunity to push for women's voting rights. In 1929 both Conamu and the Alianza came together for the final offensive of women's suffrage, and together organized a large university conference in favor of women's political rights. The movement had consciously decided to use the upcoming (1930) Centennial celebrations as the moment for the final offensive on women's suffrage. The conference itself serves as testimony to the ground gained by Uruguayan women in the professions. The featured speakers were women physicians, lawyers, educators, authors, journalists, and notaries. Subjects of the presentations included a discussion of the struggle for women's political and civil rights in Uruguay and internationally, and lectures on women in history, work, education, the professions, and the arts. Following the conference, the proceedings were compiled and published, and the book, entitled *La mujer uruguaya reclama sus derechos políticos* (The Uruguayan Woman Demands Her Political Rights), became an important source of liberal feminist propaganda. It is noteworthy that, at this event, the Alianza was given top billing, and that Isabel Pinto de Vidal did not speak at the conference. In many ways, the 1929 conference represented the apex of the women's suffrage movement in Uruguay. Most newspaper coverage assumed that the sanctioning of women's suffrage was imminent, and all political forces scrambled to curry female support.

Why women's suffrage was not approved in 1929 is not entirely clear, but the death of Batlle y Ordóñez and the onset of the Depression may have done much to derail the proposal. In 1931, the Alianza and Conamu began another petition campaign, ultimately presenting some four thousand signatures in favor of women's political rights to the legislature. When that tactic, too, proved unsuccessful, the Alianza took the lead in seeking the adhesion of any and all women's associations, hoping to convince legislators that women's suffrage was not a minority position. In March 1932 the Alianza created the *Comité Pro-Derechos de la Mujer* (Pro-Women's Rights Committee). Also known as the "Mixed Committee," this group included Conamu and many longtime Conamu affiliate organizations as well as some new ones like the *Escuela Feminista* (Feminist School), whose names had never previously appeared.[39] Finally, in December 1932, both houses of the legislature voted to sanction women's suffrage at the municipal and national level. The law should be understood as the result of a combination of pressures from the

Figure 16:
The Uruguayan Woman Demands her Political Rights, 1929.

"I'm hurrying to finish my [house]work, so I can go to the women's rights conference today at the University."

"Yes, Doctor Paulina Luisi (the most intelligent of the family), Juana de Ibarbourou [a well-known poet who did not speak at the conference], Elisa Barros Daguerre [another physician/obstetrician] and others will be speaking."

"Ah, when we vote they will look at us differently."

Political Cartoon reprinted from *Tinta China*, 5 December 1929. Archivo Paulina Luisi, Archivo General de la Nación, Montevideo.

liberal feminist movement and the political parties themselves, all of whom were attempting to court women's political favor in hopes that it would tip the delicate balance of forces that characterized Uruguayan politics in the last months before the coup d'état of March 1933. In fact, among at least the more progressive of the liberal feminists, there was by this point a great deal of disillusionment about the impact of women's suffrage on Uruguayan society, as much of the heady optimism about the "civilizing hand of woman" had faded by that point.[40]

Talk of forming a separate Women's Party had circulated among liberal feminists since 1919 when Julieta Lanteri Renshaw founded a National Feminist Party in Argentina.[41] Once Uruguayan women won the vote, this issue resurfaced, with no less controversy than it had encountered in earlier years. In January 1933, shortly after women's suffrage was approved, Paulina Luisi (writing from Madrid) sent a letter to the secretary general of the Alianza, Sara Rey Álvarez. Luisi congratulated Álvarez on the final attainment of women's suffrage, but voiced concerns about her decision to found the *Partido Independiente Democrático Femenino* (Women's Independent Democratic Party). Luisi wrote:

> You talk to me with much enthusiasm of the women's party that is forming.... I don't think I can accompany you there since I am absolutely opposed to this method and, as you know, to certain aspects of the program... I can say that, as to the formation of a women's party, I will not voice any opposition—but neither will I be a part of it.[42]

In a response letter to Luisi, Álvarez argued that a Women's Party was "the only effective means to realize feminist goals. Up to now, you know as well as I do that all the parties have given to feminism and to women are empty promises." Álvarez complained that, for some time now, the political parties had been actively trying to co-opt liberal feminism, voicing feminist rhetoric with no real intention of implementing reform. "The sad reality," she wrote, "is this: the vast majority of women are entering the parties, especially the Civic Union [Catholic political party], like the great ovine mass you spoke about."[43] Paulina Luisi, it seems, was not alone in her opposition to this strategy. When asked whether Paulina or her mother Fanny Carrió de Polleri had anything to do with the *Partido Feminista* (as it came to be known), Amalia Polleri responded: "nobody had anything to do with it. It was an invention. An invention against Paulina.... They got no votes. Nobody voted for it. If they got votes it would have only been ten."[44] Polleri was only slightly exaggerating: the party received 122 votes in the 1938 elections. Indeed, it is difficult to imagine that, after so many struggles where partisan loyalties lay just under the surface, liberal feminists would abandon their party affiliations at the very moment when they first won the right to vote.

Liberal Feminism, la mujer obrera, and the Uruguayan State:

La mujer obrera—or the working-class woman—presented difficulties for all of the organizations being studied here, and was in many ways the most illusive sector of society in terms of political organization. Many liberal feminists may have had good intentions regarding the integration of working-class and poor women into their groups, but often their assumptions and desire to maintain control over the movement prevented them from overcoming class obstacles.[45] Of course, the presumptions of middle- and upper-class liberal feminists were only some among many obstacles preventing working-class women's participation in feminist groups: many proletarian women were already overburdened with a double workday and simply lacked the time and support to engage in political activity. And not all liberal feminists were alike in this regard. In general, Conamu supported and campaigned for what were largely protective and piecemeal reforms. But in the face of more militant activity, or any action or proposal that directly threatened their class interests, Conamu retreated to a position of ambivalence and, sometimes, outright hostility. The more middle-class Alianza had a stronger commitment to cross-class organizing and adopted a somewhat less paternalistic approach than Conamu, but they too continued to view working-class women as auxiliary members and second-class feminists. Inter-feminist competition was also an important factor shaping recruitment strategies in working-class communities. Many understood that the group that successfully won working women's allegiance could shape the direction of women's integration into the political system. Thus, the goal in many cases was as much to neutralize working women and prevent them from joining up with the Communists or Catholics as much as it was to incorporate them into the liberal feminist project.

The question of liberal feminist outreach to working-class women seems to have blended with mounting Batllista/anti-Batllista tensions in 1918–1920. In 1918, during the height of the postwar economic crisis, Isabel Pinto de Vidal—then president of Conamu's Labor Committee—spoke of plans to expand the committee's work to better include working-class women and to direct conferences more specifically at workers. But this was not the appropriate moment to embark upon such a project, she wrote, given "the latest working class agitations that have so profoundly shaken our city."[46] Thus, precisely at a moment when working-class militancy was on the rise, Conamu shied away from recruiting working-class women. In the meantime, Paulina Luisi was embarking on her first direct experience with women's labor organizing, at the same time as she was taking the steps toward the Socialists mentioned above. One of the earliest and most sustained connections between liberal feminists and women workers was via the telephone operators (*telefonistas*). By the late 1910s, both the telephone and the telephone operator had made their way into the culture of the Montevidean middle and upper classes. With more than ten thousand phone subscribers in Montevideo by this time, "the families of the upper and ruling class had already incorporated it into their habits and status," making an average of four phone calls a day.[47] Telephone operators were almost all young women. In 1918, the operators at "La Uruguaya" telephone company began to organize, protesting low wages and poor working conditions stemming largely from the fact that the number of telephone operators employed was not keeping pace with the increasing number of telephones and telephone calls in the city. The early initiative for Conamu's involvement with the telefonistas came in a letter to Paulina Luisi from Socialist Party head Emilio Frugoni, dated November 29, 1918:

> I want to take this opportunity to ask for your help. It has to do with the telefonistas ... [who are trying] to improve their working conditions.... Could you go and see them, if you agree to lend them your help and influence? I think that your intervention would be very helpful; can we count on the union of your good heart?[48]

Luisi followed up on this request. The December 7 issue of *El Día* reported on the activities and demands of the telephone operators at "La Uruguaya" telephone company. The workers were demanding a salary increase from twenty-three to thirty pesos per month, and a reduction in the number of phone lines for which each operator was responsible (from one hundred to eighty). The article also spoke of the "mediation" being offered by Conamu and by Luisi in particular. "Paulina Luisi" the paper said, "had several meetings with the Manager of the Company and some members of the local Board."[49] In mid-December, Frugoni wrote to Luisi again, thanking her for her participation with the telephone workers. In fact, the Telephone Workers' Union spent a short period of time as an affiliate organization with Conamu, the only group of working women to do so.

But this relationship between the telefonistas and Conamu changed, as the workers became more radicalized in the years between 1918 and 1922. A 1919 letter from Fanny Carrió de Polleri to Paulina Luisi a few months before the Conamu/Alianza split described what was clearly becoming a troubled relationship: "Dra. [Isabel Pinto de] Vidal did some great work for the telefonistas, keeping them from having to go on strike, and as usual... they did not even thank her. Some women deserve the beatings they get."[50] But whatever "great work" Vidal and Conamu did for the telefonistas, it appears to have done nothing to improve their working situation, since the complaints and concerns of the telefonistas remained largely unchanged after Conamu's intervention. While for women like Pinto de Vidal avoiding a strike may have been seen as the ultimate success, this might have been viewed very differently by the telefonistas themselves, especially since it seems to have yielded few concrete results. The other noteworthy aspect of Carrió's comment is the offense taken by what was construed to be a lack of requisite gratitude on the telefonistas' part. They had, in essence, violated the paternalistic code, whereby social superiors exchange protection in exchange for grateful obedience on the part of subordinates. That Carrió uses a metaphorical allusion to domestic violence—a "corrective" measure for women who challenge patriarchal control—is particularly telling (and disturbing). It is not surprising, perhaps, that the telefonistas ultimately gravitated toward the Communists and away from liberal feminists in seeking to improve their labor conditions.

This tendency to blame working-class women for their lack of interest in Conamu persisted beyond the foundation of the Alianza. In the September-December 1922 issue of *Acción Femenina*, (now President) Pinto de Vidal lamented Conamu's inability to organize working-class women, showing frustration and a certain disdain:

> I have seen proof of how difficult it is to find new recruits, since, even working women, those who need legislative and social changes most... don't even think about associating themselves and even less about affiliating themselves with we who are always in the breach when it comes to seeking just solutions for women and children.[51]

Working women, in other words, were portrayed as apathetic, apolitical, and (once again) unappreciative of the work more privileged women had done on their behalf. Here Pinto de Vidal cast herself and others as martyrs, sacrificing themselves on behalf of unresponsive and indifferent working-class women. Rather than provoke a critical self-evaluation, working women's lack of response to Conamu was blamed on working women themselves. No wonder there was little communion between Conamu and women of the popular classes during the post-1919 years. Ironically, the issue of *Acción Femenina* from which the above quote was taken was published on the eve of one of the most important women's labor actions of this era: the strike of the telephone operators. In early September 1922, workers at the *Companía Telefónica de Montevideo* went on strike.[52] This was one of the most successful labor actions of the era. The strike was so prolonged (forty-five days), so disruptive, and so violent that the government was eventually forced to intervene on the side of the strikers. Workers who struck demanding a raise from about thirty-two to forty pesos a month ended up with fifty pesos a month. While the union denied charges of sabotage in the pages of the (now) Communist paper *Justicia*, the wording of such denials suggests that in fact such sabotage did take place (the cutting of wires, the downing of telephone poles, etc.).[53] There were numerous arrests of striking telefonistas, and *Justicia* reported that a woman was injured in a knife fight between striking female telephone operators and the father of a strikebreaker.[54] While nearly daily reports on the strike appeared in *Justicia*, *Acción Femenina* made no mention of the telephone workers' union after the strike began. Indeed, Conamu seems to have gone to some lengths to distance itself from an organization that had moved closer to the Communist unions.

The telephone workers' strike was not the only event forcing the women of Conamu to tread gingerly between their feminist ideals and their class interests. While in the case of the telefonistas Conamu was and could be supportive (at least initially), their position was quite different when it came to a labor issue that was literally closer to home: legislation regulating domestic service. In 1921 there was a proposal to extend the six-day workweek to domestic workers, providing them a mandatory day off away from their place of employment. This proposed law was significant for at least two reasons: first, it was the clearest example of the state intervening in the private sphere of the household; and second, it potentially pitted the interests of upper- and middle-class women directly against those of working-class women. Even more than with the telephone operators, the position taken by Conamu on this proposed legislation illustrates that class interests could and did trump gender interests when the two came into conflict.

As an organization representing women's interests, Conamu was not infrequently asked for its opinion on proposed legislation that touched on such issues. The proposed domestic worker law was one such instance, and in January 1921 Conamu sent its official response to the Ministry of Labor. While the letter recognized that after six days of work, one certainly needed to rest, and that "the body and spirit needed to recover its strength," it then went on to identify several potential problems with the legislation as it was written. Many domestic servants were foreigners, they explained, or migrants from the countryside, with no other home in the capital than that of their employer. Under such circumstances, such a law could threaten the servants' (and her employers' honor), since a full day off could "give rise to temptations that in most cases could produce a threat to their own decency [and] that, if it became public, could be damaging to the stability of the servants in their places of employment." Furthermore, servants might choose to use their day off working for someone else, hence undermining the very intent of the law.[55] The final recommendation of the leadership of Conamu was in favor of "two half days of rest, allowing the employer the choice whether or not to authorize nighttime outings."[56] While it is true that a mandatory day out of the employer's home could have posed problems for live-in servants with no family or friends nearby, the Conamu position shows a reluctance to allow domestic servants to make their own choices about how mandatory rest should be enforced, and their counterproposal reflects traditional paternalistic ideas that employers should be able to control any activity that could threaten the honor of the patrons' household.[57]

As an organization ostensibly speaking on behalf of all women, this proposed legislation placed Conamu members in a somewhat awkward position. As middle- and upper-class women dependent on domestic servitude and as women who maintained all the prejudices and particularistic interests of their class, they were deeply ambivalent about the proposed change. The resolution was to maintain a lukewarm public support for the law despite private reticence. During that same month, the Directive of Conamu in Montevideo sent a letter to its Departmental Committee in Durazno, informing them of the position that the leadership had taken on this proposed legislation:

> This being one of those problems that by its nature deals with the internal order of the home, and could intensely impact on more than one occasion its internal functioning... the feminine interest must always be of primordial attention, we have felt it best to urge all women that they not see in this law a conflict of interests but something that discretely applied could be beneficial.[58]

Conamu, in other words, urged its members to put their commitment to women's issues above their class interests, something that many were clearly wont to do. It seems that it was not only the women of Conamu who were rubbed the wrong way by the proposed law, since it was not until 1931 that a law requiring a rest for domestic workers was passed. This legislation, which instituted a six-day workweek, made a specific provision for domestic workers, allowing an arrangement where the employee took only a half-day off per week, with the remaining time accumulating as vacation time.[59]

In keeping with its more popular membership base, the Alianza seems to have made greater efforts than Conamu at attracting working-class women, even if these efforts also yielded minimal results. Amalia Polleri explained that there were some Alianza efforts to recruit working-class women, but they were not wholly successful, due largely to the time and economic constraints of women trying to manage a double workday:

> They went to speak to the women workers at the doors of the factories. But, the women workers had all the work of the factory, the eight hours, and had their own lives and their own obligations. Thus the working women did not really participate in the feminist movement. Which does not mean that they were not feminists. When one spoke with them they were in

agreement and it seemed disgusting to them what men did with their lives. But they had no time. Thus they did not take part; in general they did not take part.[60]

Alianza members did, in fact, go to factories and talk to workers, and apparently they did occasionally enjoy moderate success. Polleri's account of Alianza contact with working women may have been a version of an incident that her mother Fanny Carrió related to Paulina Luisi in a 1922 letter. "Yesterday (Saturday)," she wrote, "we went to a conference that Miss Falco gave in order to 'pillage' signatures from the working women in the factories of Paso [Molino]. And between Vitale (excellent *compañera*), Devita, *et moi* we made these girls members of the Alianza."[61] According to María Devita, one of the few Socialists in the Alianza, these events took place at a meeting of the *Comité Magisterial* (Teachers' Committee) held in Paso Molino, and the workers were from the Salvo and Martínez factories.[62] The fact that Luisi received two letters about this incident from Alianza leaders suggests that it was an unusual accomplishment. Another, perhaps related, success story came in 1924, with the creation of the short-lived *Comité Seccional de la Alianza* (Sectional Committee of the Alianza). In September 1924, a woman by the name of María Soliverri sent a letter to acting Alianza president Fanny Carrió, expressing her support for the ideas of the Alianza. She spoke of the way Carrió and the others had inspired her:

> uniting with your worthy project is a duty to justice. And believe *señora* that from the bottom of my soul I do it as a woman and as a worker. As a woman to defend the rights of the sex, and as a worker to safeguard the collective interests.... Let us struggle then for in the struggle is the secret of triumph.[63]

Attached to this letter was a list of names, with the heading Comité Seccional de la Alianza. In December 1924 Carrió wrote to Luisi about the event:

> María, this *señora* that is a seamstress at the J. de Guerra that has brought about 120 supporters [to a meeting of the Alianza]. But they are our people, that respond to us and when the D[irective] meets we will propose the formation

> of a Sectional Committee with this element...we will give them lectures, conferences, etc.[64]

Here these women are still cast in a largely passive role, as women whom the leaders of the movement can educate. Indeed, the fact that these women were incorporated into the Alianza as a "sectional committee" and not as full members is telling. From all available documentation, it appears that not much ever came of this project, and not one of the names on this list ever appears in the later membership lists of the Alianza. In sum, while both Conamu and to a greater extent the Alianza sought the participation and inclusion of working-class women in their organizational projects, neither had much success, in part due to members' inability to overcome class bias and the desire to maintain hegemony over their respective organizations. Elite and middle-class women could not, or were unwilling, to see ways to create a more inclusive movement. Liberal feminists were not alone, however, in their inability to attract sustained attention and allegiance of working women, as we will see in the following chapters.

Conclusion

Conamu in this era should be understood as a transitional organization between the older nineteenth-century beneficent societies and anticlerical associations, and twentieth-century women's political organizations centered on issues of secular social and political reform. In this the history of liberal feminism in Uruguay echoes European (and to a lesser extent, U.S.) patterns, but bears the unmistakable markings of local history and political context as well. In addition to providing an overview of the history of liberal feminist organizing from 1916 to 1932, this chapter also underscores the need to merge the history of feminism with the story of state formation and the development of civil society. Civil society was never exclusively masculine, and feminists were not above or outside partisan politics, competitions, and rivalries. This analytical approach also helps us to place the story of Uruguayan liberal feminism within a comparative regional and international context. Earlier chapters have speculated as to the influence of "late institutionalization" and "early modernization" on women's politics; and to the way in which the particularities of Batllismo shaped and were shaped by women's political activity. A study of the women themselves helps us to further localize Uruguayan feminism, most specifically by pointing out that most of the women who became active in these organizations were in fact locally born and not recent immigrants.

Both Conamu and the Alianza were officially nonpartisan organizations, but this did not mean that women left their political colors at the door, or that party rivalries did not inform political coalitions or strategies. On the contrary, this chapter has shown that, particularly in the politically tumultuous years from 1916 to 1921, local party rivalries and competitions played an important role in these international organizations ostensibly above politics. Party affiliations shaped individual liberal feminists' outlook. But just as feminists shaped Batllismo at the same time that Batllismo shaped feminism, feminists' relationship to party politics could sometimes move in the other direction. Fanny Carrió de Polleri was apparently able to influence her husband, Riverista leader Félix Polleri, with her feminist politics: "I have my husband catechized," she wrote. This influence became more important when Félix Polleri went from newspaper editor to congressman. In 1923 Fanny reported that Félix had been convinced to present "one of my wife's crazy ideas [chifladuras]" to leading congress members.[65] Not unrelated to the issue of party politics, of course, was the question of class. The Alianza not only reflects the partisan divisions in Uruguayan liberal feminism, but also the demographic growth and expanding political influence of the middle sectors. The older, more conservative Conamu had the hardest time transcending the class interests of its members, but a limited ability to reach out to working-class women characterized both Conamu and the Alianza. Liberal feminists, in Uruguay as elsewhere, claimed the right to speak on behalf of all women, and enjoyed some moderate successes in their campaigns to organize working-class women, but they were never fully able to bridge the class gap. In the process, important opportunities to forge a cross-class feminist organization were lost.

This leaves us with Paulina Luisi, the enigmatic heroine of Uruguayan feminism. A pioneering woman of tremendous energy, Luisi was motivated by conviction but also by obligation, and she struggled with physical illness as well as her own ego in her attempts to forge a unified and well-balanced feminist movement.[66] Following the advice of those who came before her, she sought to avoid the conflicts and divisions that had weakened similar movements elsewhere. But some of these fights were probably unavoidable, part of the inevitable growing pains of the movement. The successes of Uruguayan liberal feminism were not due to Luisi's efforts alone.

Chapter Four

Women like Fanny Carrió de Polleri, the seamstresses of J. de Guerra, and other (named and unnamed) members of Conamu and the Alianza were driven by political conviction and their passion for justice to dedicate their time and energies to addressing and overturning women's second-class political, economic, and social status. Neither Paulina Luisi nor future generations of women, in Uruguay and elsewhere, could have done it without them.

Chapter Five
The Catholic Ladies' League after Batlle, 1916–1932

> ...no new project like women's suffrage can [again] take us unaware and without having all of our soldiers under [our] flags. Happily, this premature initiative will not succeed, but a similar project, for better or for worse—only God knows!—is coming soon and we must be prepared.
> — El Eco (de la Liga de Damas Católicas), *1921*

Changes in the woman question and the discourse of feminism, as well as the growing strength and coherence of the anti-Batllista right shaped the politics and priorities of the Catholic Ladies' League (Liga) from 1916 to the early 1930s. Liberal feminist activity during those years appears to have reenergized Catholic women, who sought to deny liberal feminists the hegemony they sought over women's political discourse. In their earlier appropriation of and identification with "feminism," perhaps the women of the Liga (and the men behind the project) hoped to preemptively monopolize the term, and undermine its attachment to liberal, anticlerical ideologies. But from 1916 onward, it was clear that the "Christian feminists" were losing that battle, leaving the Liga to reevaluate and redesign its rhetoric and approach. Lastly, the perception that women's suffrage was coming sooner rather than later gave an urgency to Catholic organizations' efforts to win the sympathies of women from varying social classes.

Liga orientations, strategies, and even leadership were also shaped by the changing nature of conservative politics in Uruguay. As we saw earlier, the years 1910–1915 saw an awakening of Uruguayan civil society, marked especially by a flowering of conservative self-organization and militancy that culminated in the "alto de Viera" of

1916. The Bolshevik Revolution of 1917 and the general upsurge in working-class and revolutionary activism in Europe and beyond added new urgency to the conservative Catholic cause. At home, these events also galvanized the Left, and the foundation of the Uruguayan Communist Party in 1921 gave Liga women and other conservatives a new adversary in the propaganda battles being waged in working-class communities. The political Right became more overtly nationalistic during these years, a trend that continued during the 1920s, and was clearly reflected in Liga discourse and strategies.[1] This chapter will focus on the Catholic Ladies' League from 1916 to its apparent dissolution during the Terra dictatorship. During that time, the group moved away from an exclusive focus on traditional gendered activities ("women's social action") and into a more overtly political domain ("Catholic social action"). During this era, the Liga became more directly connected to the conservative wing of the Blanco Party, and to the Catholic nationalist and fascist doctrines that were gaining in popularity both in Europe and elsewhere in South America during the 1920s and early 1930s.[2] The result was that the Uruguayan Liga came to play an important role in far-right politics in the early 1930s, contributing in its own way to the construction of the female citizen and a gendered conceptualization of nationalism on the eve of women's attainment of political rights.

Liga Leaders: Political Parties and Neighborhood

While evidence is sketchy and incomplete, by the 1920s the Liga was a large organization that controlled a substantial budget, and whose leadership represented some of the most prominent conservative and elite families in the country. By 1929, the Liga claimed to have 536 "local, departmental, and sectional committees."[3] Members paid dues, and donations were constantly solicited from readers of *El Eco*, which was clearly aimed at affluent women. The group managed budgets in the thousands of pesos (many times the annual salary of the average working-class male), and these substantial resources clearly enabled the Liga to make its presence known.[4] Unlike the liberal feminists, there are no general membership lists for the Liga; only the names of the group's leaders are known. Thus, while we cannot say anything about the Liga's rank-and-file membership, biographical data compiled for a total of ninety-three of the Liga's leaders using records of the Civil Registry and various social guides of the time reveals a profile of the 'average' Liga leader. In contrast to the liberal feminists, all of the Liga woman were married, and an average age of 43.5 years of age when they first appeared in leadership rosters. She was generally a native-born Uruguayan married to a man with a similar profile who was probably a physician, lawyer, or hacendado.[5] She did not come from the newly emerging ranks of professional women (none were listed as having a profession), but instead dedicated herself exclusively to the church and charitable activities. In sum, the leadership of the organization was of a privileged socioeconomic status, born and/or married into some of the wealthiest and most aristocratic families of the city, and occupied rather traditional social and familial roles.

Residential patterns for this group are striking. The Liga leader was most likely to have lived in the *Ciudad Vieja* ("Old City") section of Montevideo, home to much of the old moneyed aristocracy at that time. Of the sixty-three for whom a home address was obtainable, nearly half lived within an approximately fifty-square-block area of the Old City. This concentration, at a time when only a minority of the so-called conservative classes still lived in this zone, suggests that Old City residents were disproportionately represented in the leadership of the Liga.[6] This could indicate the importance of personal and community ties and networks in the formation of the group, and it could also suggest the role of neighborhood in reflecting or even shaping a particular political and cultural perspective. Their physical location in the city would likely have reinforced their feelings of being overcome by the forces of modernization and secularism. They were, after all, living in a sector of the city that was literally being left behind as the twentieth century progressed. At the same time, the choice to remain in the Old City might indicate a stronger desire to hold onto tradition than others of their socioeconomic peers.

Liga leaders were also politically very well connected: many of the fathers, brothers, and especially husbands of Liga leaders were among the most important members of the opposition Blanco and *Unión Cívica* (Catholic) parties. Some were related by blood or marriage to men such as Luis Alberto de Herrera, Leandro Gómez, and Duvimosio Terra, distinguished and decorated veterans of the 1897 and 1904 armed Blanco uprisings against the Colorados. The Liga lists also abound with names like Gallinal, Ponce de Leon, Rodríguez Larreta, and Aguirre, surnames synonymous with the conservative Blancos at this time. Margarita Uriarte, a founding member and Liga president from about 1919 to 1933, was married to two prominent conservatives: Arturo Heber Jackson and (after her first husband's death) Luis Alberto de Herrera. Families associated with leading conservative Catholics were also well represented: the wives of Jacinto Casaravilla, Antonio Rius, and Carlos Ferrés all held leadership positions within the Liga. Faustina García Gómez de Secco Illa, a Liga leader until at least the mid-1920s, was the wife of prominent Catholic politician Joaquín de Secco Illa (and probably a cousin of María García Lagos de Hughes, the Liga's first president).[7] Liga women, in other words, were even more politically connected than their liberal feminist counterparts. And unlike the liberal feminists, Liga leaders proudly proclaimed that they were representing not their individual views, but those of their family. In a 1929 history of the Liga's foundation, it was explained that

> Every woman brought with them the tacit opinion of the men of their house, whether they were Catholic or well-intentioned liberals, and in this way [the Liga] exercised a feminism that did not mean emancipation, but the opposite, the intelligent exercise of what the old saying calls "vox populi, vox Dei."[8]

Changes in Liga leadership during these later years were a reflection of the changing political scene in Uruguay generally. In late 1919, María García Lagos de Hughes, who had been the Liga's president since its foundation in 1906, resigned her post. Sometime after that, Margarita Uriarte de Herrera became the new president of the Liga, a post she held until shortly before the 1933 military coup.[9] Margarita Uriarte was a veteran of Catholic women's organizations; a member of the Señoras Cristianas in 1897, she was a founding member of the Liga and an organizer of the antidivorce petition drive of 1906. She was also the wife of Luis Alberto de Herrera, the most important Blanco conservative politician of the era, associated with a more secular nationalist current within the party. During the 1910s struggles within the Blanco party between more secular, pro-business commercial and landed elites on the one hand, and conservative Catholics on the other led to the formation of the pro-Catholic conservative *Unión Cívica* (Civic Union) in 1912, leaving the former in charge of the Blanco (or National) Party. Whereas García Lagos de Hughes had ties to the leadership of the Unión Cívica, Margarita Uriarte's occupation of the top post established a direct link between the Liga and the newly emergent Blanco Party leadership.

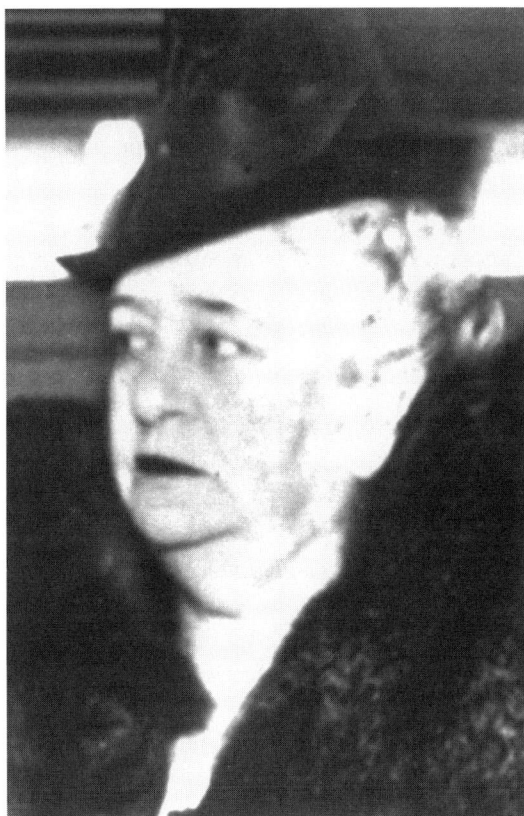

Figure 17:
Margarita Uriarte de Herrera. Founding member of the Uruguayan Catholic Ladies' League and Liga President from 1919 to 1933. Reprinted with permission from the Archivo Nacional de la Imagen, Montevideo.

While a lack of proper documentation means that any assertions about internal political divisions within the Liga must remain speculative, evidence suggests that political struggles within the Uruguayan Right made their way into the Liga.

The Liga and Its Political Rivals: Liberal Feminists and the Left Respond

After 1916, competition between Catholic and liberal feminists became an important factor shaping the strategies, campaigns, and recruiting efforts of both groups. In 1918, the Liga launched a campaign against a legislative proposal that sought to ban priests and religious instruction from the public schools. In May of that year, the Liga publication *El Eco* announced the formation of a new commission in favor of "freedom of education," aimed at combating any further secularization of schools in

Chapter Five

Uruguay. This association represented itself as ecumenical, and as having formed "without distinction of beliefs or parties," but trumpeted the fact that its membership "includes the most prestigious surnames in Uruguayan Society."[10] Anticlericals were quick to respond to this new campaign. In May of that year an article published under Paulina Luisi's pseudonym, "Ananké," criticized the formation of this new "Women's Commission." She mocked the notion that anything resembling freedom would be supported by such women of "fortune and social position, neither of which is acquired by struggling for the immortal principles of liberty." Ananké warned her readers that the whole project was nothing but a front for the Catholic Ladies League: "The whole Women's Commission, the whole thing, you understand?... belongs entirely to the Catholic Ladies' League, directed... by its gray eminences."[11]

Liberal feminists were clearly concerned about Liga and other Catholic activities aimed at women, and feared that those activities were being undertaken in surreptitious, behind-the-scenes ways. Indeed, liberal feminists seemed to have seen a conspiratorial Catholic hand at work against them, in much the same way that Catholics saw Masonic (and Jewish) conspiracies behind the actions of the state. In 1919, a few months before the foundation of the Alianza, Fanny Carrió de Polleri expressed her concerns about Catholics and the expanding women's suffrage campaign in a letter to Paulina Luisi:

> When Conamu began its campaign in favor of women's emancipation and there was a possibility of getting the vote, the German bishop got a group of women and men together to decide how to respond to this outrage. But it seems that instead of getting angry they quietly realized the advantages that women's suffrage could bring to the Catholic cause and decided to prod [Conamu] from time to time to get us to work more diligently.[12]

The belief that women's suffrage would most benefit Catholic parties was prevalent in Latin America. Carrió was worried, apparently, that Conamu had become an unwitting puppet serving the Catholic cause. But rather than abandon the suffrage campaign, Carrió sought to step up liberal feminist activity and not cede ground to the Liga. Another of Carrió's letters, written less than a month later, implies that the threat of Catholic activism may have even forced the issue of women's suffrage and thus been a factor in the Conamu/Alianza separation of that same year:

> I am so discouraged. You know how much love I have for the woman's vote. Since you left I find nobody to share it with in [Conamu]... Us with our arms folded while the Catholics organize under the leadership of the German priest... extending their tentacles into the Women's University... they have formed a students' league under the direction of M[aría] García Lagos de Hughes.[13]

The Liga had indeed begun a campaign to recruit female university students in 1919, hoping to gain the loyalty and affiliation of soon-to-be female professionals while they were still young.[14] This project necessitated some modification of the Liga's traditional suspicion that educated, professional women were betraying their natural, motherly destiny. Around 1923, the Liga began publicly defending and lauding women's pursuit of higher education, arguing, for example, that university women ran no risk of moral damage if their higher education had been preceded by a "solid religious instruction."[15] The Liga's Student Association seems to have had some short-term success, but it is interesting to note that two of the women listed as early members of this association went on, not to join the Liga but to become leaders in the liberal feminist Alianza. Both Sofia Álvarez Vignoli, the first president of the association, and Rosa Mauthone Falco, another early member, went on to become lawyers and Alianza leaders (and, in the case of the former, a Colorado senator). That both of these women's early political experience was with the Liga may also suggest that the Alianza was not as active in its recruitment of promising female students as it might have been. In any case, there seems to have been a good deal of competition between liberal and Catholic factions to win the best and the brightest of Uruguayan women over to their side.

While the Socialists and Communists occasionally complained about the interference of "Catholic ladies," it seems that they were not overly preoccupied with Liga disruptions. When the Left press mentioned the *"damas católicas"* (which did not always refer exclusively to the Liga), it was generally to ridicule their pretensions and false charity, as well as the hypocrisy of wealthy women's work on behalf of the poor: "The ladies that make up the Catholic League," the Communist newspaper *Justicia* exclaimed sarcastically, "who have always worried about the fate of the disenfranchised, have promised to remember them in their prayers and hand out... medals for the Virgin of Luján."[16] The only reference to direct interference in Communist Party work is in 1925, when *Justicia* complained that an attempt to forge a union of mostly women shoe-makers failed in part due to the "intervention of a few *damas católicas* who offered the workers many things (including heaven) if they would forget about the union."[17] It is difficult to evaluate how the Liga message was received, or the effectiveness of the Liga's projects among women of the Montevidean proletariat. It is possible that Catholic ladies' presence in working-class communities was indeed minimal; yet if Communists had felt seriously threatened by Liga activities in working-class communities they would have been wont to admit it publicly (only private letters reveal these preoccupations on the part of liberal feminists). Regardless, any appearance of Catholic success in this regard could only have served to reinforce ideas held by some Communists that working-class women were potentially treacherous members of the proletarian community, an idea we will return to in the next chapter.

Liga Activities during the 1920s

In her study of the Liga's Chilean counterpart, Ericka Kim Verba distinguishes between *acción social femenina* (women's social action) and *acción social católica* (Catholic social action). The former category comprised women's work reserved for the Liga, constituting "their gender-specific part in the larger project of re-Christianization of Chilean society."[18] Women's social action mostly meant work with other women and children, while projects targeting men or the state, or which were not so gender-specific were considered "Catholic social action" and left to men's groups. Utilizing this framework helps explain the shifts that took place in the Uruguayan Liga during the 1920s when Liga activity became less gender-specific. While the early Liga had mostly confined itself to "women's social action" by the mid 1920s, it had begun to cross the line, moving into the territory of "Catholic social action" and projects that might have been seen previously as men's work. One can connect this change both to the fact that the Liga sought to distance itself from any appearance of "feminism," which by this point was associated with liberal feminists, and to the fact that the Liga was becoming an organization of increasing importance in the battle to defend and expand Catholicism in Uruguay.

This changing orientation coincided with a gradual warming up to the idea of women's suffrage, reflecting changes at both the international and the local level. Initially, the Liga had expressed its opposition to women's suffrage, except in cases where a woman was unmarried or widowed (and thus had no male household head to represent her). In 1921, *El Eco* referred to the 1917 proposal to include women's suffrage in the new Constitution as a "premature initiative" that "happily" did not succeed.[19] The modification in *El Eco's* official position on the issue seems to have emanated as much from changes in the position of the Vatican and the Liga's French counterparts than from changes in local conditions. In 1923, at a conference of the International Catholic Women's Union, the French *Ligue* declared that they "would not oppose the attainment" of the vote and called on their members to "prepare to exercise [their] civic rights."[20] This position was seconded in a document of the International, which welcomed a change in the official position of the Vatican on an issue "which I assume that we are all supporters of, because if it is true that at the beginning some of us doubted that the Church would support women's political emancipation, it has been some time now since our Catholic writers have set our minds completely at ease on this subject." The implication was that many Catholic League women had long held suffragist ideals but kept them to themselves awaiting official Vatican approval. This same document clearly stated that even though they supported suffrage for women, Catholic Women's Associations were not to cooperate in the work of Alianza branches, because its program is "contrary to established principles of the Catholic Church" and because of a general policy of noncooperation with any "neutral, non-confessional, or protestant" organization.[21]

In Uruguay, Liga activities were still largely concentrated in the areas of women's social action and the production and diffusion of Catholic propaganda. The two categories often overlapped, of course, since assistance from Liga committees were often accompanied by, and predicated on, the receipt of pro-church messages. By the mid-1920s, however, Liga projects also involved poor men as well as women and children. The *Liga pro-trabajadores de la tierra* (Farm Workers' League), for example, practiced a combination of charity and propaganda in rural areas.[22] Founded in 1924, the group sought to educate rural peoples about farming, and it distributed seeds and other materials to poor families with the goal of keeping the rural poor out of the city. The Pro-Illiterates Committee, founded in 1928, provided free adult-literacy classes and other activities. The stated goal of the organization was to eliminate illiteracy in the country by 1930, for the "glory of [our] Religion and our Nation." Both of these projects represent important steps outside of the gender-segregated realm of "women's social action." They also reflect the fact that Catholicism and nationalism were being linked in increasingly explicit fashion by this time, an issue we will return to below.

The Liga continued to work in more traditional areas as well. One among them was the campaign against what they saw as immoral theatrical and film productions. Concerns about the impact of modernity on morality and social ties led the Liga, like other Catholic groups elsewhere, to censor spectacles perceived as objectionable or threatening. The Liga had been involved in reviewing public spectacles for their moral acceptability since 1908, but this activity became more important in the 1920s, as film became an increasingly visible aspect of life in Montevideo. Since the earliest days of silent film, religious leaders and others had raised concerns about the content of films and the impact that movie images could have on viewers. The Liga was concerned about the impact of media on adults and children alike and advocated boycotts and censorship of both stage and screen productions that it considered immoral or contrary to church teachings.[23] Censorship of "dangerous" productions was increasingly also about the fight against Communist influence and Marxist ideas. In 1919, for example, the Liga issued a strong protest against a fundraiser for the Unión Jeanne D'Arc. The event, not surprisingly, was mostly a French production, but it was also scheduled to feature some Russian dances, and herein lay the source of the controversy. The Liga publicized a statement issued by the Catholic hierarchy, threatening anyone who attended the performance with excommunication. This stronger-than-usual-condemnation reflects the anti-Russian position of the Catholic right (and the church itself) in the wake of the Bolshevik Revolution. On the pages of *El Día*'s theater column the reaction was one of surprise and indignation, given what was said to be the Liga's silence on earlier similar performances. "Only since yesterday" the writer exclaimed, "have Russian dances been considered immoral."[24] *El Día* reported that attendance at the performance was high, but that the decision whether or not to attend was the cause of much discussion and hand-wringing for Catholic women. The president of the Jeanne D'Arc resigned her post over this issue.[25]

The incident above makes clear both that the church continued to exert no small degree of influence over (especially elite) society in Montevideo, and that the Liga functioned as effective public enforcers of the Catholic right. In 1925, the Liga created a "League of Decency," which sought to increase the pressure on cinema houses and movie audiences. Members of this Decency League pledged to walk out of a theater if they saw any kind of "immoral spectacle."[26] Like other Catholic organizations at this time, the Liga also publicized reviews and ratings of films; while it is possible that the Liga prepared their own evaluations, it is more likely that film reviews and ratings came from further up the church hierarchy, or even from abroad. The entry in *El Eco* from September 1930 serves as an example.

> "Noah's Ark": Can be viewed by all.
> "The Kiss": Greta Garbo. In other words, improper.
> "Our Modern Maidens": Joan Crawford. Immodest, immoral, dangerous.
> "The End of St. Petersburg": Dangerous.
> "Galloping Justice": Cowboys. Acceptable.
> "Sin Town": Russian, profoundly immoral.[27]

By the 1930s it was becoming increasingly possible for groups like the Liga to produce their own media and to take the campaign to diffuse the "good press" to the airwaves. In 1932, with women's suffrage now imminent, the propagandizing aspect of Liga work had become paramount. *El Eco* defined the campaign of that year as focused on three projects: press, catechism, and radio. In this same year, "Radio Jackson" was reinaugurated (it had originally opened in 1928 and closed again) and declared "the only Catholic radio station in South America."[28] The Liga, which broadcast an hourly program every Sunday at 11:15 A.M., called Radio Jackson a "powerful propaganda agent of the Liga." Catholic women's groups of various stripes continued to broadcast on Radio Jackson until at least 1936, although their time slot moved to early Friday evenings. Conservative Catholic women, in sum, were dedicated and effective propagandists, and were quick to adapt to new realities in their quest for adherents to the "good cause."[29]

As earlier noted, the Liga perspective contained a certain nostalgic longing for a more paternalistic past and reflected the anxieties that modernization provoked among traditional elites. In some instances, these discourses took on more overtly racialized tones. Uruguayan reformers by and large avoided specific discussions of race in their reform discourses, but in the writings of Augusto Turenne and others one does find examples of the "whitening" discourses common among Latin American reformers of the era.[30] Meaningful documentation of the impact of mass European immigration and corresponding demographic change on the Afro-Uruguayan minority during these years has yet to be brought to light, but surely the impact was not small. There is little doubt that nonwhite Uruguayans faced new competition from European immigrants.[31] But one can look at race and modernization in Uruguay from another angle as well: that of elite nostalgia for a phenotypically distinct poor. The upsurge of European immigration after 1900 gave rise to an urban poor with light hair, skin, and eyes—clearly anxiety-provoking to an elite more comfortable with a phenotypically distinct subaltern class. Nostalgia for a romanticized past was a prominent feature of the literary production of one of the leaders of the Liga, Delia Castellanos de Etchepare. Castellanos worked for years as the editor of the woman's page of *El Bien Público*, the principal Catholic newspaper. She was married to Julio Etchepare, a distinguished physician-surgeon. In 1921, Castellanos published *Mariposas* (Butterflies), a collection of her works that had been previously published under her pseudonym "Madre."[32] *Mariposas* is structured almost like a diary, with short prose entries, presented as observations on daily life, set against the backdrop of the sometimes inhospitable Montevidean weather. From these essays emerge images of both alms-giver and receiver and the sacred place that Castellanos grants to private charity generously given and humbly received. The charity receivers in her stories are both male and female, and often very old or very young. The elderly poor especially tend to be described as having "dark" features: dark hair, eyes, and skin while the young poor are generally more European in appearance.[33] The charity givers, on the other hand, are always female (of any age, but special emphasis seems to be placed on the young), and they are always attributed "light" features: blond hair, blue eyes, and light skin.

Perhaps most interesting in Castellanos's writings is her construction of the deserving and undeserving poor. Castellanos's depiction of the grateful and humble poor implies the threat of its opposite: the ungrateful, dirty, violent, and shameless poor who live off of public charity and agitators who might join the ranks of the revolutionaries. While the dark-complected elderly are often represented as "humble, but clean," the (generally lighter-skinned) poor children are often described as dirty people who need to be saved by charity before they turn into the other, unspoken ranks of the undeserving (and dangerous) poor. Thus the dichotomy of humble and deserving poor and the ungrateful, dangerous poor breaks down generational and racial lines. The older, darker poor in Castellanos's stories seem to know and accept their place in the social hierarchy, while the younger, whiter poor are less accepting of their subordinate status. Perhaps the mere fact of their resemblance to the well-to-do upset traditional paternalistic relationships and threatened disorder. Although Castellanos recounts with heartfelt emotion these daily scenes of misery and poverty, she never questions the reasons for such poverty and never implies that this is something society should strive to eliminate. The poor in her stories seem as much a part of the natural landscape as the weather conditions (the sun, the rain, the bone-chilling wind) with which she begins many of her accounts. Social inequality, thus, is a given and natural part of existence, and it is both the moral duty and in the best self-interests of the wealthy to provide for the poor in the form of alms. There is also a sense of racial nostalgia at play here as well, and one gets a sense of lament for an earlier time when the lines between rich and poor were clearer and more visible.

The Patriotic Catholic Ladies' League as the "Paladin of Catholicism," 1930–1933

Liga discourse had long highlighted elite women's role in minimizing class conflict and bolstering traditional paternalism. By the late 1920s, the Liga would unfurl a far more ambitious banner: defender of the nation. Since the 1910s, church officials and lay leaders had been sharpening the discursive links between religion and patriotism, arguing that: "defending Catholicism was defending the 'true patriotism' against false 'Jacobin' nationalism."[34] The essence of the nation was Catholic, they argued, and only Catholicism could save Uruguay from its crisis of identity. This Catholic nationalism, merged with other Right-wing doctrines, was fueled by the economic crisis of the Depression era, giving rise to a more formidable and cohesive political Right. Many were inspired by the rise of fascism in Europe, which was embraced as the ideal solution to Uruguay's domestic crisis. The *Comité de Vigilancia Económica* (Committee of Economic Vigilance), founded in 1929, represented an important consolidation of conservative economic groups.

Chapter Five

Headed up by Joaquín de Secco Illa, the first president of the conservative Unión Cívica, this group reflected the changing political strategies of Uruguayan integralism at a time when Right-wing vigilante groups, such as the Patriotic Association and the Vanguards of the Nation, were also becoming important in Uruguay. One sees these shifts in the changing discourse of the Liga. In its last few years of publication, *El Eco* was filled with anti-Soviet propaganda and called on readers to buy only national products. There were also increased attacks on the activities of Protestant groups like the YWCA and the Salvation Army, and one can clearly recognize the anti-Communist nationalism associated with the South American Right of this era.

During this time the Liga began to assert its central role in fortifying Catholic principles and, by extension, the nation. If defending the ideological borders was now paramount, women, as the traditional bearers and transmitters of religious belief and practice in the home and within society at large, had a central role to play in preserving the nation. Thus although Liga politics became more rightist during this era, there is an assertion of citizenship and growing sense of autonomy in its discourse that marks a distinct turn from the earlier era. When in 1931 the Liga changed its name to the *Liga Patriótica de Damas Católicas del Uruguay* (Patriotic Catholic Ladies' League of Uruguay), it further underscored these links between religion and nation. With this name change came a corresponding shift in the discourse of *El Eco*, reflecting a further politicization and an even closer affinity with the "counterrevolutionary."[35] Catholicism, the publication now explained, should be associated with nationalism and the principal defense against domination by foreign elements, which were seeking to conquer Latin America through the importation of both Protestantism and Communism. Unlike other far-right groups in the region, there was little overt anti-Semitism in the Liga's rhetoric, although it was often implied in its anti-Communism.[36]

Catholic nationalism was also presented as the best weapon against United States' designs for greater regional domination. A series of articles in late 1931 justify the name change and signal the Liga's new direction. First, Liga's work was now being defined as "eminently patriotic": "Consider... the words Mr. Roosevelt used to answer Mr. Onelli, in Patagonia, when the latter asked him if he thought North American penetration of the South American nations was possible: 'I think it is impossible as long as they remain Catholic.'"[37] The sexual metaphor implicit here is noteworthy: imperial domination is equated with rape and sexual dishonor. South America, in this image, is gendered feminine, subject to forcible "penetration" by the predatory and immoral (Protestant) debaucher to the north. As long as *she* remains Catholic, Uruguay remains virtuous and able to defend her honor, which in this case is its national sovereignty. Connections between personal and national honor were underscored again in "A Call to Modesty," where readers were urged to cover their bodies on the beaches and dance floors: "Rome and Greece signed their death sentence in the middle of an orgy, in the scandal of their theaters and their baths."[38] Immorality—linked to secularism and neglect of Catholic teachings—creates national weakness, and leads ultimately to dishonor and domination. Who better than the Catholic damas to restore national purity and strength? Taking this argument to its logical conclusion, the Liga went so far as to declare itself "the paladin of Catholicism in Uruguay [and]...the defender of the borders."[39] This statement is not only important because of the connections made between Catholicism and national defense; it also reads almost like a declaration of independence, with no sign of the deference that the Liga had always paid to male clergy in the past. When the modern age demanded not simply the defense of physical borders—the responsibility of the (male) armed forces—but the defense of a nation's cultural and ideological borders, it was (elite) Catholic women who assumed the dominant role. Finally, this statement can be read as an assertion of female citizenship, when Uruguayan women were on the eve of winning the vote.

With the sanctioning of women's suffrage in December 1932, the Liga wasted no time, ardently encouraging women to exercise their new right in defense of Catholic principles. The January 1933 issue of *El Eco* was full of articles that amounted to a call to action for the Catholic woman in the electoral arena, stating: "the Uruguayan woman has the vote and must use it with conscience. She must use it to demand her rights, to demand the rights of God and of the Church, of the Home and of the Country." Reversing their earlier position, *El Eco* assured readers that the vote would not "damage the spirit of the family nor weaken the life of the home."[40] They also sought to underline the urgency in Catholic voting, emphasizing that

> The Batllista woman, the Communist woman, the Socialist woman will go to the polls, and will go with a fervent calling, a calling that will erase the Catholic

woman from the scene, if the Catholic woman does not prepare herself for the vote and go to the polls with the same firmness.[41]

But, as with many feminist organizations of the era, the Liga as an independent organization had difficulties surviving the combination of economic crisis, dictatorship, and women's suffrage, which pulled women into the traditional party structure. The organization also underwent a new change of leadership. In January 1933, around the time of the *Terrista* coup, longtime President Margarita Uriarte de Herrera suddenly tendered her resignation. No reasons for this move were given: the resignation may have been due to internal differences over the military coup itself, or perhaps the result of emerging debate over the necessity of the group's continued existence given women's suffrage and, more importantly, the debate over which political faction (Blanco or Civic Union) the group was to align itself with should it remain intact. Whatever the circumstances, Uriarte de Herrera's resignation signaled the beginning of the end for the Liga. After the coup, repeated claims in *El Eco* for financial support from readers points to a crisis within the organization. *El Eco* stopped publishing in June 1934 with no explanation. While the actual fate of the Liga remains somewhat of a mystery, the final issues imply political infighting as well as the unwillingness of many members to remain within an organization that forbid them to engage in overt partisan politics. In 1933, for example, a "Women's Assembly of the Civic Union" was founded, with many of the same names appearing in its leadership, including the Liga's first president, María García Lagos de Hughes.[42] Thus like the liberal feminists, partisan politics became a decisive factor in Catholic women's organizing. This, in combination with international policies, competition with other feminist groups, and local political conditions, worked to shape the leadership, ideology, and actions of the Uruguayan Liga.

Conclusion

The story of the Liga de Damas Católicas in Uruguay needs to be integrated into the history of both the political Right and first-wave feminism in Uruguay. Historians who study the Latin American Right have correctly pointed out that a general neglect of studies of right-wing organizations has left a distorted historical record, underplaying the significant impact that such groups have had on Latin American politics during the twentieth century.[43] Uruguayan historians have noted that, despite the nation's strong secular character, Catholics were not unsuccessful in imposing their will on Batllista Uruguay. While it seems clear that the Right exerted far less influence over Uruguayan politics than it did in Argentina, for example, much more work on this topic needs to be done to fully understand the impact of conservative politics on the Batllista project. Moreover, when the history of right-wing politics is discussed, as in the case of Uruguay, those histories often neglect or omit altogether the role played by women in right-wing political circles and organizations.[44] As the history of the Uruguayan Liga makes clear, that role could be substantial.

This history also contributes to our understanding of Uruguayan feminism by broadening the category to encompass a variety of distinct feminist trajectories, and also by underscoring the importance of inter-feminist competition in shaping organizational strategies and ideological orientation. Classifying the Liga as a feminist organization gives us a better understanding of the plurality of feminisms in existence in the early years. Simply defining the Liga as reactionary or retrograde does nothing to further our understanding of the profound changes taking place in gender ideologies and relations during these years. Secondly, excluding the Liga from the feminist category also tends to overstate their ideological differences from their liberal feminist counterparts, especially its most conservative sectors. After all, it was not just the Catholics who were employing an essentialized gender ideology; conservatives in Conamu were oriented around a maternalist feminism based on similar assumptions (of women's inherent moral superiority, for example). The Liga sought to reinforce traditional paternalism, in which elite women occupied a liminal space between *patrona* and dependent. Conamu's position, as we have seen, was not so different.

It is true that after 1916 the Liga was less self-identified with feminism than it had been in earlier years. This perhaps makes it more difficult to sustain the idea of the Liga as a feminist organization, but the group's overall actions and political discourse still compel us to consider the classification. The Liga underwent some important changes in the 1920s, most notably in moving away from its focus on "women's social action" into a broader, less gender-specific frame of operations, crossing over into arenas of activity formerly reserved for men. At the same time, the Liga became more confident and less obviously deferential to the male leadership than it had been in the past.

Chapter Five

Lastly, although their feminist self-identification had faded, the later Liga adopted a more openly suffragist position and became more supportive of women's pursuit of higher education. Even if one does not accept this author's taxonomy of feminism, the history of the Liga remains crucial to any understanding of early feminism in Uruguay, since Liga activities shaped the strategies and priorities of other feminisms (and vice versa). Liberal feminists, in particular, felt threatened by Liga activities among young university students and working-class women. The perceived need to counter that influence helped reenergize liberal feminist activities and contributed to the formation of the more middle-class Alianza in 1919. Furthermore, important liberal feminist leaders like Sofía Álvarez Vignoli cut their political teeth not with Conamu or the Alianza, but with the Liga, underscoring the role that the Liga played, albeit inadvertently, in opening the doors of political activism to women who would spend much of the rest of their lives championing women's rights in Uruguay.

This history underscores the point that we cannot understand one branch of political activity in a vacuum, or a political organization as a freestanding entity disconnected from surrounding social forces. If we want to understand the full range of women's political activism during this era, political parties need to be considered as well. Just because women could not vote during the years in question does not mean that they existed outside of partisan politics. It is logical that the women who headed up the Liga would find a way to involve themselves politically prior to women's suffrage. Many were members of families whose lives revolved around party politics and, in some cases, led and fought in armed uprisings against the ruling Colorado Party, the last of which took place only three years before the Liga was founded. The church gave them the legitimacy to step outside the boundaries of women's traditional activities without losing respectability so important to elite, aristocratic families. Evidence suggests, moreover, that, similar to the liberal feminists, struggles between Blanco and Civic Union partisans played a role in Liga leadership and activities. That the Liga struggled to survive after women's suffrage testifies to the important pull of party politics once women received the vote.

Chapter Six
Socialists and Communists, 1916–1932

> You didn't see women around anywhere in those days.... It was a powerful thing because there were no women.... Afterwards Julia [Arévalo] went into the countryside.... and there was me and another woman.... People gathered on the sidewalk...it seemed strange to them that a woman was speaking.... It was shameful, there were no women.
>
> — *Isabel Fernández de Sala, Communist Party organizer, Interview with Fernando López D'Alesandro, 1991*

Uruguay's more open and democratic political climate meant that, compared to its South American neighbors, Left groups enjoyed a nearly unparalleled freedom to operate for much of the twentieth century. Anarchists in Uruguay, for example, did not suffer under the residence laws that were used to expel immigrant activists in early twentieth-century Argentina and Brazil. The Uruguayan Communist Party, founded in 1921, was one of the first in Latin America, and in 1926 Uruguay became the second Latin American nation to officially recognize and establish diplomatic relations with the Soviet Union (after revolutionary Mexico in 1924). Lastly, and perhaps most importantly, Uruguay was also the only Latin American nation where, until the 1960s, the Communist Party was never illegal.

By the 1920s the activities of the Catholic Ladies' League were as much about undercutting Communist influence in working-class communities as it was about winning over new recruits. Liberal feminists, too, competed with Communists for the hearts and minds of working-class women. All of this, in turn, shaped the politics and policies of

Chapter Six

Socialist and later Communist drives to incorporate women into their organizing efforts. The Marxist vision clashed directly with that posited by conservative Catholics, as well as many liberals. Marxists held that class struggle was the defining feature of society and the principal engine of history. Here the ruling elites were not protectors, but oppressors. Social and economic inequality were not natural and inevitable in this view, but rather the product of constructed relations of production wherein one class systematically exploits another for its own benefit. Both Catholics and Marxists dealt in utopias, but whereas that vision for the Catholic Right was one of class cooperation and a well-ordered, hierarchical and paternalistic model of society based on mutual obligation and respect, Marxists envisioned a world in which all would participate equally and reap equal benefit, without distinction as to birth or wealth. Marxist politics were also atheistic, of course, and viewed the church as complicit in the class oppression they sought to destroy.

We have seen that liberal feminists had difficulties incorporating working-class women into their ranks due to their inability (or unwillingness) to bridge class gaps and break with ingrained class-borne prejudices. The Catholic Liga probably reached more working-class women, but they too were uninterested in incorporating them as equal partners in their organization. We might expect Socialists and Communists to have had more success. The truth, however, is that Left groups also had problems organizing working-class women, due to an inability to bridge the gender gaps and an overall conceptualization of the Communist vanguard in masculine terms. In general, it can be said that all of the organizations in question approached poor and working-class women as outsiders and others and tried to compel them to participate on the terms of the dominant group, whether that was elite women or the male leadership of Left parties. The nature of Left party structure should have favored women's greater participation. The Socialist and Communist parties differed from traditional political parties like the Blancos and Colorados in that electoral politics was a smaller part of overall focus and strategy. That control of the state through electoral means was not the only or even the primary goal of Left and/or revolutionary parties opened up a space for women that barely existed in the traditional parties before 1932. But although Socialist and Communist women participated in party activities and leadership to a greater extent than within other traditional parties, women still struggled to gain respect from male colleagues and to draw attention to issues specifically affecting working-class women. While there were numerous attempts to form women's groups on the Uruguayan left, most seemed to be little more than ad hoc committees with a handful of members. Many of these groups were unstable, dissolving and reforming in a fairly short cycle, and to an even greater degree than the liberals or Catholics, Marxist women's organizing remained centered around one or two important women within the party.

Like the Catholic Liga, we lack the internal documentation of Socialist and Communist women's organizing that gave more depth to our analysis of liberal feminists. Nevertheless, we do see debates about the role of women in the party, the economy, and proletarian culture in the Socialist and Communist press. At issue was nothing less than the place of women in the proletariat, the gendered construction of the revolutionary vanguard, and the place of sexual equality in the socialist utopia.[1] In examining the discourse and debate on the woman question in the Socialist and Communist press of these years, one can identify two tendencies—not always internally coherent or consistent—struggling for ascendancy throughout the period in question.[2] A paternalistic strain, which can be labeled "family wage socialism/communism," defended the working-class family and saw women as a distinct, often retrograde, element within the working class. Here the construction of a socialist society was an essentially male task, and in turn the vision of a communist utopia was one where domestic politics and relations of reproduction would remain largely intact. Women were best mobilized, therefore, in auxiliary fashion, to "neutralize" them to Communist propaganda, but with no expectation that women would enter into the party on the same terms as men. One can also identify a different tendency, an antipaternalistic "feminist socialism/communism"—linked to earlier anarchist worker feminist strains—which saw women's oppression in the workplace and in the home as an unjust consequence of an exploitative capitalist system. In this view, women's subordinate position in society was socially and culturally constructed, and their emancipation understood as an integral part of the anticapitalist project. This tendency even went so far as to criticize working-class gender relations and identify male hostility and resistance as an obstacle to women's full participation in the Communist cause. This faction supported organizing women on equal terms with men, yet recognized at the same time that the demands of the double workday on working women often limited their ability to participate on an equal basis. This latter tendency, not surprisingly, was espoused most clearly by the leading women in the party. Following the discourse on the pages of the Socialist (and later Communist) press, one can trace an ongoing debate between these two tendencies. Most importantly, one can hear the voices of the handful of Socialist and Communist women leaders, who stubbornly insisted on women's equality, criticized the intransigence of their male comrades, and understood class emancipation as fundamentally connected to gender emancipation, and vice versa.

This chapter looks at women and gender issues on the Marxist Left from 1916 to 1932. It follows the history of women in the Socialist Party from 1916 to 1921, when the Communist Party was founded. Because the Uruguayan Socialist Party all but dissolved at that point, the focus then shifts to the Communists, the largest and most important Left group on the Uruguayan political scene in the 1920s and 1930s. This speaks to the unusual constitution of the Uruguayan Left, where the reformist environment of Batllismo both encouraged the Left to abandon the anarchists' abstentionism and created a space for the development of radical politics. The shift in importance from anarchism to Socialism and then to Communism also reflected the process of industrialization in Uruguay, which encouraged a change of focus from small-scale and artisan producers to a focus on the formal industrial proletariat. The abandonment of the utopian, community-based politics of the anarchists in favor of the shop floor-based orthodoxy of the Communists also meant that working-class women became less visible.[3] Finally, Left politics were also shaped by the continuing arrival of waves of European immigrants, many of whom brought their radical (increasingly Marxist) political sympathies with them. Mostly Jewish immigrants from Eastern Europe played a singularly important role here, especially in the various debates over the woman question in the Communist Party.

Socialist Women, 1916–1921

As we saw in Chapter 1, Socialist women had been organizing themselves, in fits and starts, since the party's foundation in 1911. By 1916 the fragile attempts at cooperation between anarchist and Socialist women had been replaced by public attacks and separation. In these years, Left women continued to face numerous obstacles in their organizing efforts, namely a general inflexibility of party rhetoric on gender issues, and the very real obstacles of the demands placed on the time of working-class women, for whom the double work day often left very little time for political activity. Unlike their liberal or Catholic counterparts, Left women were unlikely to have the domestic servants that often helped free up more affluent feminists for political activism and organization. Male party members often perceived this low level of activity as lack of interest or political disengagement. The Socialist press during these years recorded women's organizing efforts, called for greater female participation in party activities, and attempted to analyze why that participation was not forthcoming. Within this discourse we can also hear the frustrations of the few women who were party militants, and who struggled to create space for women in a party structure that spoke of women's oppression and necessary liberation, but which still maintained the working*man* firmly at the center of its analysis.

In 1916, there were some important changes in the feminist landscape, which affected Socialist women in direct and indirect ways. We remember that in this year universal male suffrage was established, an important victory for the Socialists, who saw their potential electoral base grow significantly with the incorporation of many previously disenfranchised working-class men. This change, coupled with the pending Constitutional Convention, gave rise to a campaign to extend the vote to women as well. We recall also that Conamu presented a petition in favor of women's suffrage to the Convention in 1917, and that the recently constituted *Centro Socialista Femenino* (Socialist Women's Center) presented its own document calling for women's expanded political rights. Julia Arévalo (now eighteen years old) and her sister Hortensia were once again listed among the leaders of the new group. Comparing available information on the signatories of these two petitions gives us a sense of the very different class base of the liberal feminist Conamu and the Centro Socialista. Although we are limited by the existing documentation to the use of husbands' or fathers' occupations as our primary indicator of women's class status, we can nevertheless see a marked contrast between these two groups. The women who signed the Conamu petition tended to be the wives and/or daughters of physicians, lawyers, bankers, industrialists, and mainstream politicians. Additionally, some of the women were themselves professionals, and one finds physicians, lawyers, and schoolteachers among the signatories as well. In contrast, although far less information was available on the signers of the Centro Socialista petition, the available data suggests a group of women linked directly or via male family members to the social class from which the Socialist Party drew much of its support: skilled laborers. The fathers and especially the husbands of the women for whom information was available were metalworkers, stonemasons, carpenters, mechanics, and electricians.[4] It is likely, furthermore, that many of these women were themselves engaged in wage work outside the home, of a very different sort than the university-trained professional activity associated with many liberal feminists.

Corresponding with the Socialist support for the women's suffrage proposal before the Constitutional Convention, starting in mid-1917 there was a flurry of activity targeting women and discussions of the woman question in the official party paper, *El Socialista*. It became obvious that there was no clear consensus on this issue among Socialist Party members. While the party leadership voiced its support for women's voting rights, it seems that not all members and sympathizers were so enthusiastic. During this time, Julia Arévalo published a piece in *El Socialista*, attempting to convince the paper's readership to support women's political rights. One by one she addressed the objections to women's suffrage: that women were not capable of voting; that the vote would disturb the home and family; that women would vote the way the church asked them to; and so on. Arévalo was, in essence, responding to the objections and concerns of family wage socialism, a tendency that sought to transform the relations of production outside the home, but was uneasy about any proposals that might alter the relations of reproduction inside the home.[5] Arévalo's argument, in contrast, is undergirded with a belief in women's equal capacity to participate in politics, and a belief that women's emancipation should accompany, not follow, the transition to socialism. It is likely for this reason that Socialists like Arévalo continued to quietly maintain contacts with liberal feminists (especially Paulina Luisi). Even if they objected to the principles upon which groups like Conamu were constituted, they likely understood that some independent agitation around gender issues was necessary.

Those supporting a more feminist socialism and asserting women's equality with men were dogged by the lack of a consistent presence of more than a handful of women in the party. A persistent problem in working-class feminist circles seems to have been that of maintaining any kind of sustained level of activism. Spurts of activity were followed by long dry spells, and these lulls were often met by hostility from party leaders, rather than any attempt to analyze the possible impediments to women's fuller incorporation. Articles published in *El Socialista* in late 1916, for example, sought to cajole women into taking a more active role. The rhetorical strategy was to link a woman's duty as a mother with her duty to join the struggle, by arguing that her separation from and indifference to labor activism was tantamount to neglecting her obligations to her own children. These and other articles tended to blame women for their lack of participation, and rarely stopped to examine the structural obstacles within working-class communities that may have discouraged women's political activism. Moreover, these pieces argued that factory work itself was harmful to women, and undermined their ability to perform their natural maternal duties. Women were thus given a mixed and contradictory message: they should get involved in workers' struggles within their place of employment, or they should leave the workforce altogether. The underlying message is one of hostility toward women workers generally and a particular discomfort with their presence in the industrial workplace. The revolutionary proletariat, in other words, was unreservedly male, and women's presence, it seems, was a constant source of apprehension among elements of the party leadership.

While women's absence from party ranks and activity was seen as evidence of her backward status by some, other articles in *El Socialista* sought to identify and analyze a number of factors seen as contributing to women's low level of participation. The double workday, cultural pressure and prejudice against women's public activity, and male hostility were all cited at one point or another, but only rarely did the analysis go beyond the superficial, or attempt to examine personal and familial relations in working-class communities. Bourgeois capitalist society was blamed for women's oppression, and women themselves were criticized for not doing more to liberate themselves, but rarely were gender relations within the working-class family and between working men and women placed under scrutiny. For example, in a 1917 article in *El Socialista* entitled "Feminine Improvement," the issue of the double workday for women is addressed, and subsequently dismissed, as a valid reason for women's noninvolvement in party activities:

> We women must try and attend the events organized by our *compañeros*, since we know that these events take place at times when we are not at work. Perhaps some woman will say to herself that women's work is never

Chapter Six

done, and that is true; but if one puts one's mind to it surely it is possible to dedicate a few moments to our own moral betterment.[6]

Women, in other words, were simply urged to try harder. At no point was it suggested that working-class men might assist their wives or partners in the home, in order to facilitate their greater participation in working-class struggles. Nor, in this case, is "feminine improvement" defined in terms other than the support of the political activities of male family members. Social stigma against woman's engagement in political activity outside the home was also identified as a factor in women's staying away from party work. The belief that "it is not right for a woman" to participate in politics was acknowledged.[7] Yet once again, women were encouraged to simply overcome or ignore these pressures—with an insinuation that women were more vain and frivolously concerned about the opinions of others than men. No real analysis was made as to the source of these pressures: was it the community as a whole, other women, or male family members (some of whom may even have been Socialists) who exerted that pressure? Furthermore, the implication of this and similar articles is that, in essence, gossip and reputation were all in a woman's head, without any recognition that for women rumors of dishonorable behavior, for example, could have potentially serious consequences.

Among the factors identified as contributing to women's nonparticipation in party politics, the issue of male resistance to women's activity within the working-class household was by far the most sensitive. It was largely left to women in the party to point out male intransigence as an obstacle to women's engagement in working-class struggles, but male party leaders occasionally voiced these concerns as well. At a 1918 Socialist women's conference, two different male party leaders used the conference as a platform to criticize members who might be hostile to feminist ideas. One took to the podium to "use this occasion to strongly condemn those within our ranks who belittle the women's movement, and those who do not put into practice the doctrines of equality supported by the party with which they are affiliated." Another male party leader then "affirmed that those men whose wives defend their own rights, far from being 'unfortunate husbands' as some think, should consider themselves lucky."[8] But again, this analysis rarely went beyond an identification of the problem: clearly the hope was that women could be convinced to participate in Socialist activity without provoking any substantial reevaluation of gender relations in working-class communities. But in these statements we do see an acknowledgement that Socialist men themselves may have been an obstacle to women's participation in party activities.

Communist Women, 1921–1929

We have already seen how the particular political climate in Uruguay shaped the ideology and political positioning of the Socialist Party. It also gave a unique shape to the Socialist/Communist split that emerged in the wake of the Russian Revolution. In Argentina a 1921 vote within the Socialist Party on whether to affiliate with the Third International was voted down by a majority, and the Argentine Communist Party was initially the result of a minority split from the Socialists. In Uruguay, in contrast, the overwhelming majority of party members voted in favor of affiliation, and in 1921 the Socialist Party changed its name to the Communist Party of Uruguay, with some two thousand members.[9] The Socialist Party newspaper—which had changed its name to *Justicia* in 1919—became the Communist Party newspaper at this time. Based on a vote taken in the recently formed Socialist women's group, the Rosa Luxemburg Center, women appear to have voted similarly to their male counterparts. In April 1921, when Socialist party members voted to accept the Twenty-One Conditions of Lenin and affiliate with the Third International, the women of Rosa Luxemburg voted ten to one in favor of affiliation (it does appear that other women opposed to the change simply abstained). Communist affiliation was accompanied by an unusually direct critique of the position of the "old party" on the woman question. The Luxemburg Center concluded its report with a resolution to "call on the Executive Committee to urge party members to concern themselves with women's emancipation, [an issue] completely neglected until now."[10]

Shortly thereafter, the *Agrupación de Mujeres Comunistas* (Communist Women's Association) replaced the Rosa Luxemburg Center. This new group sought to capture the momentum and excitement surrounding the political change, and dove right in to active organizing. The first serious campaign of the Communist Party of Uruguay aimed at working women was a campaign to organize domestic servants, in response to legislation initially proposed in early 1921 to grant domestic workers a mandatory day of rest. The proposed legislation was mocked in the Communist press as an unenforceable provision that did nothing to improve the position of domestic servants or to lessen the near total domination that employers had over them. A campaign to organize domestics to demand real reform was kicked off in the pages of *Justicia*, with an article written by Isabel Fernández, a new voice in feminist socialist circles. Fernández appealed to the domestic servant directly, addressing her as "you who are the most mistreated, the least appreciated by this cursed society... you, who endure with humiliating resignation the most cruel threats and insults and sometimes the most shameful propositions of the 'boss.'"[11] The project began with a great deal of enthusiasm, and several assemblies were held between July and September, when it was announced that the "Union of Servants, Maids, and Affiliates" was "definitively constituted."[12] But once again, problems of sustainability and stamina appear to have emerged. Soon after the formation of the group was announced, the tone of the articles changed to reflect concern with lack of participation; concern became chastisement when one article asked "are you afraid of being unionists fighting for your liberty?"[13]

The failure of the domestic-servant campaign prompted a serious debate on the woman question within the party. Once again, some blamed women themselves for the lack of energy, while others sought to identify structural obstacles to greater feminine participation. In July 1922, a series of articles appeared in the *"Tribuna Femenina,"* a regular column in *Justicia* overseen by someone using the pseudonym "Butterfly" (in English in the original). "Butterfly" often engaged liberal feminists in debates, and criticized feminist politics generally for dividing the working class and fostering hostility between the sexes. In this case, under the heading "How to propagandize among women," the debate started with an unsigned article, which was both a critique of targeting domestic servants for a proletarian movement, and a broader reproach of women generally. The anonymous author characterized some women (especially housewives and domestic servants) as

> house proletarians [*proletarios a domicilio*] who, due to the nature of their work and their mentality can be best compared to peasants, and as peasants are not admissible within our Party; but since they could constitute an impediment in future working class struggles, they need to be neutralized to our propaganda... they can never be communists, but they can in some way be attracted

toward communism by the fact that they live with workers and are part of the working class.[14]

The above characterization speaks to the ways in which party members sought to incorporate gender into the rigid class analysis of orthodox Marxism. In this lies an important point, traceable throughout Communist Party rhetoric in the 1920s: a suspicion that not just housewives and domestic servants, but probably all women were simply unfit to be full party members, and thus part of the proletarian vanguard.[15] This was a key component of "family wage" (now) communist' ideology: women are like peasants, and as such cannot be fully incorporated into the party, but need to be "neutralized," lest they pose an active impediment to party organizing and the establishment of a communist society. Neutralization also meant preventing working-class women from associating with anti-Communist groups like the Catholic Liga. This position was not often so openly expressed, but it surely represented a strong current within the party, one with which women party members constantly had to grapple.

In response to this salvo, Julia Arévalo once again stepped up to defend female party members and women in general. While she too voiced her concerns with the lack of female militancy in the party, Arévalo defended her female comrades from criticisms about their lack of action, writing that "there are very few and in addition they can do very little in the area of propaganda, given that almost all are mothers. It is bad thus for others who combat and criticize from the outside the lack of action of this group."[16] Women's nonparticipation, in other words, was not due to her place in the relations of production, but to her place in the relations of reproduction, where she was expected to bear a substantial burden. Here Arévalo refrained from pointing the finger at working-class men, but a second piece published later that month (unsigned, but Arévalo may well have been the author) took a stronger stand. "It is true that women have been very much on the margins of the social struggle," the author stated, "but it is no less true that the hostile attitude is all but fomented by men who call themselves revolutionaries, [but] cooperate in the work of bourgeois society."[17]

It is worth underscoring the fact that both sides in this debate used the vocabulary of Marxist orthodoxy to shape their arguments. In the first example, inactive proletarian women are virtual peasants—Marx's "potatoes in a sack," unorganizable and potentially treacherous.[18] In the latter case, working-class men hostile to women's equality (and those harboring the ideas expressed above) are crypto-bourgeois, undermining the proletarian struggle with their anachronistic views and continued desires for domination. What is common to both positions is the use of class terminology to describe women's place in the party and in the working-class community. This inability, and lack of vocabulary, to engage in a specific gender analysis further weakened the party's capacity to reach out to working-class women.

Any counter that Arévalo was able to provide to the attitudes of her male comrades was diluted after 1922, when she left Montevideo with her husband and children and settled in Lavajella, in the Uruguayan interior. While she continued to be active in the party, and enjoyed a certain degree of success in organizing laundresses, meatpacking workers, and other working women, Arévalo remained on the margins of party politics for at least a decade. Women's organizing—and resistance to the misogynistic views of some party members—continued, however, now increasingly under the leadership of Isabel Fernández. It is also during these years that we see a definitive break between Communist women and liberal feminists (in particular, the Alianza), with whom the "old party" had maintained tentative yet cordial relations.

The campaign to organize domestic servants was quickly replaced by the campaign and strike of the telefonistas, which once again renewed hopes among party members about the militancy of female workers. *Justicia* reported faithfully on the daily happenings of the 1922 strike, and printed the names and addresses of women accused of being strikebreakers. This was the high-water mark of women's labor activity during this era, and everybody wanted to be a part of it. We remember that during this strike the liberal feminist Alianza embarked on a more aggressive program to recruit working women. This direct competition engendered greater animosity between liberal feminists and Communist women. Shortly after the telephone operators accepted Communist affiliation, new attacks on liberal feminists began to appear in the pages of *Justicia*, criticizing them as bourgeois reformists whose programs promised nothing to working-class women. In 1924 an attack on the Alianza was published in *Justicia* under the same penname "Butterfly." The attack was answered by "Zoraída" in the more mainstream newspaper *El Siglo*, thus beginning a debate over the role of a moderate liberal feminist organization in the struggle for radical social change. "Butterfly" urged her female readers, and working-class women generally, "not to uselessly waste their energies... with those who mutilate the woman problem." [19] "Zoraída" responded to these criticisms by the Communists, accusing them of "revolutionary impatience." She described the majority of the membership of the Alianza as "degree holders and intellectuals," and argued that "the fact that they are not active in workers' parties does not mean that they oppose their demands, because they form a part of the intellectual proletariat and advanced doctrines do not frighten them."[20] This use of the term *intellectual proletariat* was taken directly from the vocabulary of the Uruguayan Socialist Party, who often used that term to describe its members.[21] "Butterfly" rejected the notion that the "intellectual proletariat" was an ally of the working class in any way. "We know perfectly" "Butterfly" wrote, "that class prejudices and concern for comfortable situations are rooted more strongly in these 'degree-holders and intellectuals' than in anybody."[22] Liberal feminism, in other words, was identified with the politics of the "old party" (i.e., the Socialists). This new harder line with regard to cooperation with "petit bourgeois" elements was also part of the drive to centralize, purify, and "Bolshevize" the party.

Perhaps as a means to head off any potential liberal or Catholic feminist campaigns in working-class communities, the Communist Party created a *Comité Central Femenino* (Women's Central Committee, or CCF) in 1924. The CCF was a small executive body, with both female and male members, in charge of overseeing the creation of women's neighborhood, ethnic, and other committees and in formulating party strategy with regard to women. The CCF was also supposed to encourage the formation of women's committees in response to high rates of unemployment, especially in neighborhoods dependent on the crisis-ridden meat-packing industry. These groups mostly organized cooperatives and raised funds to help those who were out of work. The members of these women's committees (many of whom were family members of party militants) were not fully party members either in terms of duties or ideology, and the groups functioned more like a women's auxiliary of the party in working-class neighborhoods. This represented a fundamentally distinct strategy for recruiting women from that used for recruiting men. As opposed to the vanguard party model, where party members were recruited selectively based on specific qualities and potential contributions, the model used here for women was more that of a mass party, where sheer numbers of recruits was the goal and little emphasis was placed on ideological orientation or the disciplining of members. This is in essence a new version of the family wage communist model, with a renewed drive to bring women into the party fold but always in a subordinate and secondary way. The pivotal question remained whether or not working-class women were truly part of the proletariat, or whether they were impure elements within working-class communities that needed to be organized into auxiliaries so as to "neutralize" them to Communist propaganda.[23]

The CCF campaign enjoyed some short-term success, but some female militants clearly understood the implications of this recruitment model, and voiced their concerns about the strategy. In May 1924, the women's column in *Justicia* decried the new policy, writing that "among us there are many who believe that the propaganda among women should have as its immediate result the attraction of a large number of women to our ranks... that they come, whatever their ideology, whatever their education, whatever their aptitudes for struggle." "We believe that this point of view signifies a great error," the writer continued. "It is not an issue of many coming, but that those who are on our side be real Communists."[24] While the organization of dances, theater, and other cultural events to woo women into the party may bear short-term fruit, the article continues, the party risked creating a false impression as to what being a Communist really meant. The article concluded by arguing that same selective vanguard party approach used in the recruitment of men should be applied to women as well, but stopped short of criticizing the mass party strategy as condescending to women generally.

In keeping with the Left's short attention span when it came to women's issues, the CCF strategy, and the debate surrounding it, quickly subsided. In the years between 1924 and 1929 the woman question largely faded into the background, a reflection of both local conditions and conditions within the larger Communist International (Comintern). In her study of women and the Comintern, Elizabeth Waters wrote that "the international apparatus of the Communist women's movement all but disappeared by the mid-1920s."[25] We recall that these were also years of downturn in liberal feminist organizing in Uruguay, and a time when the Liga was moving away from its earlier Christian feminist orientation toward a broader right-wing nationalist politics. Among Communists during these years, one observes a continuing cyclical pattern of temporary excitement around International Proletarian Women's Day and May Day, with women's groups forming and disbanding, short-lived campaigns, and the occasional complaint by a female militant about the lack of dedication of their male comrades to the work of bringing more women into the party.

By the late 1920s, however, political and economic conditions once again brought gender questions to the forefront. Much of this impetus toward organizing women seems to have come from the Comintern itself, but it was also a response to changing conditions which made the organization of Communist women both easier (in some cases) and more necessary (in others). The circumstances of the Great Depression, as noted in Van Gosse's study of Communist politics in the United States, convinced the party to "double back" and resuscitate old strategies for community-based organizing that necessarily brought women back into its sight lines. At the same time, it was during these years that the so-called Bolshevization of the Latin American Communist parties starts to become a reality, greatly impacting both the policies and practices of Latin American Communism.[26] Not only did these changes lead to a greater centralization and a lessened ability to mold campaigns and policies to fit local conditions, it also resulted in what can best be called the "Stalinization" of Communism where, as Isabel Fernández herself put it, "the party was always right."[27]

Local conditions also drove the evolving discourse over the woman question. During these intervening years, the size and composition of the female workforce had changed. In earlier years, women had been largely relegated to home work (mostly sewing); in semi- to non-skilled manufacturing (cigarettes, matches, beer, etc); and in service jobs (maids, laundresses, and the like). They were not often working in the same places as men and, with a few notable exceptions such as the telephone operators, rarely in the spotlight as far as labor struggles were concerned. But in April 1929 *Justicia* noted some changes in the workforce, stating that because of "the industrial backwardness of the country, only in the last few years have a considerable number of working women begun to appear."[28] The most notable of these changes was the entry of women into the meatpacking plants, or frigoríficos. Like Argentina, beef was at the center of the Uruguayan export sector, and meatpacking workers held a pivotal place in working-class struggles. As early as May 1923, the anarchist-oriented *La Batalla* discussed "the work of women in the frigoríficos," claiming that the work force was approximately 35 percent female.[29] The first mention of women in the frigoríficos in *Justicia* occurred in 1924.[30] Yet despite these earlier acknowledgments, it was not until the late 1920s that the issue of women in the meatpacking industry began to gain significant attention in the Communist press. It is hard to say whether the timing of this new campaign was the result of economic crisis and reaching a critical mass as far as the number of women in the plants, or a response to international directives. But in any case, during these years the Communist women's group began to regularly remind both its male and female audiences of the significant percentage of women working in the frigoríficos. An article in *Justicia* in early 1930 stated that in the Swift plant seventeen hundred out of five thousand workers were female, and that in the Artigas plant (both in Montevideo) one hundred out of three thousand workers were women. A year later, *Justicia* claimed that one-third of the frigorífico workers in the city's meatpacking district were female.[31] The paper also noted that women working in these plants were earning far less than their male counterparts, roughly .8 pesos per day as opposed to the 1.76-peso average earned by men.[32] The pages of *Justicia* in 1929–1930 were filled with condemnations of the treatment of women in the plants, and with calls for equal pay for equal work.

The ethnic composition of the female proletariat was changing as well. Specifically, it seems that a relatively large number of those female meatpacking workers were mostly Jewish Eastern European immigrants, as opposed to the Italian, Spanish, and native-born women who dominated the female workforce in earlier years. The Jewish immigrant community, which first began to establish itself in Uruguay in the early years of Batllismo, saw another growth spurt in the 1920s, in response to the economic crisis and anti-Semitism plaguing postwar Europe. Most came from Russia, Lithuania, Hungary, and other parts of Eastern Europe.[33] By the late 1920s Jewish immigrant women had also established a strong presence within the ranks of the Communist Party. The names of women like Rosa Ghelman, Sonia Epstein, and Julia Stern began to appear in the pages of *Justicia*. The most prominent Jewish woman in the party was Sara Abramovich de Dubinsky, born in Argentina in 1898 to Russian parents. She appears to have begun her activity in the Socialist Party in 1921. When the Rosa Luxemburg Center voted to accept Communist affiliation, Sara Abramovich was named as the alternate to Julia Arévalo at the Party Congress, and in November 1921 she became the Center's secretary. Sometime in the following few years, she married Luis Dubinsky, a Russian immigrant and important leader within the Uruguayan Communist Party. Dubinsky was working as a petty trader at the time that he and Sara's first child, Lenin, was born in 1924. He also oversaw and ran a Jewish library in Montevideo, which provided reading materials in Yiddish,

Russian, and other languages to the Eastern European immigrant community in the capital.

The increasing visibility of these new immigrants within Communist women's networks provoked a number of articles on the activism of Jewish women. When the *Centro Femenino Clara Zetkin* was founded in April 1929, *Justicia* reported that: "almost all of the *compañeras* who came to the meeting were *israelitas*."[34] A week later, *Justicia* continued on this theme, stating that a "large number of *compañeras israelitas* have entered [the party] since in general these workers are accustomed to revolutionary militancy and are already free of many of the prejudices that still bind the Latin American woman worker."[35] The Jewish woman, in other words, was held up as a model of the ideal Communist woman. Again the onus was placed on the "backward" Latin American woman, without any exploration as to what this pattern might suggest about the Latin American male worker, family structures, etc. In her study of Jewish immigration to Uruguay, Teresa Porzecanski offers her own cultural analysis as to why Jewish immigrant women may have been involved in party activities in large numbers. "The *ashkenaki* family," she claimed, "permitted a greater degree of gender equality and a more democratic decision-making system than the classic western patriarchal family of the era."[36] Whether we attribute the differences to cultural, economic, or other factors, the makeup of Communist women's groups changed significantly, and the entry of relatively large numbers of Eastern European Jewish women changed the structure of Communist women's organizing.

The party tried to respond to these changes in the makeup of the working class, and to overcome the language barriers involved, by organizing so-called idiomatic groups, almost all of which were aimed at Eastern European immigrants. Some of these groups organized women's sections. In March 1930, the Women's Section of the party published the resolutions of its previous session. One of these resolutions stands out, in that it is reflective of the changing nature of the Uruguayan working class:

> 4. Insist to the idiomatic groups that they intervene in the campaign, distributing leaflets... among the women of their language, holding rallies in their offices, etc.
> Especially we point out that the Lithuanian needs to work intensely among the women in the *frigoríficos* of the Cerro, given that 60% are workers of this language.[37]

There appears to have been some response to this call. In August 1931, the *Sección Femenina de la Agrupación Lituana* (Women's Section of the Lithuanian Group) was founded, and in the next month the formation of a *Sección Femenina del Club Húngaro* (Women's Section of the Hungarian Club) was announced. It is not known how successful, large, or long lasting these groups were. Yet, in any case, the activism of Eastern European immigrant women undermined any argument about women's inherent conservatism or political apathy and served as an example that it was possible to rally women to the Communist cause, challenging the party to reevaluate its gender politics and strategies for organizing women.

Stalinization, Women's Suffrage, and the Expulsion of Isabel Fernández, 1929–1933

By the late 1920s, it was increasingly apparent that women's suffrage was a short-term inevitability. Yet the Stalinization of the party (i.e., its growing centralization and authoritarianism) meant that open debates over the woman question were more difficult and less tolerated than they were earlier. Thus began a series of events that culminated in the expulsion of one of the party's most important women, Isabel Fernández. Her expulsion can be explained in part by the fact that she never ceased to be a *woman* party militant, and a proponent of "feminist communism." This perspective left her vulnerable to suspicions of disloyalty and lack of total commitment to the Communist cause.

In November 1929, *Justicia* published an article calling on party members to prepare for the eventuality of women voting, writing that "it is evident that now more than ever we must dedicate even more attention in order that, under our banner, she is transformed into a conscious element in the class struggle."[38] The party was rarely this candid about the links between campaigns to organize women and the desire to capitalize on upcoming women's suffrage. Renewed discussion about women's suffrage came at a moment when the Comintern leadership had committed itself to tightening the reins on the Latin American parties, a process that would create further problems for women and for the woman question within the Uruguayan Communist Party. The 1929 First Latin American Communist Conference, held in Buenos Aires in June 1929, was aimed in large part at bringing Latin American Communists closer to the Moscow line. This conference generated a document, a *Carta Abierta* (Open

Letter), which outlined problems and suggested strategies for Latin American Communist parties. In keeping with the language of the era, the aim of the document was to help local parties purge themselves of "right-wing deviations" (meaning in this case Social Democratic politics), and to forge a disciplined vanguard capable of undertaking the revolutionary struggle that was believed to be in ascension. Among other topics, this document addressed strategies for integrating more marginal groups into the party: nonwhite populations, peasants, youth, etc.[39] The document prompted another round of internal debate over the role of women in the party, as well as some change in the recruitment strategies of the mid-1920s.

There was an open discussion of the "*Carta Abierta*" in the pages of *Justicia*. Understanding what went on here exactly necessitates a great deal of reading between the lines, especially in a moment when internal dissent was being severely curtailed. It appears, however, that Isabel Fernández criticized the party for its inattention to women's organizing and lack of commitment to women's emancipation. An unnamed contributor wrote: "I am with *compañera* Fernández because she clearly pointed out the men in the party pay little attention [to women's issues], and that they have the women bound [and] enslaved (of course with exceptions)."[40] Fernández's criticisms of the party clearly went far beyond the issue of organizing women, which she saw as symbolic of the problems of the party and of what she termed its "right-wing deviation...which have as one of its principal causes the lack of authentic proletarians in the party in general as well as in the leadership."[41] Once again, the neglect of the woman question was attributed to inauthentic (crypto-bourgeois) elements in the party leadership. Yet others strongly criticized Fernández for "having lost the line" of the party, and the following weeks saw a series of rather vicious public attacks on Fernández and her views. One of the strongest criticisms came from Félix Ramírez, who accused Fernández of elite vanguardism and disloyalty to the party based on the fact that "she said that the Party was not interested in the wives of Communists and as a consequence members needed to dedicate themselves to recruiting outside of the home...that the wives of Communists were of no use to the Party."[42] This publicly aired hostility would come to a head several years later in Isabel Fernández's expulsion from the party. Before discussing these events, it is worthwhile to say a few words about one of the party's most prominent women and her experiences as a Communist militant.

Chapter Six

Born in Spain in 1901, Isabel Fernández joined the Uruguayan Communist Party around 1921. In 1925 she had a child, Rusia Luz, with Leopoldo Sala, who was also a Spanish immigrant and a party leader. Although she was not officially licensed until a few years' later, Fernández declared her occupation as *partera* (midwife) on Rusia's birth certificate. Advertisements for "Isabel Fernández de Sala—Partera" first appeared in *Justicia* in early 1929, and in the following year these advertisements indicated that Fernández was working at the State Maternity Hospital in addition to maintaining an office on Rivera Street. In a later interview, Fernández explained that many of her clients were the wives and partners of party members, many of whom came to her seeking abortions, which were, of course, illegal. Her profession put her in a position to know a good deal about the gender politics of working-class families, as well as the political commitment and orientation of the "wives of Communists."

Fernández was at the forefront of almost every major campaign and debate involving women and the Communist Party for most of the years under examination. But her militancy came to a temporary end in 1933. In a 1991 interview, she spoke of the difficulties women Communists faced: "You didn't see women around anywhere in those days... it was shameful, there were no women."[43] She spoke also of the hardships faced both by Communist Party women and by the wives of party members, both of whom were still in charge of caring for their families. "I got married," she said, "and afterwards I had my daughters. Also my mother was very old. So I was in a very compromised situation.... I had my daughters, my mother, my work."[44] On numerous occasions, Fernández emphasized how difficult it was to be a party militant (male or female) during these years. The party demanded so much of one's time that members were constantly forced to choose between dedication to the Communist cause and familial responsibilities.

Fernández experienced this conflict personally when, in 1932, the party sent her to Europe. At the time she was juggling political work with her work as a midwife and taking care of her daughters. She returned from work to find two party members at her home with ship passages and orders for her to leave the next day for Germany to attend a conference. Fernández was forced to take one daughter with her, because she was too young (eighteen months) to be left behind. While in Europe, the child contracted measles, and fell seriously ill. After the Congress in Germany was over, Fernández and her daughter were sent on to Moscow, where the child's condition worsened. After her work in the Soviet Union was completed, the two had to stay an additional month in Moscow, because her daughter was far too sick to travel. The girl barely survived the journey. When they finally returned to Montevideo, the Central Committee informed Fernández that she was to leave right away on a tour of South America to talk about her experiences in the Soviet Union. "I told them no," she said, "I explained what had happened with the girl...that I needed time to recuperate...and they expelled me." And so, Isabel Fernández was expelled in 1933 for failing to obey the orders of the party, in a situation where she was forced to choose between her responsibilities as a mother and her duties as a Communist.[45]

In December 1932, in *Justicia* as in all Uruguayan newspapers, there was a flurry of articles on the sanctioning of the women's-suffrage law and, like most papers with partisan affiliations, speculation as to how the vote would affect the party and calls to recruit women into their ranks. The Communist Party adopted an interesting strategy of simultaneously saying the women's suffrage meant nothing—that it was a ruse to strengthen the hand of the bourgeoisie—and urging women to vote Communist. The party was clearly concerned about how working-class women would vote, and called on working women to "vote for the Party of your class, the Communist Party."[46] It is interesting to note that now that they were to have the power of the vote in their hands, working-class women were once again full members of the proletariat. Women were no longer peasants or wives, or even workers, but voters. And that required a whole new strategy.

Conclusion

From this material we see that feminist activism was not limited to the circle of professional women and their allies that made up the membership and supporters of liberal feminist organizations, or to the elite women of the Liga who sought to mobilize women to defend the "holy cause" of Christian feminism. Indeed, the woman question was widespread across Uruguayan society and political discourse. Different political tendencies discussed women and their place in politics and society in different ways, but they were all talking about it, illustrating the important and profound changes that were occurring in gender relations during that era. The Uruguayan Communist Party benefited both from a relatively high degree of freedom to operate and the influx of thousands of already politicized immigrants from Eastern and Southern Europe. Yet, with the prominent exception of the Eastern

European Jewish immigrant community, those realities did not translate into a particularly progressive agenda on gender issues, and Communist women continued to struggle under the weight of a male-dominated party structure and a rigid ideology that was severely limited in its ability to incorporate gender issues into its analysis.

Both the Liga and the Communists were different from the liberal feminists in that they maintained a more adversarial position toward the state. They were, in other words, outside of the constitutive agenda of the Batllista state. Like the liberal feminists, women's groups of the Left and Right were connected with local party politics to greater or lesser degrees, and with varying consequences. Left women were always more integrated into the broader (male) party networks. This had both positive and negative consequences. Because the strategies of the Socialist and Communist parties were not exclusively electoral, there was room for women in a way not found in other party arenas before 1932. This likely contributed to the fact that the Communist Party was one of the first to run women for political office after women's suffrage was passed. On the other hand, this integrated agenda may have created a somewhat claustrophobic environment for women activists, who often lacked the autonomy to create networks, alliances, and strategies independent of the male leadership and masculinist dogma. Studies of Chile in a later era by Tinsman, Power and others have noted the celebration of masculinity and male autonomy that was at the center of Left discourse, and that the socialist vision was construed as the full realization of manhood. Women's agency and assertions of independence could be perceived as a threat to that vision.[47] Uruguayan Communism during the Batllista era reflects similar patterns.

Tracing the history of women and Communism in early twentieth century Uruguay, it becomes clear that one of the obstacles never overcome and never really confronted was the simple reality of the double workday for working-class women. Middle- and upper-class liberal feminists generally had domestic servants to help take care of the children, freeing up more time for political activism. As alluded to by Julia Arévalo in the early years of the party, such was not the case for women of the popular classes, who often worked and had children to take care of, leaving them little time for political work. This was probably more true for the Communist Party, which demanded substantial time commitments and the unwavering loyalty of its members. Women in the party had a clear understanding of the sexual division of labor as an obstacle to women's liberation from oppression. For many men in the party, on the other hand, this same division of responsibilities allowed them to dedicate the kind of time being a Communist demanded. To support this structure, women's inequality was constructed as a fixed material condition—where women are only capable of integration into the party in a marginal way—rather than as a by-product of an oppressive society, one which men participated in and benefited from. The history of Uruguay during these years clearly demonstrates the ways in which working-class women's fate was intimately tied up with the revolutionary agenda of the labor movement, and how with the adoption of a more rigidly class and shop floor-based analysis, feminist rhetoric (no matter how shallow) began to fade.

Conclusion

> That sex [women] now enjoys a greater degree of social and economic emancipation in Uruguay than in any other Latin American county primarily because of the impetus Batlle gave that emancipation.
> — *Russell Fitzgibbon*, Uruguay: Portrait of a Democracy, *1956*

> The feminists at this point knew that the vote was not going to change the panorama very much. They knew it and they said it; until one arrives at equal coparticipation. ... this is adornment. And it was true, it's adornment. The proof is that we are still in the same situation.
> — *Amalia Polleri, interview with the author, 1995*

The *época batllista* was a time of dramatic political, social, economic, and demographic change in Uruguay. These and the immediately preceding years witnessed mass European immigration, urbanization, and the rise of the labor movement: changes associated with the era of the social question to which the woman question was intimately linked. It was also a time when one saw the rise of the Uruguayan welfare state, for which Uruguayan women were both major boosters and beneficiaries. Whether it was Catholic women protesting divorce, liberal professional women demanding the vote, or telephone operators striking and sabotaging phone lines, women of all walks of life were demanding that their voices be heard in a way that had not previously occurred.

What provided the initial catalysts for each group? For the Catholics, it was the attack on church privilege launched by liberal Batllistas and others; for liberals and Socialists, the 1916 *alto de Viera* and the upcoming Constitutional Convention. The Russian Revolution had a dramatic impact on all of these groups, but none more so than the Left, and the Uruguayan Communist Party (obviously) was a direct product of these events and crisis of the postwar period. Lastly, the

Conclusion

years 1929–1932 were important for all the groups involved. The liberal feminists were able to reconcile their differences enough to present a united front to take advantage of the "second reformist impulse" in Uruguay as well as suffrage victories in the United States and Europe. For Catholics and Communists, on the other hand, one sees a radicalization partially in response to events in Europe: the Stalinization of the Comintern on the one hand, and the rise of fascism and its corresponding anti-Communism on the other.

None of the organizations studied here were mass movements in any sense of the word. These were relatively small associations populated by women who were clearly exceptional in their political dedication, and led by women who, in different ways and to varying degrees, violated the existing norms of behavior of the era. Paulina Luisi, Laura Carreras de Bastos, and Isabel Fernández all chafed under the restrictions of a society that thought them inferior beings, and who judged them unqualified—based on their gender—to address the challenges of their age. They identified very different root causes of that subordination, and the visions of an ideal society that guided these women were radically different as well. But it is crucial to emphasize that these plural feminist tendencies were not simply parallel tracks, responding to the same or similar historical forces but never making contact with each other. On the contrary, I have tried to show in preceding chapters that all of these groups were very aware of each other's presence and existed to some extent in dialogue with each other. Catholic women clearly responded to the campaigns of the Communists and vice versa, not only on the international level but on the local level as well, and it seems no coincidence that the campaign on the pages of *Justicia* against the Alianza coincided with the latter's accelerated campaign to bring working-class women into their organization. Uruguayan feminisms, in other words, were relational.

By early twenty-first-century standards, the limitations of the Batllista state are clear; but judging it within its own historical context we must acknowledge that Batllismo represented an important step in the history of Latin American democratization. For while Batllismo may have reformulated, rather than challenging, paternalistic relationships and social hierarchies, it simultaneously shaped a discourse of inclusiveness and civil equality (the Uruguayan notion of *"mesocracia"*), and a political environment open to experimentation and innovative ideas, all of which had a profound effect on women and gender ideologies. Batllista state formation helped to shape and catalyze Uruguayan civil society, and provided opportunities for otherwise disenfranchised groups to insert themselves into the public arena. In evaluating whether the Batllista state served to preserve traditional gender roles or undermine paternalism, one must consider what may have been (for some) the unintended consequences of these reforms. Through the sponsorship and subsidy of women's education and elite women's social assistance, the Batllista state constructed platforms from which some more privileged women were able to develop a feminist consciousness and enter the political fray. We also have to consider the class/gender dimension of this problem, and understand the ways that middle-class and affluent women supported and promoted the class-based paternalism of the Batllista project, through which they were able to gain status and position as the "mothers" of their less fortunate "sisters." This project has demonstrated that the early development of the Uruguayan welfare state served to institutionalize the compensation politics of Batllismo. Making poor women wards of the state and elite women its agents transformed the nature of elite women's charity work and, in so doing, influenced the germination of a moderate liberal feminism. But as we have seen, even some subaltern women (working-class women, juvenile wards) were occasionally able to use the new infrastructure and resources of the state to gain some control over their lives.

This history provides us with a gendered look at the formation of civil society in early twentieth-century Uruguay. Powerful economic interests mobilized and entered the political fray in new critical ways during this era, while universal male suffrage and the rise of labor unions signaled the entry of the previously disenfranchised into the political process. By including women's political awakening in this picture, we can more fully appreciate the significance of the transition that took place during these years. After the first women's suffrage bill was presented to the Constitutional Congress in 1917, all sides knew that it was only a matter of time before Uruguayan women were granted the vote, and all political parties began preparing for that eventuality. This gave the context of women's organizing—and the competition between liberal, Catholic, and Socialist women—an urgency perhaps not felt in other national contexts. Calls for women's political action were constructed in distinctly gendered ways. Women physicians, for example, were compelled to get involved because they felt and understood the pain and deprivation suffered by the masses of people; Catholic women felt a duty to get involved because defense of womanhood was intrinsically linked to defense of the church; and Communist women were called to defend their proletarian families and communities from the rapacious assaults of the capitalist class.

Working-class women were in many ways the "golden fleece" for all of the groups under examination here. None were entirely successful in organizing them, because they were really never able to identify with the specific issues and perspective of this societal group or come to terms with the burdens of the double workday. Taking the middle- and upper-class leadership of the Liga, Conamu, and the Alianza and the male leadership of the Socialist and Communist parties as a group, all seemed to view "la mujer obrera" as an incomprehensible aberration. Most in one way or another bought into the concept of the family wage and the male breadwinner even if, in the case of professional women, they did not necessarily see it as applying to themselves. In general, men encountered fewer difficulties in combining work, family, and political activity than women who were subjected to the burdens of the double workday and for whom, in effect, political activism meant a triple workday. Fifty years later, similar issues persisted. A survey of Uruguayans imprisoned during the military dictatorship of the 1970s and 1980s for their political activities revealed that "most men were married at the time they were arrested, most women single or without family responsibilities."[1] This suggests a persistence of older patterns and an environment that continued to discourage women from combining political and familial responsibilities. Women, in other words, were expected to participate in Left politics on largely male terms; an environment far from inviting for women who were also wives and mothers.

For those of us with commitments to inclusive and democratic social change these are not merely academic exercises. This study points to the possibilities, limitations, and obstacles in forging broad coalitions for change under relatively favorable conditions. The Uruguayan Communist Party, for example, enjoyed an environment mostly free of the repression encountered by their counterparts elsewhere in the region; yet they were still unable to overcome gender barriers within working-class organizing. The consequences of progressive forces not creating cohesive unified communities can be disastrous. Margaret Power's *Right Wing Women in Chile*, for example, which examines the history of anti-Allende women's groups, shows the legacy of the Left's inattention to working-class women (especially housewives) and its lack of vocabulary to speak about gender issues. In Chile in the 1970s, the revolution was still fundamentally a male affair, and the result was that the right wing was able to effectively organize working-class women in ways that the Left was not.[2]

※ ※ ※

What does this study of feminism and Batllismo contribute to our broader understanding of gender, feminism, and state formation in Latin America? Comparative work on gender and state formation has thus far largely focused on Europe, the United States, and to a lesser extent, Australasia.[3] Koven and Michel, for example, have suggested an inverse relationship between state formation and (liberal) feminism, arguing that: "the strength and range of women's private sector welfare activities often varied inversely with the strength of the state."[4] The Uruguayan case certainly seems to complicate this model.[5] Unlike some of the "stronger" European states like Germany and (to a lesser extent) France, Uruguay did not possess a vital civil society and/or a well-established bureaucracy by the early twentieth century. But unlike some of the "weaker" states, such as the United States and (to a lesser extent) Britain, the Batllista state aspired to universal protections and, ultimately, to the creation of a centralized state providing universal or near-universal social assistance to those in need. With a centralized apparatus and an active core of state-centered reformers, political and economic constraints nevertheless compelled a more pluralistic solution that, in turn, gave individual women reformers and women's associations input and power in the implementation of social assistance (if not in the formulation of policy), at least temporarily. One could argue, at the risk of oversimplifying, that what we see in the Uruguayan case is a partially successful attempt at implementing a "European" welfare state in an exaggeratedly "American" (frontier) setting—a part of the Americas with a particularly weak colonial and policy legacy that meant that twentieth-century reformers were, in many ways, starting from scratch.

Previous work on gender and state formation elsewhere in Latin America also allows us to place the Uruguayan case within a larger regional framework. This study has shown, for example, that women who operated as agents of the state, in direct and indirect ways, were a fundamental element in the development of liberal feminism. The Uruguayan case resembles both the Brazilian and Chilean cases in this respect, where Besse and Rosemblatt have noted connections between liberal feminism and women in public-sector employment. Both Brazilian and Uruguayan liberal feminist umbrella organizations

Conclusion

brought together women with particular relationships to the state. In 1922, Bertha Lutz helped found the *Federacão Brasileira pelo Progresso Feminino* (Brazilian Federation for the Advancement of Women, or FBPF). Like its Uruguayan counterpart, Conamu, the FBPF had an important component of upper-class leadership, but was, over time, increasingly oriented toward middle-class female professionals, many of whom were "government employees" like Lutz.[6] The FBPF, furthermore, had affiliations with groups like the Association of Women Civil Service Workers and the Professional Women's Association, and they lobbied heavily for women's increased presence in the paid public sector (as social workers, police, etc.). The parallels with the Uruguayan case are apparent and intriguing, and future research on the issue of feminism and women as state agents in Brazil will hopefully allow for more in-depth comparisons with the Uruguayan and other cases.

Karin Rosemblatt's *Gendered Compromises* looks mostly at a later era, when both women's presence in the Chilean social service sector and Chilean feminism was more established. More radical politically and reflecting a more popular and cross-class membership base, the *Movimiento pro Emancipación de la Mujer Chilena* (Movement for the Emancipation of Chilean Women, or MEMCh), founded in 1935, was a very different type of organization from either Conamu or the FBPF. "Although an elite brand of feminism devoid of concern for the social and political rights of the poor had existed in Chile, by 1935 it was mostly defunct," Rosemblatt wrote.[7] As key female agents of the state, social workers are an important part of Rosemblatt's gendered examination of Popular Front politics. She underscores how the work experiences of especially middle- and working-class social workers inspired many to become active in Communist and/or feminist ranks, as well as the ways in which those ideological affiliations shaped their approach to their professional work. For its part, MEMCh appears to have placed some emphasis on organizing state agents, including social workers, nurses, and schoolteachers.[8]

One sees a very different relationship between elite women, the state, and liberal feminism in Uruguay. This is largely attributable to the earlier date of reforms, and the particularities of Uruguayan modernization. By the era of the Popular Front (1938–1952), the change from private beneficence to public social assistance was largely complete in Chile. Rosemblatt implies a smooth transition: "Social workers stepped in where aristocratic ladies had exercised philanthropy."[9] Indeed, Chile was the first Latin American country to begin to train social workers, and by and large their professional existence predated significant state-building efforts, so perhaps the shift from private philanthropy to social work was cleaner there. In Uruguay, however, this transition took place over a generation, and involved an important intermediary phase where aristocratic "ladies" operated as parastatal agents, running ostensibly private organizations while receiving significant public subsidies and under the increasing control of state agencies.

Batllista Uruguay invites perhaps its most intriguing comparisons with revolutionary Mexico. Like Uruguay, feminism in Mexico did not significantly predate reform, and both state-building projects emerged from periods of violence and instability (although the violence and bloodshed of the Mexican Revolution far surpassed what Uruguayans had experienced). Women's desires for greater autonomy and citizenship grew out of this period of violence, but was tempered by the desire to forge a new "national family," a highly gendered metaphor based on unequal paternalistic relations. Both countries saw an upsurge of feminist activity in 1916 in anticipation of upcoming Constitutional Conventions. In Uruguay in 1916, Conamu was founded, while in Mexico a series of feminist conferences in the state of Yucatán (where especially progressive and feminist-friendly governments were in place) discussed everything from the vote to sex education. Although women were unsuccessful in securing equal citizenship rights in either case, their efforts were not entirely in vain: the Uruguayan Constitution of 1917 was the first in Latin America to include the possibility of women's suffrage, and the 1917 Law of Family Relations in Mexico granted married women new property and civil rights.

There are at least two important differences in the Mexican and Uruguayan cases, however. In Mexico, deep cleavages along lines of race and class made the creation of a multiclass, secular liberal feminist organization extremely difficult, and political violence and the upheavals of the Mexican Revolution made for a distinctly different political climate. Unlike Mexico, the Catholic Church in Uruguay was weak, and the perception that women were hostile to the liberalizing anticlerical policies of reformers was nowhere near as pronounced as it was in the Mexican case. Catholics resisted, but Uruguay had no equivalent to the Cristero Rebellion, and after 1904, the Batllista state faced no significant armed resistance. This may help to explain why Uruguayan women gained the vote at the end of the reform period in 1932, while Mexican women waited until 1953 to see full enfranchisement.[10] Although they represent two of the earliest, most comprehensive social-reform projects

Conclusion

in twentieth-century Latin America, little comparative work on Batllista Uruguay and revolutionary Mexico has been done to date. To what extent did the Mexican and Uruguayan models shape subsequent reform efforts elsewhere in Latin America? Were either of these reformist projects directly influenced by the other, or did they develop along independent trajectories, looking to Europe and the United States for guidance rather than other nations in Latin America? Future researchers will hopefully take up these questions, and yield important new understandings about state formation and gender politics in twentieth-century Latin America.

One important way that the Uruguayan case differs from that of Mexico and many other Latin American countries is on the question of race, a thread left largely unexplored in the present study. The Uruguayan population was (and is) overwhelmingly of European descent, but it has never been nearly as white as official imagery would have us believe. And more importantly, just because the population was mostly European does not mean that race was not a factor in political discourse. Batllismo was about whitening the polity literally through encouragement of European immigration, and culturally and discursively by imposing "discipline" on a previously "savage" and "barbaric" population. In this, Batllista modernization was part of the "whitening" project that dominated Latin American intellectual and political thought from the late nineteenth through early twentieth centuries. Jerry Dávila's study of Brazilian racial discourses and education policy forcefully establishes the idea that "whitening" in Brazil was both literal and metaphoric. Most importantly, Dávila demonstrates that racial discourses and the discourse of progress overlapped in many ways, encouraging us to read modernization as whitening (and vice versa).[11] His discussion of schoolteachers and teacher training (which not only whitened, but feminized the profession) speaks to a gendered dimension of these discourses and policies as well. How much did the perception of whiteness in Uruguay influence the Batllista project? In her comparative study of gender, race, class, and reform in Puerto Rico and Belize, Anne MacPherson has concluded that "the perception of racial similarity may have helped to bridge cultural differences of class, making Puerto Rican leaders more likely to attempt a populist alliance with Puerto Rican workers than their counterparts in the British Caribbean."[12] To what extent did these perceptions facilitate the growth of organized feminism, and to what extent was "whiteness" part of feminist discourses in early twentieth-century Latin America? The continued cross-fertilization of these areas of historical inquiry—gender and state formation on the one

Conclusion

hand, and race and nation on the other—will surely yield significant insights into this formative period in the region's history.

Finally, this study also contributes to our understanding of women's right-wing political activity in Latin America, by suggesting some comparisons both with other branches of the Damas Católicas and other right-wing movements in which women participated. I suggest that there are two variables worth highlighting: the perceived strength of anticlerical forces, and the perceived proximity of women's suffrage in a given national context. Comparing the histories of the Damas Católicas in Uruguay, Chile, and Mexico is instructive. In the 1910s and 1920s, anticlerical politics in Chile were nowhere near as menacing, from a Catholic perspective, as they were in Batllista Uruguay and revolutionary Mexico. This goes a long way toward explaining the fact that the Uruguayan Liga, and eventually its Mexican counterparts, were more confrontational with the state, justifying their transgression of traditional gender roles (via petitions, street marches, etc.) by the dire urgency of defending the place of religion in their respective societies. The Chilean Damas, in contrast, were more traditional in their methods, leaving the lobbying of parliament largely to the men and reserving most of their efforts to reforming the upper-class society to which they belonged.

Another by-product of Batllista reform was the language in the 1917 Constitution regarding suffrage and the consequently perceived proximity of women's vote in Uruguay. This added another element to women's activism, and required male political figures to take women's citizenship issues seriously, perhaps more so than in neighboring countries (like Chile and Argentina) where women's suffrage was on a more distant horizon during the 1920s and early 1930s. Here the Brazilian case is useful. Like Uruguay, women's suffrage came comparatively early to Brazil (1932, a few months before Uruguay), and was certainly perceived as imminent by the late 1920s. According to Sandra McGee Deutsch, this altered the place that women held in far-right politics, where she observes that the Brazilian Right had to "reconcile itself with the reality of women's suffrage."[13] Because of this combination of an early anticlerical assault and the place of women's suffrage in politics, in the story of the rise of the Right in the 1930s Southern Cone, it is tempting to think—but premature to assume—that Uruguayan women played a more prominent role than in other neighboring countries.

Notes

Introduction

1. Eduardo Galeano, *Memory of Fire*, Vol. 3: *Century of the Wind* (New York: Pantheon, 1988), 35.
2. Franklin Martin, *South America from a Surgeon's Point of View* (New York: Fleming H. Revell, 1922), 118. See also Simon G. Hanson, *Utopia in Uruguay: Chapters in the Economic History of Uruguay* (New York: Oxford University Press, 1938); and Milton Vanger, *The Model Country: José Batlle y Ordoñez of Uruguay, 1907–1915* (Hanover, NH: University Press of New England, 1980).
3. Russell Fitzgibbon, *Uruguay: Portrait of a Democracy* (London: Allen and Unwin, 1956), 128.
4. "El memorable discurso de Batlle," *Mujer batllista* (September 1946): 20.
5. See, for example, Carol Brown, "Mothers, Fathers, and Children: From Private to Public Patriarchy," in *Women and Revolution: A Discussion of the Unhappy Marriage of Marxism and Feminism*, ed. Lydia Sargent (Boston: South End Press, 1981); Eileen Boris and Peter Bardaglio, "The Transformation of Patriarchy: The Historic Role of the State," in Irene Diamond, ed., *Families, Politics, and Public Policy: A Feminist Dialogue on Women and the State* (New York: Longman, 1983), 70–93; Linda Gordon, ed., *Women, the State, and Welfare* (Madison: University of Wisconsin Press, 1990); Mimi Abramowitz, *Regulating the Lives of Women: Social Welfare Policy from Colonial Times to the Present* (Boston: South End Press, 1988).
6. Ann Orloff, "Gender in the Welfare State," *Annual Review of Sociology* 22 (1996): 51–78. See also Julia O'Connor, Sheila Shaver, and Ann Orloff, *States, Markets, and Families: Gender, Liberalism and Social Policy in Australia, Canada, Great Britain and the United States* (Cambridge: Cambridge University Press, 1999).
7. Sueann Caulfield, "The History of Gender in the Historiography of Latin America," *Hispanic American Historical Review* 81: 3–4 (May 2001), 475. See also Elizabeth Quay Hutchison, "Add Gender and Stir?: Cooking up Gendered Histories of Modern Latin America," *Latin American Research Review* 38, no. 1 (2003): 267–87.
8. Susan K. Besse, *Restructuring Patriarchy: The Modernization of Gender Inequality in Brazil, 1914–1940* (Chapel Hill: University of

North Carolina Press, 1996); Mary Kay Vaughan, "Modernizing Patriarchy: State Policies, Rural Households, and Women in Mexico," in *Hidden Histories of Gender and the State in Latin America*, ed. Elizabeth Dore and Maxine Molyneux (Durham, NC: Duke University Press, 2000). For a discussion of similar patterns in a more contemporary historical setting, see Maxine Molyneux, "Mobilization without Emancipation? Women's Interests, The State, and Revolution in Nicaragua," *Feminist Studies* (Summer 1985); Heidi Tinsman, *Partners in Conflict: The Politics of Gender, Sexuality, and Labor in the Chilean Agrarian Reform, 1950–1973* (Durham, N.C.: Duke University Press, 2002).

9. Elizabeth Quay Hutchison, *Labors Appropriate to Their Sex: Gender, Labor, and Politics in Urban Chile, 1900–1930* (Durham, N.C.: Duke University Press, 2001); Thomas Miller Klubock, *Contested Communities: Class, Gender, and Politics in Chile's El Teniente Copper Mine, 1904–1951* (Durham, N.C.: Duke University Press, 1998); Ann Farnsworth-Alvear, *Dulcinea in the Factory: Myths, Morals, Men and Women in Colombia's Industrial Experiment, 1905–1960* (Durham, NC: Duke University Press, 2000).

10. Much of the recent scholarship on gender in Latin American history continues to address feminism and feminist politics, but not as a central area of focus. See, for example, Besse, *Restructuring Patriarchy*; Hutchison, *Labors Appropriate to Their Sex*; Eileen Suárez Findlay, *Imposing Decency: The Politics of Sexuality and Race in Puerto Rico, 1870–1920* (Durham, NC: Duke University Press, 1999); Karin Alejandra Rosemblatt, *Gendered Compromises: Political Cultures and the State in Chile, 1920–1950* (Chapel Hill: University of North Carolina Press, 2000); Katherine Elaine Bliss, *Compromised Positions: Prostitution, Public Health, and Gender Politics in Revolutionary Mexico City* (University Park, PA: Pennsylvania State University Press, 2001); Anne S. MacPherson, "Citizens v. Clients: Working Women and Colonial Reform in Puerto Rico and Belize, 1932–1945," *Journal of Latin American Studies* 35 (May 2003), 279–310.

11. For national and comparative histories of Latin American feminism, see Marifran Carlson, *Feminismo!: The Woman's Movement in Argentina from Its Beginnings to Eva Perón* (Chicago: Academy Chicago Publishers; 1988); June Hahner, *Emancipating the Female Sex: The Struggle for Women's Rights in Brazil, 1850–1940* (Durham, NC: Duke University Press, 1990); Asunción Lavrin, *Women, Feminism, and Social Change in Argentina, Chile, and Uruguay, 1890–1940*

(Lincoln: University of Nebraska Press, 1995); Francesca Miller, *Latin American Women and the Search for Social Justice* (Hanover, NH: University Press of New England, 1991); K. Lynn Stoner, *From the House to the Streets: The Cuban Woman's Movement for Legal Reform, 1898–1940* (Durham, NC: Duke University Press, 1991). For relations and interactions between feminists in the Pan-American arena, see Donna Guy, "The Politics of Pan-American Cooperation: Maternalist Feminism and the Child Rights Movement, 1913–1960," 449–69, and Christine Ehrick, "Madrinas and Missionaries: Uruguay and the Pan-American Women's Movement," 406–24, both in *Gender and History* 10, no. 3 (November 1998).

12. Marianismo became an important paradigm for understanding Latin American women's history in a comparative context. See, for example, Evelyn P. Stevens, "Marianismo: The Other Face of Machismo in Latin America" in *Female and Male in Latin America*, ed. Anne Pescatello (Pittsburgh: University of Pittsburgh Press, 1973), 89–101; Elsa Chaney, *Supermadre: Women in Politics in Latin America.* (Austin: University of Texas Press, 1979).

13. Internal organizational records and membership lists were available for the National Women's Council and the Women's Suffrage Alliance, the two principal liberal feminist groups in Uruguay at this time, in both the Paulina Luisi archives and the private archives of the National Women's Council. A lack of equivalent documentation for the Catholic Ladies' League and/or the Communists and Socialists meant that data was mostly limited to the leadership of these organizations.

14. Francisco Panizza, "Late Institutionalisation and Early Modernisation: The Emergence of Uruguay's Liberal Democratic Political Order," *Journal of Latin American Studies* 29 (October 1997): 667–91; Fernando López-Alves, *Between the Economy and the Polity in the River Plate: Uruguay, 1811–1890* (London: University of London Institute of Latin American Studies, 1993). See also Fernando López-Alves, *State Formation and Democracy in Latin America, 1810–1910*, (Durham, NC: Duke University Press, 2000); and David Rock and Fernando López-Alves, "State Building and Political Systems in Nineteenth-Century Argentina and Uruguay," *Past and Present* 167 (May 2000): 177–202.

15. Rebecca Earle, "Rape and the Anxious Republic: Revolutionary Colombia, 1810–1830," in Dore and Molyneux, eds., *Hidden Histories of Gender and the State in Latin America*, 129; Ariel De la Fuente, *Children of Facundo: Caudillo and Gaucho Insurgency during the*

Argentine State-Formation Process, La Rioja, 1853–1870 (Durham, NC: Duke University Press, 2000), esp. 92.

16. See Carlos A. Forment, Democracy in Latin America, 1760–1900, Vol. 1: *Civic Selfhood and Public Life in Mexico and Peru* (Chicago: University of Chicago Press, 2003). Although women and gender analysis receive minimal attention in this ambitious reevaluation of democratic legacies and nineteenth-century politics in Latin America, Forment's study does attest to women's participation in civic organizing in Mexico and Peru during this era. Especially in the Peruvian case, it seems, women were auxiliary but nonetheless active participants in postindependence associational activity. Forment's upcoming volume on Argentina and Cuba will doubtless have more direct relevance to the Uruguayan case.

17. Gerardo Caetano, *La República Conservadora*, 2 vols. (Montevideo: Fin de Siglo, 1992–1993). See also Aimee Verdisco, "Between Accountability and "Reivindicación": Development and Intra-National Differentiation in Uruguay." (Ph.D. diss, State University of New York, Buffalo, 1996).

18. For scholarship on Uruguay from independence through the Batllista era that does touch on areas of gender, see the extensive work of José Pedro Barrán, especially *Amor y transgresión en Montevideo, 1919–1931* (Montevideo: Ediciones de la Banda Oriental, 2001) and *Historia de la sensibilidad en el Uruguay*, 2 vols. (Montevideo: Ediciones de la Banda Oriental, 1991–1992). See also Lucía Sala de Tourón and Rosa Alonso Eloy, *El Uruguay comercial, pastoríl y caudillesco*, Tomo 2, *Sociedad, Política e Ideología* (Montevideo: Ediciones de la Banda Oriental, 1991); Gerardo Caetano and Roger Geymonat, *La secularización uruguaya (1859–1919)*, Tomo 1 *Catolicismo y privatización de lo religioso* (Montevideo: Ediciones Santillana, 1997).

19. Gerda Lerner, *The Creation of Patriarchy* (New York: Oxford University Press, 1986), 239.

20. See Sandra Lauderdale Graham, *House and Street: The Domestic World of Servants and Masters in Nineteenth-Century Rio de Janeiro* (Austin: University of Texas Press, 1988), 91–107. Kim Butler uses the term *patronage* to describe a similar system of relations, looking fundamentally at the construction and preservation of racial inequalities. See *Freedoms Given, Freedoms Won: Afro-Brazilians in Post-Abolition São Paulo and San Salvador* (New Brunswick, NJ: Rutgers University Press, 1998), 16–24.

21. Félix V. Matos Rodríguez, *Women and Urban Change in San Juan,*

Puerto Rico, 1820–1868 (Gainesville: University Press of Florida, 1999). See also Teresita Martínez-Vergne, *Shaping the Discourse on Space: Charity and Its Wards in Nineteenth-Century San Juan, Puerto Rico* (Austin: University of Texas Press, 1999).

22. See, for example, Carlson, *Feminismo!*; Lavrin, *Women, Feminism, and Social Change*; Miller, *Latin American Women and the Search for Social Justice*. Stoner, *From the House to the Streets*.

23. Studies on right-wing women and conservative politics in Latin America include Sandra McGee Deutsch, *Las Derechas: The Extreme Right in Argentina, Brazil, and Chile, 1890–1939* (Stanford, CA: Stanford University Press, 1999); Margaret Power, *Right-Wing Women in Chile: Feminine Power and the Struggle against Allende, 1964–1973* (University Park, PA: The Pennsylvania State University Press, 2002); Patience Schell, "An Honorable Avocation for Ladies: The Work of the Mexico City Unión de Damas Católicas Mexicanas, 1912-1926." *Journal of Women's History* 99, no.10 (Winter 1999): 78–103; and Ericka Kim Verba, "Catholic Feminism and *acción social femenina* [Women's Social Action]: The Early Years of the Liga de Damas Chilenas, 1912–1924," (Ph.D. diss., University of California, Los Angeles, 1999). For studies of left feminisms and working-class women, see Maxine Molyneux, "No God, No Boss, No Husband: Anarchist Feminism in Nineteenth Century Argentina, " *Latin American Perspectives* 13, no.1 (Winter 1986): 119–45; Elizabeth Hutchison, "From 'La Mujer Esclava' to 'La Mujer Limón': Anarchism and the Politics of Sexuality in Early-Twentieth-Century Chile" *Hispanic American Historical Review* 81, nos. 3–4 (August/November 2001), 519–53. See also sections on worker feminisms in Rosemblatt, *Gendered Compromises*; Hutchison, *Labors Appropriate to Their Sex*; Findlay, *Imposing Decency*. Shirlene Soto, *Emergence of the Modern Mexican Woman: Her Participation in Revolution and Struggle for Equality, 1910–1940* (Denver, CO: Arden Press, 1990).

24. Besse, *Restructuring Patriarchy*, 164. Shirlene Soto's *Emergence of the Modern Mexican Woman* also looks at women's participation across the political spectrum, from the *soldaderas* to women participants in the conservative Cristero Rebellion. She does not, however, engage in discussing the competing definitions of feminism. For an overview of the plurality of French feminisms in the early twentieth century, see Jennifer Waelti-Walters and Steven C. Hause, eds., *Feminisms of the Belle Epoque: A Historical and Literary Anthology* (Lincoln: University of Nebraska Press, 1994), 42–57.

25. For more on Left and worker feminisms, and gender within working-class communities, see Hutchison, *Labors Appropriate to Their Sex*; Klubock, *Contested Communities*; Molyneux, "No God, No Boss, No Husband"; Farnsworth-Alvear, *Dulcinea in the Factory*; MacPherson, "Citizens v. Clients."
26. Nancy Cott, *The Grounding of Modern Feminism* (New Haven, CT: Yale University Press), 1987, 4–5.
27. Karen Offen, *European Feminisms, 1700–1950: A Political History* (Stanford, CA: Stanford University Press, 2000), 21–22. Molly Ladd-Taylor, in contrast, does not see maternalism as feminism per se, because her definition of maternalism includes support for the family wage, and thus women's dependence. See Molly Ladd-Taylor "Toward Defining Maternalism in U.S. History," *Journal of Women's History* 5, no. 2 (Fall 1993): 110–13.
28. Seth Koven and Sonya Michel, eds., *Mothers of a New World: Maternalist Politics and the Origins of Welfare States* (New York: Routledge, 1993), 4.
29. Offen, *European Feminisms*, 170.
30. See, for example, Hahner, *Emancipating the Female Sex*; Besse, *Restructuring Patriarchy*; Findlay, *Imposing Decency*; and Miller, *Latin American Women and the Search for Social Justice*.
31. Sonia E. Álvarez, *Engendering Democracy in Brazil: Women's Movements in Transition Politics*, (Princeton, NJ: Princeton University Press, 1990), 24.
32. See ibid., esp. 19–36. See also the discussion of "practical" and "strategic" gender interests in Orloff, "Gender in the Welfare State," 69–70; and in Molyneux, "Mobilization without Emancipation?"
33. Rebecca Edwards, *Angels in the Machinery: Gender in American Party Politics from the Civil War to the Progressive Era*, (New York and Oxford: Oxford University Press, 1997), esp. 51–58. For more on women and party politics in the pre-women's-suffrage United States, see Melanie Gustafson, Kristie Miller, and Elisabeth Israels Perry, eds., *We Have Come to Stay: American Women in Political Parties, 1880–1960* (Albuquerque: University of New Mexico Press, 1999); and Melanie Gustafson, *Women in the Republican Party, 1854–1924* (Urbana: University of Illinois Press, 2001).
34. Corinne Antezana-Pernet, "Peace in the World and Democracy at Home: The Chilean Women's Movement in the 1940s," in *Latin America in the 1940s: War and Postwar Transitions*, ed. David Rock (Berkeley and Los Angeles: University of California Press, 1994), 166.

35. Rosemblatt's *Gendered Compromises* focuses on the struggles between Communists and non-Communists in Chilean feminism, underscoring the way that the complicated and contentious party politics of the Popular Front were echoed in internal feminist politics.
36. Miller, *Latin American Women and the Search for Social Justice*, especially her discussion of Peruvian feminism, 79–82; Lavrin, *Women, Feminism, and Social Change*, 16–20.
37. For more on feminism and internationalism, see, for example, Leila J. Rupp, *Worlds of Women: The Making of an International Women's Movement* (Princeton NJ: Princeton University Press, 1997); and Nitza Berkovitch, *From Motherhood to Citizenship: Women's Rights and International Organizations* (Baltimore: Johns Hopkins University Press, 1999).
38. See Miller, *Latin American Women and the Search for Social Justice*, 71. June Hahner makes a similar observation in *Emancipating the Female Sex*, 20–25.
39. Leading Brazilian liberal feminist Bertha Lutz, for example, was also a pioneer in women's education, who maintained official ties with the state while she headed up the main women's-rights organization. Similar to Miller's assessment of schoolteachers, Besse notes that "Lutz's position as a government employee provided opportunities for her to establish formal contacts with women's organizations throughout Europe and the Americas" (Besse, *Restructuring Patriarchy*, 167). But Besse does not elaborate on the ways in which Lutz's education or relationship to the Brazilian state may have influenced the tenor or orientation of her feminism.
40. Some scholars of United States history and politics have written about women's private and church-based reform activity in the United States, while others have noted the links between this activity and organized feminism. See, for example, Theda Skocpol, *Protecting Soldiers and Mothers: The Political Origins of Social Policy in the United States* (Cambridge: Harvard University Press, 1992); Mary P. Ryan, *Cradle of the Middle Class: The Family in Oneida County, New York, 1790–1865*. (New York: Cambridge University Press, 1981).
41. Gisela Bock, *Women in European History* (Oxford: Blackwell, 2002), 111. In *Protecting Soldiers and Mothers*, Theda Skocpol identifies the rise of voluntary associations, along with expanded higher education, as "conditions that favored the organization and civic engagement of American women" (318).
42. See Linda L. Clark "Feminist Maternalists and the French State: Two

Inspectresses General in the Pre–World War I Third Republic," *Journal of Women's History* 12, no.1 (Spring 2000): 32–59. Here, Clark also emphasizes the connections between feminism and French state formation under the ideology of "solidarism," which served as a model for Batllista state-making in Uruguay. See also Linda L. Clark, *The Rise of the Professional Woman in France: Gender and Public Administration since 1830.* (Cambridge and New York: Cambridge University Press, 2000).

43. See Linda L. Clark "Bringing Feminine Qualities into the Public Sphere: The Third Republic's Appointment of Women Inspectors," in Elinor A. Accampo et al. *Gender and the Politics of Social Reform in France, 1870–1914* (Baltimore: Johns Hopkins University Press, 1995), esp. 149–54.

44. George Steinmetz, *Regulating the Social: The Welfare State and Local Politics in Imperial Germany* (Princeton, NJ: Princeton University Press, 1993); O'Connor et al. *States, Markets, and Families*; Julia Adams and Tasleem Padamsee, "Signs and Regimes: Rereading Feminist Work on Welfare States," *Social Politics* 8, no. 1 (2001): 1–23; Margaret Weir, Ann Orloff, and Theda Skocpol, eds., *The Politics of Social Policy in the United States* (Princeton, NJ: Princeton University Press, 1988). Much of this scholarship is influenced by Foucaultian understandings of the state, including the view that power is not coterminous with the state apparatus. See, for example, Michel Foucault, *Power/Knowledge: Selected Interviews and Other Writings, 1972–1977* (New York: Pantheon, 1980), 55–62.

45. Janet R. Horne *A Social Laboratory for Modern France: The Musée Social and the Rise of the Welfare State* (Durham, NC: Duke University Press, 2002).

46. For information on the Argentine system, see María Herminia Di Liscia and José Maristany, eds., *Mujeres y estado en la Argentina: educación, salud y beneficencia* (Buenos Aires: Editorial Biblos, 1997), esp. 134.

47. In *Women and Urban Change in San Juan, Puerto Rico*, Matos Rodríguez makes a similar argument about links between elite beneficence and feminism, but does not really develop or explore this connection.

Prologue

1. Gerardo Caetano and José Rilla. *Historia contemporánea del Uruguay moderno: de la colonia al Mercosur* (Montevideo: CLAEH/Fin de Siglo, 1994), 54.

2. John Charles Chasteen, "Fighting Words: The Discourse of Insurgency in Latin American History," *Latin American Research Review* 28, no.3 (Summer 1993), 86. For more on gauchos, caudillos, and nineteenth-century politics in the Rio de la Plata region, see Ariel de la Fuente, *Children of Facundo: Caudillo and Gaucho Insurgency during the Argentine State-Formation Processs (La Rioja, 1853–1870)* (Durham, NC: Duke University Press, 2000).
3. Cited in María del Carmen Ortíz de Terra and Rosario Quijano, "Las mujeres durante la revolución lavallejista de 1832," *Hoy es Historia* 4, no. 23 (September-October 1987), 25.
4. Antonio N. Pereira, *Cosas de antaño: Bocetos, perfiles y tradiciones interesantes y populares de Montevideo* (Montevideo: El Siglo Ilustrado, 1893), 264–65.
5. Lucía Sala de Tourón and Rosa Alonso Eloy, *El Uruguay comercial, pastoríl y caudillesco*, Tomo 2: *Sociedad, Política e Ideología* (Montevideo: Ediciones de la Banda Oriental, 1991), 98.
6. J. A. B. Beaumont, *Viajes por Buenos Aires, Entre Rios y la Banda Oriental (1826–1827)* (Buenos Aires: Librería Hachette, 1957), 65–66.
7. Tomás de Iriarte, *Memorias: El Sitio de Montevideo* Vol. 11 (Buenos Aires: Editorial Goncourt, 1969), 24.
8. Iriarte, cited in Aníbal Barrios Pintos, *El Silencio y la voz: Historia de la mujer en el Uruguay* (Montevideo: Linardi y Risso, 2001), 121–22. For a discussion of women's participation in the independence wars in South America, see Evelyn M. Cherpak, "The Participation of Women in the Wars for Independence in Northern South America, 1810–1824," *Minerva: Quarterly Report on Women and the Military* 11, no.3 (December 1993): 11–28; Rebecca Earle "Rape and the Anxious Republic: Revolutionary Colombia, 1810–1830" in Dore and Molyneux, eds. *Hidden Histories of Gender and the State in Latin America* (Durham, NC: Duke University Press, 2000), 127–46.
9. Augusto I. Schulkin, *Historia de Paysandú: Diccionario biográfico*, Tomo 3 (Buenos Aires: Ed. Van Roosen, 1958), 171–73. See also chapter 10 in Barrios Pintos, *El Silencio y la Voz*.
10. John Charles Chasteen, *Heroes on Horseback: The Life and Times of the Last Gaucho Caudillos* (Albuquerque: University of New Mexico Press, 1995), 195 n. 9.
11. Rosario Quijano, "Ana Monterroso de Lavalleja," in *Mujeres Uruguayas: El lado femenino de nuestra historica*, ed. Blanca Rodríguez and Cielo Pereira (Montevideo: Alfaguara, 1997), 1:179.
12. María del Carmen Ortíz de Terra, "Bernardina Fragoso de Rivera," in

Rodríguez and Pereira, *Mujeres Uruguayas*, 1: 124.
13. Cited in Ortíz de Terra and Quijano, "Las mujeres durante la revolución lavallejista de 1832," *Hoy es Historia* 4, no. 23 (September-October 1987), 27.
14. Oscar Padrón Favre, *Durazno Antiguo* (Durazno: Mlm Pesce, 1991), 1:14–17.
15. Milton I. Vanger, *José Batlle y Ordóñez of Uruguay: The Creator of His Times, 1902–1907* (Cambridge: Harvard University Press, 1963), 10.
16. Cited in Mónica Szurmuk, *Women in Argentina: Early Travel Narratives* (Gainesville: University Press of Florida, 2000), 20.
17. Hermán C. Kruse, "Las damas de la caridad y los caballeros de la filantropía: Un estudio sobre caridad, filantropía y beneficencia en el Uruguay del Siglo XIX" (Master's thesis, University of the Republic, Montevideo, 1994), 44.
18. Iriarte, *Memorias*, 11:552.
19. Ortíz de Terra, "Bernardina Fragoso de Rivera," in Rodríguez and Pereira, *Mujeres Uruguayas*, 1:132. See also José Salgado, *Las Damas Orientales en la Beneficencia Pública* (Montevideo: Impresora L. I. G. U., 1942).
20. Nicolás Sánchez-Albornoz, "Population," in *Latin America Economy and Society, 1870–1930*, ed. Leslie Bethell (New York: Cambridge University Press, 1989), 88–89.
21. See, for example, Luis E. González, *Political Structures and Democracy in Uruguay*, (Notre Dame, IN: University of Notre Dame Press, 1991), 13.

Chapter One

1. In 1907, Chile reported a literacy rate of only 40 percent; even in the city of Rio de Janeiro only slightly more than half (52 percent) of residents were literate by 1906.
2. José Pedro Varela, *Obras Pedagógicas: La educación del pueblo* (Montevideo: Ministerio de Instrucción Pública y Previsión Social, 1964), 216.
3. Varela, *Obras Pedagógicas*, 210–16.
4. An equivalent school for boys was not opened until 1891.
5. See Carlos Zubillaga and Mario Cayota. *Cristianos y cambio social en el Uruguay de la modernización (1896–1919)* (Montevideo: CLAEH/Banda Oriental, 1988), 40–47.
6. Cited in María Julia Ardão, *La creación de la Sección de Enseñanza Secundaria y Preparatoria para Mujeres en 1912* (Montevideo:

Editorial Florensa y Lafon, 1962), 15.
7. Cited in Virginia Cánova, *Por una fortuna una Cruz y Los orígenes del feminismo en Uruguay* (Montevideo: Biblioteca Nacional, 1998), 192.
8. Asociación de Señoras Cristianas; *Memoria presentada a la Asociación de Señoras Cristianas en la Asamblea Extraordinaria el 22 de agosto de 1897* (Montevideo: Marcos Martínez, 1897).
9. Russell H. Fitzgibbon, *Uruguay: Portrait of a Democracy* (London: George Allen and Unwin, 1956), 232.
10. Studies of Freemasonry in both France and United States cite the era of the late nineteenth through early twentieth centuries as a time when women became more directly integrated into Masonic activities, although they were generally incorporated in an auxiliary fashion. See Janet M. Burke and Margaret C. Jacob, "French Freemasonry, Women, and Feminist Scholarship," *Journal of Modern History* 68, no. 3 (September 1996), 513–49; Lynn Dumenil, *Freemasonry and American Culture, 1880–1930* (Princeton, NJ: Princeton University Press, 1984); Mildred J. Headings, *French Freemasonry under the Third Republic*, (Baltimore: Johns Hopkins University Press, 1949); María De Letre, *La masonería y la mujer* (Mexico DF: Editorial Herbasa, n.d.).
11. Oscar Padrón Favre, *Durazno Antiguo* (Montevideo: Mlm Pesce, 1991), 1:44–46.
12. "Las Damas del Durazno" *El Argos* (Durazno, Uruguay) 782 (16 January 1896), 1. Archives of Oscar Padrón Favre, Durazno, Uruguay.
13. Oscar Padrón Favre, interview with the author. Durazno, Uruguay, June 7, 1998.
14. For more on anarchist feminism in Latin America, see Maxine Molyneux, "No God, No Boss, No Husband: Anarchist Feminism in Nineteenth-Century Argentina," *Latin American Perspectives* 13, no.1 (Winter 1986), 119–45. Elizabeth Quay Hutchison, "From 'La Mujer Esclava' to 'La Mujer Limón': Anarchism and the Politics of Sexuality in Early-Twentieth-Century Chile," *Hispanic American Historical Review* 81, nos. 3–4 (August/November 2001), 519–53. For information on women and anarchism in Spain, see Temma Kaplan, *Anarchists of Andalusia, 1868–1903*, (Princeton, NJ: Princeton University Press, 1977); Temma Kaplan, *Red City, Blue Period: Social Movements in Picasso's Barcelona* (Berkeley: University of California Press, 1992); Martha A. Ackelsburg, *Free Women of Spain: Anarchism and the Struggle for the Emancipation of Women* (Bloomington: Indiana University Press, 1991);
15. "A las mujeres," *La Aurora*, Montevideo, September 1899, 1. UCLA

Special Collections, Labor Newspapers Collection, Box 21.
16. "Matrimonio y prostitución," *Derecho a la Vida*, January 1895, 3. UCLA Labor Newspapers, Box 46.
17. "La mujer: su vida y su esclavitud," *La Verdad*, 8 September 1897, 3. UCLA Labor Newspapers, Box 177.
18. In "From 'La Mujer Esclava' to 'La Mujer Limón,'" Hutchison notes that men frequently assumed female pseudonyms in discussions of the woman question printed in the anarchist press.
19. "Grito de la mujer rebelde," *Derecho a la Vida*, July 1896, 1. UCLA Labor Newspapers, Box 46.
20. Hutchison, "From 'La Mujer Esclava' to 'La Mujer Limón,'" 553.
21. Yamandú González Sierra, *Del hogar a la fábrica: deshonra o virtud?* (Montevideo: Ed. Nordan, 1996), 74.
22. "Progresando," *La Aurora*, September 1899, 4. UCLA Labor Newspapers, Box 21.
23. Universindo Rodríguez Díaz, *Los sectores populares en el Uruguay del novecientos, primera parte (1907–1911)*, (Montevideo: Editorial Compañero/Tristán, 1989), 1:92.
24. Francisco Pintos, *Historia del movimiento obrero del Uruguay* (Montevideo: n.p., 1960), 57.
25. "1901 Balance general del movimiento obrero," *Tribuna Libertaria*, 7 January 1902, 2. UCLA Labor Newspapers, Box 170. Emphasis in original.
26. Carlos Zubillaga and Jorge Balbis, *Historia del movimiento sindical Uruguayo*, 4 vols. (Montevideo: Ediciones de la Banda Oriental, 1985–1992), 3: 131.
27. This *La Voz de la Mujer* should not be confused with the late-nineteenth Argentine anarchist feminist paper of the same name, although the use of the same name may not have been a coincidence. See Molyneux, "No God, No Boss, No Husband."
28. "Las corseteras," *La Voz de la Mujer*, 15 April 1905, 1.
29. Haiti was the first Latin American country to legalize divorce, following independence. The Dominican Republic, Venezuela, Ecuador, and all of the Central American nations except Panama had some form of legal divorce before 1907. As late as the 1950s, neighboring Chile, Argentina, Brazil, and Paraguay still had no legal divorce. See Ricardo Gallardo, *Divorcio, separación de cuerpos, y nulidad de matrimonio en las naciones latino-americanas* (Madrid: n.p., 1957). Susan K. Besse, in *Restructuring Patriarchy: The Modernization of Gender Inequality in Brazil, 1914–1940* (Chapel Hill: University of North

Carolina Press, 1996), mentions that affluent Brazilians would sometimes travel to Uruguay to secure divorces, which were still unobtainable in Brazil in the 1920s and 1930s (55).

30. *Registro de Leyes y Decretos*, 1907:606. Like much of Latin America, Uruguayan law was based on the Napoleonic Code. For more on the women and the Napoleonic Code in Europe, see Claire Goldberg Moses, *French Feminism in the Nineteenth Century* (Albany: State University of New York Press, 1984), 18–20; Gisela Bock, *Women in European History* (Oxford: Blackwell, 2002), 62–78. For the Napoleonic Code and Latin American women, see Maxine Molyneux, "Twentieth-Century State Formations," in *Hidden Histories of Gender and the State*, ed. Elizabeth Dore and Molyneux (Durham, NC: Duke University Press, 2000).

31. In her study of the Damas Católicas Mexicanas, Patience Schell makes a similar analysis about the later Catholic women's response to the anticlericalism of the Mexican Revolution. See Patience Schell, "An Honorable Avocation for Ladies: The Work of the Mexico City Unión de Damas Católicas Mexicanas, 1912–1926." *Journal of Women's History* 99, no. 10 (Winter 1999): 78–103.

32. Joaquín de Secco Illa, "El Divorcio," *El Bien Público*, 15 August 1905. Reproduced in Joaquín de Secco Illa, *Tres Años de Periodismo: Ideas Sueltas* (Montevideo: Vita Hermanos y Cía, 1908). 84–86.

33. This kind of tactic among Catholic women was not new in the region. In Chile, for example, over seventeen thousand women signed a petition opposing civil marriage in 1883. See Erika Maza Valenzuela, "Liberals, Radicals, and Women's Citizenship in Chile, 1872–1930." Kellogg Institute for International Studies, Working Paper no. 245, November 1997.

34. *Diario de la H. Cámara de Representantes* 183 (1905), 404–5.

35. "Congreso de Sevilla: Informe presentado por la Vice Presidenta del C.S. de LDCU," *El Eco*, August 1929.

36. Laura Carreras de Bastos, *Feminismo Cristiano*, (Montevideo: Imp. de la Buena Prensa, 1907), 10.

37. See Odile Sarti, *The Ligue Patriotique des Françaises, 1902–1933: A Feminine Response to the Secularization of French Society* (New York: Garland, 1992).

38. The Chilean Liga was formally organized in 1912, as was a branch of the *Damas Católicas Mexicanas*. For more information on the Chilean *Liga*, see Ericka Kim Verba, "Catholic Feminism and *Acción Social Femenina* [Women's Social Action]: The Early Years of the Liga

de Damas Chilenas, 1912–1924" (Ph.D. diss., University of California, Los Angeles, 1999); and Schell, "Honorable Avocation for Ladies." In *Las Derechas: The Extreme Right in Argentina, Brazil, and Chile, 1890–1939* (Stanford, CA: Stanford University Press, 1999), Sandra McGee Deutsch mentions the initial formation of a Brazilian Catholic Ladies' League in 1909 and an Argentine branch in 1910–1911.

39. Zubillaga and Cayota, *Cristianos y cambio social*, 59–67, 122–43.
40. Petrona Cibils de Jackson, Luisa Gurméndez de Carve Urioste, and Estanislada Márquez de Lessa were all wives of leading bankers, developers, and industrialists. Faustina Gómez de García Lagos was the daughter of Blanco military leader Leandro Gómez, and Francisca Lacaze de Ponce de Leon's husband was an important military leader in Saravia's armies in the late nineteenth century.
41. In the membership database for the Liga, there are several mother-daughter pairs in the leadership, along with a few mother-in-law/daughter-in-law matches, and a number of cousins.
42. "La Liga de Damas Católicas: Lo que es lo que quiere," *El Eco* 1 (31 January 1907), 1. Emphasis in original.
43. Reverend Father Bettemboug, "La Mujer Cristiana," in *Conferencias pronunciadas bajo los auspicios de la Liga de Damas Católicas durante el año 1907* (Montevideo: Imp. de la Buena Prensa, 1908), 51.
44. "Las Conferencias de la Liga," *El Eco* 12 (15 May 1908), 1.
45. Carreras de Bastos, *Feminismo Cristiano*, 12.
46. Ibid. The concept of "Christian feminism" dates back to late nineteenth-century France, where Marie Maugeret published a monthly *Le Feminisme chrétien*. See Karen Offen, *European Feminisms, 1700–1950: A Political History* (Stanford, CA: University of Stanford Press, 2000), 196–200.
47. Carreras de Bastos, *Feminismo Cristiano*, 21.
48. For more on women and Catholic social action in South America, see Verba, "Catholic Feminism," 175–77.
49. Carreras de Bastos, *Feminismo Cristiano*, 21. Karen Offen reports that in 1906 (shortly before this pamphlet was published), Pope Leo XIII denounced women's political participation, a position he reasserted in 1909. (Offen, *European Feminisms*, 199.)
50. Laura Carreras de Bastos, *Acción social de la mujer ante el divorcio absoluto* (Montevideo: Imp. de la Buena Prensa, 1909), 11.
51. Liga de Damas Católicas, *Conferencias pronunciadas*, 56.
52. "Nueva Asociación," *El Eco* 19 (8 December 1908), 7.
53. "Informe del comité central de la Asociación de Matrimonios," *El*

Eco 72 (15 October 1913), 3.

54. The best example of this is found in *Estatutos de la Sociedad Femenina de Socorros Mutuos establecida en Paysandú, patrocinada por el comité departamental de la Liga de Damas Católicas*, (Montevideo: M. Martínez), 1909.
55. "Comités populares," *El Eco* 25 (15 June 1909), 1.
56. "De los comités populares y asociaciones femeninas," *El Eco* 38 (15 September 1910), 301.
57. Zubillaga and Cayota, *Cristianos y cambio social*, 75.
58. Asociación de Propaganda Liberal, "La mujer y la familia," Folleto No. 42, February 1904, cited in Caetano and Geymonat, *La secularización uruguaya* (1997), 221.
59. Ana Frega, "Redentores, amos y tutores: concepción dominante sobre el papel de la mujer en el Uruguay al comienzos del siglo XX" (GRECMU, photocopy, 1990), 22.
60. In her early years in Uruguay she was known as Belén Sárraga de Ferrero, or simply as Belén Sárraga. In 1909, she began to use Belén de Sárraga, a name that she continued to use when she was active in Chile in later years. For the purposes of simplicity, I refer to her as "Belén Sárraga."
61. See "Belén de Sárraga: Noticias de Vida" in Belén de Sárraga, *Conferencias sociológicas y de crítica religiosa* (Santiago de Chile: La Razón, 1913), 165–73.
62. The August 19, 1908, issue of *El Liberal* mentions the existence of an "Asociación de Damas Liberales de Montevideo," but no further information on the organization is provided.
63. "Nuestros propósitos," *El Liberal*, 8 April 1908, 1.
64. "Divorcio y derechos de los hijos naturales," *El Liberal*, 10 June 1908, 1.
65. Sárraga, *Conferencias sociológicas*, 24.
66. "Rusia contestando a Ferri," *El Liberal*, 25 September 1908, 1.
67. "Las asociaciones de damas liberales," *El Liberal*, 7 July 1909, 1.
68. "Movimiento obrero—las mujeres obreras," *El Liberal*, 19 April 1908, 2.
69. Sárraga, *Conferencias sociológicas*, 24.
70. "Libertad Liberticida," *El Liberal*, 22 October 1908, 1.
71. "La mujer y la iglesia," *El Liberal*, 14 February 1909, 1.
72. "Frente a la iglesia—la mujer," *El Liberal*, 29 June 1909, 1; 2 July 1909, 1.
73. "La mujer en la campaña," *El Liberal*, 17 April 1909, 1.
74. Ibid.
75. Oscar Padrón Favre, *Durazno: Bases para una identidad y un destino* (Durazno, Uruguay: Imprenta ABC, 1988), 19–20.

76. Renzo Pi Hugarte, *Los indios del Uruguay* (Montevideo: Ediciones de la Banda Oriental, 1998), 184.
77. José Pedro Rodríguez, "Las Mujeres en la historia de Durazno," Conferencia realizada en el Museo Casa de Rivera, en el programa conmemorativo del Día Internacional de la Mujer, Durazno, 1988.
78. Paulina Luisi to Otilia Schultze de Galarza, 26 December 1917. Private archives of Oscar Padrón Favre, Durazno, Uruguay.
79. Such accusations may have been accurate in Otilia Schultze's case. Years later, in 1923, Otilia received a letter signed by the *Gran Maestro* of the Uruguayan Masons, thanking her for her contribution and for her words of support, seen as a "clear and concrete manifestation that the heart of the Uruguayan woman can be inspired by the fundamental principles of our Institution." Instituto Masónico del Uruguay to Otilia Schultze de Galarza, 28 December 1923. Private archives of Oscar Padrón Favre, Durazno, Uruguay.
80. Asunción Lavrin, for example, wrote that in Uruguay, before 1915, "only one female feminist personality stands out, María Abella de Ramírez." Lavrin, *Women, Feminism, and Social Change in Argentina, Chile, and Uruguay, 1890–1940* (Lincoln: University of Nebraska Press), 322.
81. See María Abella de Ramírez, *Ensayos Feministas* (Montevideo: El Siglo Ilustrado, 1965).
82. Rodríguez Díaz, *Los sectores populares*, 92. Rodríguez Díaz reports Sárraga as honorary president, but *El Liberal* ran a correction on 22 May 1910 stating that she was in fact honorary vice president.
83. Lavrin, *Women, Feminism, and Social Change*, 261.
84. Rodríguez Díaz, *Los sectores populares*, 92. A 1913 biography of Sárraga mentions the death of her oldest child, Libertad, "a few years ago." This may explain her absence from the political scene during much of 1910–1911. (See Sárraga, *Conferencias sociológicas*.)
85. "Propaganda Liberal," in *El Día*, 29 March 1911, 2.
86. Sárraga received the warmest welcome, it seems, in Chile. Elizabeth Hutchison writes of her visit to Chile in 1913, and the significant impact of that visit, which included the foundation of several *Centros Belén de Sárraga*, which "gave a distinctly anti-clerical cast to the project of female mobilization." Hutchison, *Labors Appropriate to Their Sex: Gender, Labor, and Politics in Urban Chile, 1900–1930* (Durham, NC: Duke University Press, 2001), 126. Sárraga apparently made a second tour of Chile in 1915.
87. "A las mujeres: necesidad de organizarse," *La Nueva Senda*, April

1910, 3. UCLA Labor Newspapers, Box 91. In "From 'La Mujer Esclava' to 'La Mujer Limón,'" Hutchison refers to Juana Rouco Buela as Juana Rouco. In Uruguay she was always known as Juana Buela.
88. Rodríguez Díaz, *Los sectores populares*, 96.
89. "Esfuerzos feministas: La Federación Pan-Americana," *El Día*, 25 August 1910, 2.
90. "El feminismo entre nosotros," *El Día*, 13 March 1911, 1.
91. "Asociación Femenina Emancipación," *El Día*, 4 April 1911, 2. Belén Sárraga was still in Uruguay at this time, but appears to have been uninvolved in any stage of this process.
92. Rodríguez Díaz, *Los sectores populares*, 91.
93. Ibid., 118.
94. "Asociación Feminista Emancipación," *El Día*, 12 April 1911, 2.
95. "Asociación Feminista Emancipación," *El Día*, 25 April 1911, 3.
96. Rodríguez Díaz, *Los sectores populares*, 98.
97. Ibid.
98. "Asociación Feminista Emancipación" *El Día*, 17 June 1911, 3.
99. "Por el buen camino?," *El Socialista* 120 (13 July 1913), 2.
100. "Obreros," *El Socialista* 142 (14 December 1913), 3.
101. Julia Arévalo, "El obrero, la mujer y el socialismo—tomemos ejemplo," *El Socialista* 153 (31 April [sic] 1914), 3.
102. Rodríguez Díaz, *Los sectores populares*, 99.

Chapter Two

1. Asistencia Pública Nacional, *Publicación oficial de la dirección general* (Montevideo, 1913), 7.
2. The Uruguayan Public Assistance Law was patterned after the French "right of the poor" law of 1905, and the APN modeled after the French *Assistance Publique*. Batlle spent most of the Williman years in Europe, largely in France, and the French politics of *solidarité*, which sought to encourage class collaboration and "social peace" via an activist state, provided a particularly strong model. For more on the policies of the French Third Republic, see, for example, Sanford Elwitt, *The Third Republic Defended: Bourgeois Reform in France, 1880–1914* (Baton Rouge: Louisiana State University Press, 1986); Judith F. Stone, *The Search for Social Peace: Reform Legislation in France, 1890–1914* (Albany: State University of New York Press, 1985).
3. Miguel Becerro de Bengoa, *Los problemas de la Asistencia Pública* (Montevideo: El Siglo Ilustrado, 1922), 5.
4. "El memorable discurso de Batlle" *Mujer batllista* (September 1946),

20. Speech originally delivered via radio on December 12, 1922.
5. *Boletín de la Asistencia Pública Nacional* (hereafter *Boletín APN*) (July 1911), 23; Asistencia Pública Nacional, *Publicación oficial de la APN* (Montevideo, 1913), 21.
6. Carlos Vaz Ferreira, *Sobre Feminismo* (Buenos Aires: Editorial Losada, 1945), 37–38.
7. On the theoretical and historical links between gender, citizenship, and welfare state development, see Carole Pateman, *The Disorder of Women: Democracy, Feminism, and Political Theory* (Stanford, CA: Stanford University Press, 1989).
8. Other historians have noted the ideological and discursive inseparability of the "woman question" and the "social question." See, for example, Elinor A. Accampo et al., eds., *Gender and the Politics of Social Reform in France, 1870–1914* (Baltimore, MD: Johns Hopkins University Press, 1995); Elizabeth Quay Hutchison, *Labors Appropriate to Their Sex: Gender, Labor, and Politics in Urban Chile, 1900–1930* (Durham, NC: Duke University Press, 2001).
9. Silvia Rodríguez Villamíl and Graciela Sapriza. "Feminism and Politics: Women and the Vote in Uruguay, " in *Retrieving Women's History: Changing Perceptions of the Role of Women in Politics and Society*, ed. S. Jay Klienberg (New York: Oxford University Press, 1988), 286.
10. "Los empleos públicos y las mujeres," *El Día*, 10 April 1911, 1.
11. "A Woman Diplomat," *The Times South American Supplement*, (London), (September 1911), 30.
12. Francesca Miller observes that "normal-school graduates completed their certificates at the age of seventeen or eighteen, and they were barred from entry to universities, as their preparation was considered inferior to that of secondary, or preparatory, school students." Francesca Miller, *Latin American Women and the Search for Social Justice* (Hanover: University Press of New England, 1991), 48.
13. Benjamín Nahum, *Manual de Historia del Uruguay*, Vol. 2, *1903–1990* (Montevideo: Ediciones de la Banda Oriental, 1998), 58. See also María Julia Ardão, *La creación de la Sección de Enseñanza Secundaria y Preparatoria para Mujeres en 1912* (Montevideo: Editorial Florensa y Lafon, 1962), esp. 21; Ana Frega. "Redentores, amos y tutores: La concepción dominante sobre el papel de la mujer en el Uruguay a comienzos del siglo XX" (Montevideo: GRECMU, 1990, photocopy), 17.
14. "La Universidad para mujeres," *El Día*, 6 June 1911, 1.
15. *El Día*, 3 April 1912. Cited in Alba G. Cassina de Nogara, *Hacia una democracia integral: Apuntes para una historia del feminismo en*

Uruguay (Montevideo: Consejo Nacional de Mujeres del Uruguay, 1990), 58.

16. Cassina de Nogara, *Hacia una democracia integral*, 48.
17. By 1915 over eighty students were registered at the new Women's University. See Ardão, *La creación de la Sección de Enseñanza Secundaria*, pp.53–55.
18. Romeo Grompone, *Divorcio* (Montevideo: Edina, 1946), 206.
19. *Registro Nacional de Leyes y Decretos*, Vol. 36 (1913): 602–3. The legislation required that the couple had been married for at least two years, and mandated a one-year separation before divorce was finalized.
20. Ricardo Gallardo, *Divorcio, separación de cuerpos y nulidad del matrimonio en las naciones latino-americanas* (Madrid: n.p., 1957), 558.
21. This older legislation was based upon the Napoleonic Code, which prohibited the "investigation of paternity." See Bock, *Women in European History*, 63–64. For more on illegitimacy and inheritance in Latin America, see Ann Twinam, *Public Lives, Private Secrets: Gender, Honor, Sexuality, and Illegitimacy in Colonial Spanish America* (Stanford, CA: Stanford University Press, 1999).
22. *Registro Nacional de Leyes y Decretos*, Vol. 37 (1914): 438–39.
23. "La investigación de la paternidad," *El Día*, 21 September 1918, 4.
24. Gerardo Caetano classified the *Federación Rural* as the first "modern pressure group" in Uruguayan politics. Caetano, *La República Conservadora* (Montevideo: Fin de Siglo, 1992), 1:22.
25. "La palabra presidencial" *El Día*, 17 August 1916, 1. Cited in Caetano, *La República Conservadora*, 1:44.
26. Miller, *Latin American Women and the Search for Social Justice*, 98.
27. Asunción Lavrin, *Women, Feminism, and Social Change in Argentina, Chile, and Uruguay, 1890–1940* (Lincoln: University of Nebraska Press, 1995), 207.
28. "Un presidente feminista: Palabras del doctor Baltazar [sic] Brum," *Nuestra Causa*, July 1919, 52–53.
29. Lavrin, *Women, Feminism, and Social Change*, 217.
30. Baltasar Brum, *Los derechos de la mujer: Reforma a la legislación civil y política del Uruguay* (Montevideo: Peña Hermanos, 1925), 32–34.
31. For more on the rise of the radical right in South America during these years, see Sandra McGee Deutsch, *Las Derechas: The Extreme Right in Argentina, Brazil, and Chile, 1890–1939* (Stanford, CA: Stanford University Press, 1999).
32. Luce Fabbri, interview with the author, Montevideo, 7 June 1995.
33. For an example of this characterization, see Philip Taylor, "The

Uruguayan Coup d'Etat of 1933" *Hispanic American Historical Review* 32, no. 3 (August 1952): 301–20.

34. Gerardo Caetano and Raúl Jacob; *El nacimiento del terrismo (1930–1933)*, 3 vols. (Montevideo: Ediciones de la Banda Oriental, 1989–1991), 1:21.

35. Nitza Berkovitch, *From Motherhood to Citizenship: Women's Rights and International Organizations* (Baltimore: Johns Hopkins University Press, 1999), 2.

Chapter Three

1. By 1922 nearly 10 percent of licensed practitioners in dentistry and pharmacy were women, whereas only slightly more than 1 percent of physicians were female by that same date. Consejo Nacional de Higiene, *Nómina de los doctores y licenciados en medicina y cirugía (farmacéuticos, dentistas, parteras, veterinarios, practicantes y flebótomos) hasta el 30 de diciembre de 1922* (Montevideo: El Siglo Ilustrado, 1923).

2. For more on women's gendered professionalism and the state, see Ellen More, *Restoring the Balance: Women Physicians and the Profession of Medicine, 1850–1995* (Cambridge, MA: Harvard University Press 1999); and Linda L. Clark, *The Rise of the Professional Woman in France: Gender and Public Administration since 1830* (Cambridge and New York: Cambridge University Press, 2000).

3. Asunción Lavrin, "Paulina Luisi: Pensamiento y escritura feminista" in *Estudios sobre escritoras hispanoaméricanas en honor de Georgina Sabán Rivero*, ed. Lou Charnon-Deutsch (Madrid: Editorial Castalia, 1992), 159.

4. In a letter written to Otilia Schultze de Galarza toward the end of the First World War, Luisi spoke of having French ancestry: "Your last name is German right? If so, I ask that you ignore the international issues, since I am very French, I have it in my maternal blood." Paulina Luisi to Otilia Schulze de Galarza, 26 December 1917. Private archives of Oscar Padrón Favre, Durazno Uruguay.

5. In 1911, *El Socialista* listed Angel Luisi as a representative of the Masonic lodge "Gran Oriente del Uruguay" ("La manifestación anti-clerical," *El Socialista*, 25 June 1911, 1).

6. Paulina Luisi to Otilia Schultze de Galarza, 26 December 1917. Private archives of Oscar Padrón Favre, Durazno.

7. Enrique Méndez Vives, *La tiza y el sable: Vida cotidiana en el Uruguay de Varela y Latorre* (Montevideo: Fin de Siglo, 1993), 110–11.

8. "La mujer en las carreras liberales," *El Día*, 24 July 1924, 6.
9. Amalia Polleri, interview with the author, Montevideo, 17 March 1995.
10. "La mujer en las carreras liberales" *El Día* 24 July 1924, 6.
11. Amalia Polleri, interview with the author, 17 March 1995.
12. Petrona Eyle to Paulina Luisi, 1 May 1907, PL-BN Folder E.
13. For more on Paulina Luisi's Pan-American "pen pals" and feminist networks, see Christine Ehrick, "*Madrinas* and Missionaries: Uruguay and the Pan-American Women's Movement," *Gender and History* 10, no. 3 (November 1998): 406–24.
14. See Michel Foucault, *The Birth of the Clinic: An Archaeology of Medical Perception* (New York: Pantheon, 1973). See also José Pedro Barrán, *Medicina y sociedad en el Uruguay del novecientos* (Montevideo: Ediciones de la Banda Oriental, 1993), 1:101.
15. Donna Guy discusses the political influence and importance of women physicians in Argentina in *Sex and Danger in Buenos Aires: Prostitution, Family, and Nation in Argentina* (Lincoln: University of Nebraska Press, 1990). See also E. Moberly Bell, *Storming the Citadel: The Rise of the Woman Doctor* (London: Constable and Co.: 1953); Regina Morantz-Sánchez, *Sympathy and Science: Women Physicians in American Medicine* (New York: Oxford University Press, 1985); and Ellen S. More, *Restoring the Balance*.
16. Paulina Luisi to Eloísa Díaz, 21 October 1918, Conamu Archives, Copiador 1.
17. For more on the relationship of the Socialist Party to Batllismo, see Fernando López D'Alesandro, *Historia de la izquierda Uruguaya*, 3 vols. (Montevideo: Nuevo Mundo/Vintén, 1988–1992), 2:100.
18. "La universidad para mujeres: Lo que opina la doctora Paulina Luisi," *El Día* 27, June 1911, 1.
19. Paulina Luisi, *Movimiento Sufragista* (Montevideo: El Siglo Ilustrado, 1919), 3–4.
20. Lavrin, "Paulina Luisi," 162.
21. For more on the medicalization of social thought in early twentieth-century South America, see Dain Borges "'Puffy, Ugly, Slothful and Inert': Degeneration in Brazilian Social Thought, 1880–1940," *Journal of Latin American Studies* 25, no. 2 (May 1993), 235–56.
22. See, for example, Nancy Leys Stepan, *The Hour of Eugenics: Race, Gender, and Nation in Latin America* (Ithaca, NY: Cornell University Press, 1991); and Katherine Elaine Bliss, *Compromised Positions: Prostitution, Public Health, and Gender Politics in Revolutionary Mexico City* (University Park, PA: Pennsylvania State University

Press, 2001). Stepan generally characterizes women as marginal to Latin American eugenics circles, and thus does not really address the links between feminism and eugenics thought. In her study of prostitution in revolutionary Mexico, Bliss acknowledges that "feminist circles and the Mexican eugenics movement shared some members" (193–94), but she generally speaks of the two groups as separate entities. Future research will help determine how unusual Luisi was in the history of Latin American eugenics.

23. Lavrin notes that many feminists, especially feminist physicians, were attracted to eugenics thought, but she argues against any real compatibility between feminism and eugenics. "The discussion of eugenics as policy did not bring any advantage to feminism," she wrote, mainly because it did not challenge the bedrock of gender roles and gendered sexuality" (Lavrin, *Women, Feminism, and Social Change in Argentina, Chile, and Uruguay, 1890–1940* (Lincoln: University of Nebraska Press, 1995), p.10). This argument is repeated in Licia Fiol-Matta, *A Queer Mother for the Nation: The State and Gabriela Mistral* (Minneapolis: University of Minnesota Press, 2002), 82–83.

24. See Ann Taylor Allen, "Feminism and Eugenics in Germany and Britain, 1900–1940: A Comparative Perspective," *German Studies Review* 23, no. 3 (October 2000), 477–505; and Alexandra Minna Stern, "Responsible Mothers and Normal Children: Eugenics, Nationalism, and Welfare in post-Revolutionary Mexico, 1920–1940," *Journal of Historical Sociology* 12, no. 4 (December 1999), 369–97.

25. Lavrin, "Paulina Luisi"; Cynthia Jeffress Little, "Moral Reform and Feminism: A Case Study," *Journal of Inter-American Studies and World Affairs* 17, no. 4 (November 1975): 386–97. Although Little's article is an examination of Luisi's views on "moral reform" and "social hygiene," the term *eugenics* was assiduously avoided, and Luisi's early publications on eugenics were not mentioned or cited. Lavrin does not mention Luisi's early writings on eugenics, either, although she does refer to Luisi's endorsement of abortion on eugenic grounds. See Lavrin, *Women, Feminism, and Social Change*, 163–76.

26. There is a general consensus that positive or "soft" eugenics dominated Latin American eugenics circles. See Stepan, *Hour of Eugenics*; Donna Guy, "The Pan-American Child Congresses, 1916 to 1942: Pan-Americanism, Child Reform, and the Welfare State in Latin America," *Journal of Family History* 23, no.3 (July 1998): 272–91; Jerry Dávila, *Diploma of Whiteness: Race and Social Policy in Brazil, 1917–1945* (Durham, NC: Duke University Press, 2003). 24–25. For more on French

eugenic and neo-Lamarckian thought, see William Schneider "Toward the Improvement of the Human Race: The History of Eugenics in France," *The Journal of Modern History* 54, no. 2 (June 1982): 268–91.

27. Paulina Luisi, *Algunas ideas sobre eugenía* (Montevideo: El Siglo Ilustrado, 1916). Donna Guy mentions Luisi's speech, and the controversy surrounding it, in "Pan-American Child Congresses."
28. Luisi, *Algunas ideas sobre eugenía*, 17.
29. Paulina Luisi, *Enseñanza Sexual* (Montevideo: El Siglo Ilustrado, 1916), 5.
30. Paulina Luisi, *Para una mejor descendencia*, (Buenos Aires: Juan Perrotti), 1919.
31. Ann Taylor Allen, "Eugenics and Feminism," University of Louisville Faculty Forum, September 26, 2003; Stern, "Responsible Mothers," 369. Many thanks to Ann Allen for her invaluable assistance with this section.
32. Luisi worked closely with Argentine physician-abolitionists Petrona Eyle, and Alicia Moreau de Justo, who headed up the campaign against prostitution and white slavery in Argentina. See Donna Guy, *Sex and Danger in Buenos Aires*, 94–98; and Lavrin, *Women, Feminism, and Social Change*, 269. For more on prostitution and the debate over its regulation in Latin America, see Bliss, *Compromised Positions*.
33. Paulina Luisi, *Proyectos sobre moralidad* (Buenos Aires: J. Perrotti, 1919), 10. See also Paulina Luisi, "Una moral única para ambos sexos," *Tribuna Libre* (Buenos Aires), 25 February 1920.
34. Other Latin American physician-reformers made similar arguments in less explicitly gendered ways. Katherine Bliss refers to Mexican physician-reformer Dr. Bernardo Gastelum, and his and others efforts to "strip sexuality of its cloak of privacy and situate it instead within the domain of health science" (Bliss, *Compromised Positions*, 97).
35. Paulina Luisi, *Un crimen social: la trata de blancas* (Buenos Aires: Tribuna Libre, 1918), 136–37.
36. Graciela Sapriza, *Memorias de rebeldía: siete historias de vida* (Montevideo: Puntosur, 1988), 90.
37. The poem is clearly written on Luisi's typewriter, and it is signed with the pseudonym "Ananké," a penname that Luisi frequently used.
38. PL-BN Folder S. The poem was written c.1929. The phrase "Weep, weep urutaú" is an idiomatic lament from a nineteenth-century ballad written after the Triple Alliance War (1865–1870), in which Paraguay was devastated by Brazilian, Argentine, and Uruguayan armies. An urutaú is a Paraguayan bird with a mournful song. It reads in part:

237

Llora, llora, urutaú/En las ramas del yatay/Ya no existe el Paraguay/Dónde nací como tú/Llora, llora, urutaú ("Weep, weep, urutaú/Among the palm branches/The Paraguay where you and I were born/no longer exists/Weep, weep, urutaú").

39. Within Uruguayan feminist historiography, there are those, like Sapriza and Villamíl, who argue that Luisi was a Socialist, and others, like Cassina de Nogara, who argue just the opposite. See, for example, Sapriza, *Memorias de rebeldía*; and Alba G. Cassina de Nogara, *Hacia una democracia integral: Apuntes para una historia del feminismo en Uruguay*, (Montevideo: Consejo Nacional de Mujeres del Uruguay), 1990.

40. Paulina Luisi, *La lucha contra el alcoholismo y el sufragio femenino* (Buenos Aires: Revista Argentina de Ciencias Políticas, 1918), 12.

41. Luisi, *Para una mejor descendencia*, 29.

42. "Biblioteca Dra. Paulina Luisi," *El Sol*, 4 November 1929, 1.

43. *International Women's News (Jus Suffragii)* 17, Issue 9 (December 1922), 36; Sapriza, *Memorias de la rebeldía*, 107.

44. Luisi, *La lucha contra el alcoholismo*, 22–23.

45. Ibid., 48.

46. AGN-CPDM, 1919 Folder 571, 1. I use initials for both the juvenile wards and their guardians throughout this article to maintain their anonymity. Information on M. A. and other individual juveniles comes from the archives of the Consejo Patronato de Delincuentes y Menores in the Archivo General de la Nación in Montevideo, Uruguay. A small sample of twenty case files dated 1916, 1919, 1923, and 1927 was obtained, with lesser amounts of information on a number of other cases. The small number of cases does not allow for any systematic quantitative analysis of the data, but a qualitative analysis of the cases and identification of certain patterns is possible.

47. For a comparison with European cases, see, for example, Elinor Accampo et al., eds., *Gender and the Politics of Social Reform in France, 1870–1914*, (Baltimore: Johns Hopkins University Press, 1995); Seth Koven and Sonya Michel, eds., *Mothers of a New World: Maternalist Politics and the Origins of Welfare States*, (New York: Routledge, 1993); and Susan Pedersen; *Family, Dependence, and the Origins of the Welfare State: Britain and France, 1914–1945* (Cambridge: Cambridge University Press, 1993). For the U.S. case, see Linda Gordon, ed., *Women, the State and Welfare* (Madison: University of Wisconsin Press, 1990); and Theda Skocpol, *Protecting Soldiers and Mothers: The Political Origins of Social Policy in the*

United States (Cambridge: Harvard University Press, 1992).
48. *Boletín APN* (December 1913), 421.
49. Dr. Carlos Nery, "La Escuela de Nurses: Su organización y métodos," *Primer Congreso Médico Nacional, Montevideo 9–16 Abril 1916,* Tomo 4 (Montevideo: El Siglo Ilustrado, 1917), 367–68.
50. The reasons for this spelling are not entirely clear. Some reports on this organization spell the name *Mater* (Latin for mother), but the organization itself always spelled it the other way.
51. Asociación Pro-Matre, *Memoria correspondiente al ejercicio social 1915–1916* (Montevideo: El Siglo Ilustrado, 1916).
52. *Registro de Leyes y Decretos* 1916–1920. This figure represented more than Pro-Matre's entire annual budget as reported in its 1916 *Memoria* (twenty-seven hundred pesos).
53. A. N. Anké, "Mujeres del Uruguay," *Nuestra Causa*, July 1919, 58.
54. Ibid., 58.
55. "Sociedades incorporadas: Dirección del Instituto de Ciegos 'General Artigas,'" *Acción Femenina* (August 1917), 54.
56. Arturo Scarone, *Uruguayos contemporáneos: Nuevos diccionario de datos biográficos y bibliográficos*, 2d ed. (Montevideo: Barreiro y Ramos, 1937), 21. From 1917 to 1933 Juan José de Amézaga was the head of the State Insurance Bank (*Banco de Seguros del Estado*).
57. *Diario de sesiones de la H. Cámara de Representantes*, Vol. 283 (August 1920), 498–99.
58. In her study of the Mexico City Poor House during the late colonial and early national period, Silva Arrom describes a similarly complicated arrangement that relied on public, private, and ecclesiastical funds and institutions for its functioning. Silvia Marina Arrom, *Containing the Poor: The Mexico City Poor House, 1774–1871* (Durham, NC: Duke University Press, 2000).
59. Steve J. Stern discusses the concept of "patriarchal pacts" in *The Secret History of Gender: Women, Men and Power in Late Colonial Mexico* (Chapel Hill: University of North Carolina Press, 1995). I replace the word *patriarchal* with *paternalistic* for reasons explained in the introduction to this book.
60. Gabriel Haslip-Viera notes the same process of placing delinquent women *"en depósito"* with "honorable families" in eighteenth-century Mexico City in *Crime and Punishment in Late Colonial Mexico City, 1692–1810* (Albuquerque: University of New Mexico Press, 1999). Felix Matos Rodríguez discusses the "placement" of indigent girls as domestic servants in nineteenth-century San Juan, Puerto

Rico. In the 1860s, he wrote, it was "clear that the Casa was used as an employment agency of sorts for domestic workers." Felix V. Matos Rodríguez, *Women and Urban Change in San Juan, Puerto Rico, 1820–1868*, (Gainesville: University Press of Florida, 1999), 113. Tessa Bridal's *The Tree of Red Stars* (Minneapolis, MN: Milkweed Editions, 1997), a novel set in 1960s Uruguay, includes a character sent by the state to live with a neighboring family for a small wage.

61. This is similar to arrangements made in the nineteenth-century United States by the Children's Aid Society, who placed young women domestics in the homes of "good Christian families" in the Midwest. See Clay Gish, "Rescuing the 'Waifs and Strays' of the City: The Western Emigration Program of the Children's Aid Society," *Journal of Social History* 33, no.1 (Fall 1999), 121–42.
62. AGN-CPDM 1923, Folder 301, 18–19.
63. *Boletín APN* (December 1913), 420.
64. "Página Blanca," *Página Blanca*, 15 October 1915, 1.
65. Although the reasons are not clear, the *Bonne Garde* goes almost unmentioned on the pages of *Página Blanca*.
66. In 1916, the first year of the program, Elvira D. was placed with the García Lagos family, and Jacinta I. with the De María family. Both of these families were wealthy and powerful, but it should be noted, neither one were families associated or allied with the ruling Colorado Party. AGN-CPDM 1916, Folder 410, 1; Bonne Garde *Minutos*.
67. *Boletín APN* (January- February 1929), 104.
68. Augusto Turenne, *La Protección a la Madre Soltera* (Montevideo: Consejo de Salud Pública, 1932), 14.
69. Sociedad La Bonne Garde, *Libro de Actas*, entry 14 June 1922.
70. "Interesante tipo de nobleza femenina," *Mundo Uruguayo*, 31 December 1925, 61.
71. *Boletín APN* (May-June 1929), 757.
72. The program to train *visitadoras sociales* was set up in 1926 within the *Escuela de Nurses* (Nursing School) founded in 1913. See also Carolina González Laurino, "La construcción colectiva de la identidad del Trabajo Social en el Uruguay de comienzos de Siglo XXI" (Simposio Nacional transformaciones en el mundo del trabajo, Montevideo 30 de Junio al 1 de Julio, 2000)
73. Laura Cortinas, "El Buen Amor," in *Teatro del Amor* (Barcelona: Editorial Juventud, 1930), 85–157.
74. For details on this process in the United States, see Regina Kunzel, *Fallen Women, Problem Girls: Unmarried Mothers and the*

Professionalization of Social Work, 1890–1945 (New Haven, Conn: Yale University Press, 1993).

75. Matos-Rodríguez makes a similar observation about the links between elite women's beneficence and early liberal feminism. See chapter 5 of *Women and Urban Change in San Juan, Puerto Rico*.

76. See, for example, Ericka Kim Verba, "The *Círculo de Lectura* [Ladies' Reading Circle] and the *Club de Señoras* [Ladies' Club] of Santiago: Middle- and Upper-Class Feminist Conversations (1915–1920)." *Journal of Women's History* 7, no. 3 (Fall 1995), 6–33.

Chapter Four

1. For more on this historical phenomenon, see Carole Pateman. *The Disorder of Women: Democracy, Feminism, and Political Theory*, (Stanford, CA: Stanford University Press, 1989).
2. Amalia Polleri, interview with the author, 17 March 1995.
3. Índices de la personería jurídica, Archivo General de la Nación, Montevideo, Uruguay.
4. For more on the national and international politics of the International Council of Women and other international feminist organizations of this era, see Leila J. Rupp, *Worlds of Women: The Making of an International Women's Movement* (Princeton, NJ: Princeton University Press, 1997).
5. Cecilia Grierson to Paulina Luisi, 24 October 1913, PL-BN, Folder G.
6. *Acción Femenina*, Año 1, No. 1 (July 1917), 15, 34
7. *Acción Femenina* 1:1 July 1917, 40
8. Lavrin characterizes the difficulties between Luisi and Pinto de Vidal as fundamentally a clash of personalities. Silvia Rodríguez Villamíl and Graciela Sapriza identify Pinto de Vidal as a "militant Batllista" and understand the conflicts between she and Luisi in ideological terms. See Lavrin, *Women, Feminism, and Social Change in Argentina, Chile, and Uruguay, 1890–1940* (Lincoln: University of Nebraska Press, 1995); Silvia Rodríguez Villamíl and Graciela Sapriza, *Mujer, estado y política en el Uruguay del siglo XX* (Montevideo: Ediciones de la Banda Oriental, 1984).
9. In 1917, Batlle engaged in a lengthy public polemic with Socialist Party leader Celestino Mibelli, debating topics such as militarism, class relations, and international trade. See Milton Vanger, *Reforma o Revolución? La polémica Batlle-Mibelli, 1917* (Montevideo: Ediciones de la Banda Oriental, 1989).
10. "La conferencia femenina—un gran éxito," *El Socialista* 308 (14

December 1918), 2.
11. *Acción Femenina* 21 (July 1919), 115.
12. A. N. Anké [Paulina Luisi], "Mujeres del Uruguay," *Nuestra Causa*, July 1919, 59.
13. Paulina Luisi, "El Consejo Nacional de Mujeres del Uruguay," *Nuestra Causa*, July 1919, 60. Although the telephone workers' union did briefly affiliate itself with Conamu, the Socialist Women's Center never did.
14. AGN-PL Box 251 Folder 6, 57.
15. AGN-PL Box 251 Folder 6, 81.
16. "Para Nosotras," *La Mañana*, 17 March 1921, 2.
17. See Alianza Uruguaya to Presidente Cámara de Representantes, July 1922, PL-AGN Box 251 Folder 7, 32; "La mujer escribano: gestiones de la Alianza Feminista," (n.d.), PL-AGN Box 251 Folder 7, 122.
18. Cámara de Representantes, *Legislación referente a la mujer* (Montevideo: División Información y Antecedentes Legislativos, 1986), 2.
19. Edelmira U. De Márquez, "Interesante cuestión feminista," *La Noche*, 30 July 1921. In PL-AGN Box 257, Folder 3, 24.
20. See *El Día*, especially in the early months of 1918. The group is alternately referred to as the "Comité Femenino Pro Batlle" and the "Comité Feminista Pro Batlle."
21. Paulina Luisi to Fanny Carrió de Polleri, 1 December 1921, PL-AGN, Box 252 Folder 3, 6.
22. The column was signed "Fafhm." Fanny's daughter Amalia identified this as her mother's pseudonym, representing the first initials of her children, although it is possible the column had multiple authors.
23. Fafhm, "Para Nosotras: A Agreste," *La Mañana*, 10 July 1919, 5
24. Fafhm, "Equiparación de sexos," *La Mañana*, 21 May 1919, 1.
25. Fafhm, "Para nosotras," *La Mañana*, 13 July 1919, 7.
26. Carmen C. de Queirolo, "Cuestiones feministas," *La Mañana*, 9 June 1919, 3.
27. Fanny Carrió de Polleri to Paulina Luisi, 22 October 1922, PL-BN, Folder F.
28. This number is probably low because of the lack of anything approaching a complete list of members of the Socialist Party at this time. Two of the Alianza members, María Devita (de Marote) and Lola Gianelli de Miller were listed in a 1932 issue of *El Sol* (the official Socialist Party paper at the time) as having held membership

in the party for at least two years. Two other Alianza members were wives and daughters of important Socialist Party leaders.

29. Amalia Polleri, interview with the author, 17 March 1995.
30. Ibid.
31. For the first Conamu group I have date of birth information for 47 out of a total of 158, with home addresses for 144 of them. For the Alianza group I have birthdate information for 57 out of 171, with home addresses for 150 of them.
32. I include the adjacent Punta Carretas and Parque Rodó neighborhoods within the "Pocitos" category.
33. AGN-PL Box 250 Folder 7, 73.
34. Lavrin, *Women, Politics and Social Change*, 16–19.
35. Letters from Fanny Carrió de Polleri to Paulina Luisi, 9 November 1924 and 28 December 1924. PL-BN Folder F.
36. The broadened focus (and name change) was part of the changing focus and strategy of the International Alliance as well. The International Women's Suffrage Alliance suffered an identity crisis after World War I, when many women got the right to vote. Many nationals therefore, wanted to "move beyond suffrage," leading the IWSA to change its name to the International Alliance of Women in 1926. See Karen Offen, *European Feminisms, 1700–1950: A Political History* (Stanford, CA: Stanford University Press, 2000), 376–77.
37. "La mujer en las carreras liberales," *El Día*, 27 July 1924, 6.
38. See AGN-PL Box 250 Folder 7, 33–86.
39. "En pro del reconocimiento de los derechos de la mujer: Una interesante iniciativa de la Alianza U. de mujeres," *El Imparcial*, 11 May 1932. From PL-AGN Box 259 Folder 4, 18.
40. Amalia Polleri, interview with the author.
41. Fanny Carrió de Polleri to Paulina Luisi 15 May 1919, BN-PL Folder F
42. Paulina Luisi to Sara Rey Álvarez, 23 January 1933, PL-AGN Box 250 Folder 8, 141–43.
43. Sara Rey Álvarez to Paulina Luisi, AGN-PL, Box 250, Folder 8, 144–45.
44. Amalia Polleri, interview with the author, 17 March 1995. See Julio T. Fabregat, *Elecciones Uruguayas (Febrero de 1925 a Noviembre de 1945* (Montevideo: Corte Electoral, 1948).
45. Other histories of Latin American feminism have noted similar class tensions. See Eileen J. Suárez Findlay, *Imposing Decency: The Politics of Sexuality and Race in Puerto Rico, 1870–1920* (Durham, NC: Duke University Press, 1999); and Karin Alejandra Rosemblatt, *Gendered Compromises: Political Cultures and the*

State in Chile, 1920–1950 (Chapel Hill: University of North Carolina Press, 2000).

46. Isabel Pinto de Vidal, "Informe de la Comisión de Trabajo," *Acción Femenina*, 7–8 (September-October 1918), 167.
47. José Pedro Barrán and Benjamin Nahum, *Batlle, los estancieros y el imperio británico*, 8 vols. (Montevideo: Ediciones de la Banda Oriental, 1979), 1:117.
48. Emilio Frugoni to Paulina Luisi, 29 November 1918, PL-BN Folder F.
49. "Las telefonistas de 'La Uruguaya' Una justa solicitud," *El Día*, 7 December 1918, 6.
50. Fanny Carrió de Polleri to Paulina Luisi, 15 May 1919, PL-BN, Folder F.
51. Isabel Pinto de Vidal, "Palabras de la Presidenta," *Acción Femenina* 43–46 (September-December, 1922), 68.
52. Argentine socialist feminist (and friend of Paulina's) Petrona Eyle wrote to Luisi about a strike of telephone operators in Buenos Aires. See the letter from Petrona Eyle to Paulina Luisi, 14 March 1919, PL-BN Folder E.
53. On charges and denials of sabotage, see *Justicia* 22 September 1922; 23 September 1922; and 28 September 1922.
54. "Huelga de las telefonistas," *Justicia* 899 (8 September 1922), 2.
55. Conamu to Minister of Labor Eduardo Anaya, January 1921. Conamu private archives.
56. Ibid.
57. For more on relations between employers and domestics, see Sandra Lauderdale Graham, *House and Street: The Domestic World of Servants and Masters in Nineteenth-Century Rio de Janeiro* (Austin: University of Texas Press, 1988).
58. Conamu to Otilia Schultze de Galarza, January 1921, Conamu private archives, Copiador 2.
59. *Registro de Leyes y Decretos* 1931–1933: 215
60. Amalia Polleri, interview with the author.
61. Fanny Carrió de Polleri to Paulina Luisi, 25 June 1922, PL-BN, Folder F.
62. María Devita to Paulina Luisi, 7 July 1922, PL-BN, Folder D. María Devita was one of the Alianza members known to be affiliated with the Uruguayan Socialist Party.
63. María Soliverri to Fanny Carrió de Polleri, 12 September 1924, PL-BN Folder S.
64. Fanny Carrió de Polleri to Paulina Luisi, 28 December 1924, PL-BN, Folder F.
65. Fanny Carrió de Polleri to Paulina Luisi 12 March 1923. BN-PL,

Folder C.

66. In her letters to Otilia Schultze de Galarza, Luisi complained frequently about fatigue and physical ailments that made it difficult to maintain her professional and political activity. Private archives of Oscar Padron Favre, Durazno.

Chapter Five

1. See Gerardo Caetano ed. *Los Uruguayos del centenario: nación, ciudadanía, religión y educación (1910–1930)* (Montevideo: Santillana, 2000).
2. For more on right-wing politics among Uruguay's neighbors at this same time, see Sandra McGee Deutsch, *Las Derechas: The Extreme Right in Argentina, Brazil, and Chile, 1890–1939* (Stanford, CA: Stanford University Press, 1999).
3. Bettembourg, "La mujer cristiana" in Liga de Damas Católicas, *Conferencias pronunciadas bajo los auspicios de la Liga Damas Católicas durante el año 1907* (Montevideo: Imp. de la buena prensa, 1908), 51; and "Congreso de Sevilla: Informe presentado," *El Eco* 241 (August 1929), 3079.
4. In 1917 the Liga reported at its Eleventh General Assembly that it spent 3,471 pesos, and that it took in a total of 4,069 pesos (only 252 of which came from the Departmental committees). As a crude form of comparison, the 1914 Bulletin of the *Oficina del Trabajo* reported that the average salary of a working-class man was a little less than 500 pesos a year, while the average annual salary of a working-class woman was less than 150 per year. "11a Asamblea general," *El Eco* 113 (November 1917), 2014.
5. Of the thirty-two for whom I have data, nine or 27 percent lawyers; six or 18 percent doctors; five or 15 percent *hacendados/estancieros*; and eight or 24 percent listed as *comercio/comerciante/rentista*.
6. In their study of social-class and residential patterns in turn of the century Montevideo, Barrán and Nahum calculate that about 20 percent of the so-called conservative classes were still living in the Old City by 1920. José Pedro Barrán and Benjamin Nahum, *Batlle, los estancieros y el imperio británico*, 8 vols. (Montevideo: Ediciones de la Banda Oriental, 1979–1985), 1:209–11.
7. See Carlos Zubillaga and Mario Cayota, *Cristianos y cambio social en el Uruguay de la modernización (1896–1919)* (Montevideo: CLAEH/Banda Oriental, 1988). Secco Illa had earlier led the right-wing putsch in the Catholic paper *El Bien*, and in 1912 was a founding leader of the

conservative Catholic party the *Unión Cívica*.
8. "Congreso de Sevilla," *El Eco* 241 (August 1929), 3079.
9. "13a Asamblea General de la LDCU," *El Eco* 133 (November-December 1919), 2150. Information as to exactly when Uriarte de Herrera became Liga president is unavailable. She was listed as a vice president in 1915, and president in 1925, the next time a full listing of Liga leadership was published.
10. "Último Momento," *El Eco* 118 (April 1918), 2055.
11. "Cartas de Mujer," *El Día*, 12 May 1918, 4.
12. Fanny Carrió de Polleri to Paulina Luisi 15 May 1919, PL-BN, Folder F. The "German bishop" to whom she refers is probably Father Bettembourg, a conservative Catholic priest and active proponent of the active incorporation of women in defense of the Catholic cause.
13. Fanny Carrió de Polleri to Paulina Luisi, 10 June 1919. PL-BN, Folder F.
14. Ericka Verba describes a youth league founded by the Damas Chilenas in 1913, aimed mostly at upper-class daughters (rather than university students). A later Catholic Women's Youth Organization, founded in 1921, does not appear to have been directly under the auspices of the Damas Chilenas. See Ericka Kim Verba, "Catholic Feminism and *acción social femenina* [Women's Social Action]: The Early Years of the Liga de Damas Chilenas, 1912–1924," (Ph.D. diss., University of California Los Angeles, 1999).
15. "Problema femenino: estudiantes universitarios," *El Eco* 168, July 1923, 2474.
16. "La Liga de Damas Católicas," *Justicia* 15 December 1923, 1.
17. "Como se levanta la organización de las obreras alpargateras," *Justicia* 17 February 1925, 2.
18. Verba, "Catholic Feminism," 190.
19. "El Censo," *El Eco* 121 (October 1921), 2323.
20. "El voto femenino," *El Eco* 168 (July 1923), 2474.
21. "El Congreso I. Sufragista y la Unión I. Católica Femenina," *El Eco* 169 (August 1923), 2784. The Uruguayan 1917 project was sponsored by liberals, which probably helps explain Liga reluctance (or willingness to tow the official Catholic line). For a comparison with the Chilean case, see Verba, "Catholic Feminism," 378–84
22. The work of this committee likely complemented that of the Rural Federation, the conservative "pressure group" headed up by Margarita Uriarte's husband, Luis Alberto de Herrera.
23. For information on similar Catholic-led campaigns in the United States, see Frank R. Walsh, *Sin and Censorship: The Catholic Church*

and the Motion Picture Industry (New Haven, CT: Yale University Press, 1996); and Gregory D. Black, *The Catholic Crusade Against the Movies, 1940–1975* (Cambridge: Cambridge University Press, 1998).

24. "La liga que aprieta," *El Día*, 14 July 1919, 5.
25. "Entre ellas," *El Día*, 15 July 1919, 7.
26. "Importante proyecto," *El Eco* 195 (October 1925), 2698. In this the Liga seems to be following the guidelines of the International Liga.
27. "Vistas cinematográficas censuradas," *El Eco* 252 (September 1930), 3171. "Sin Town," a movie made in 1929, was a Western, with no apparent "Russian" aspect to it. The Liga was not alone among women's groups in expressing its concerns about the content of some films. In 1929, the Alianza and Conamu joined together to urge Montevideo city government to regulate cinema aimed at children, arguing that such measures would already have been taken had women been empowered to vote and serve in government. AGN-PL Box 251, Folder 7, 88.
28. "Estación Radio Jackson," *El Eco* 270 (April 1932), 3315.
29. For more on women, gender and early radio, see Kate Lacey, *Feminine Frequencies: Gender, German Radio, and the Public Sphere, 1923–1945* (Ann Arbor: University of Michigan Press, 1996).
30. See, for example, Jerry Dávila, *Diploma of Whiteness: Race and Social Policy in Brazil, 1917–1945* (Durham, NC: Duke University Press, 2003).
31. For the history of Afro-Uruguayans, see, for example, Oscar Montaño, *Yeninyanya (Umknonto II): historia de los afrouruguayos*, (Montevideo: Organizaciones Mundo Afro, 2001); Ildefonso Pereda Valdés, *El negro en el Uruguay: pasado y presente* (Montevideo: Instituto Histórico y Geográfico del Uruguay, 1965).
32. Delia Castellanos de Etchepare, *Mariposas* (Montevideo: Claudio García, 1921).
33. See, for example "Gratitud Ejemplar," Castellanos de Etchepare, *Mariposas*, 68–71.
34. Gerardo Caetano, Roger Geymonat, and Alejandro Sánchez, "'Dios y Patria': Iglesia Católica, nación y nacionalismo en el Uruguay del Centenario," in *Los uruguayos del centenario: nación, ciudadanía, religión y educación (1910–1930)*, ed. Gerardo Caetano (Montevideo: Taurus, 2000), 31.
35. It is likely no coincidence that the Liga's new name matched the right-wing Argentine organization, the *Liga Patriótica Argentina* (Argentine Patriotic League), founded years earlier.
36. For more on anti-Semitism in 1930s Uruguay, see Clara Aldrighi et al.,

Antisemitismo en Uruguay: raíces, discursos, imágenes (1870–1940) (Montevideo: Ediciones Trilce, 2000); Daniela Bouret et al., *Entre la Matzá y el Mate: La inmigración judía en Uruguay: una historia de construcción* (Montevideo: Ediciones de la Banda Oriental, 1997).

37. "Porque, después de 25 años," *El Eco* 263 (August 1931), 3257.
38. "Un llamado al pudor," *El Eco* 267 (December 1931), 3291.
39. "Importante Aviso," *El Eco* 263 (August 1931), 3261.
40. "De Actualidad," *El Eco* 278 (January 1933), 3366.
41. "Reflexionad," *El Eco* 278 (January 1933), 3366.
42. See *El Imparcial*, 21 January 1933 (AGN-PL, Box 259, Folder 4, 31).The membership list also included Juana de Ibarbourou, one of Uruguay's most important literary figures (and a noted conservative).
43. See, for example, McGee Deutsch, *Las Derechas*; Margaret Power, *Right-Wing Women in Chile: Feminine Power and the Struggle against Allende, 1964–1973* (University Park, PA: The Pennsylvania State University Press, 2002).
44. See for example, Caetano, *Los uruguayos del centenario*; Zubillaga and Coyota, *Cristianos y cambio social*; Gerardo Caetano *La República Conservadora*, 2 vols. (Montevideo: Fin de Siglo, 1992–1993.

Chapter Six

1. For a discussion of vanguardism and Left politics, see Karin Alejandra Rosemblatt, *Gendered Compromises: Political Cultures and the State in Chile, 1920–1950* (Chapel Hill: University of North Carolina Press, 2000), 16–18, 223–29.
2. Others have noted similar debates within Marxism and Communism in particular. Robert Stuart concludes that conservative and radical interpretations of the "woman question" circulated simultaneously among French Marxists during these years, with no overall historical trend toward one or the other (Robert Stuart, "Whores and Angels: Women and the Family in the Discourse of French Marxism, 1882–1905," *European History Quarterly* 27, no. 3 (1997): 339–69. See also Van Gosse, "'To Organize in Every Neighborhood, in Every Home": The Gender Politics of American Communists between the Wars," *Radical History Review* 50 (1991):109–141; Rosemblatt, *Gendered Compromises*.
3. Gosse makes a similar observation in "'To Organize in Every Neighborhood, in Every Home.'" He describes the "exceptionally masculinist character" of U.S. Communism in the 1920s, and argues that the increasingly exclusive focus on "workers" and shopfloor organizing,

to the neglect of earlier Left campaigns focused on proletarian neighborhoods, left women in a secondary, largely invisible position in the party.

4. Out of the approximately 220 signatories on the Socialist Party petition, reliable data on the father's or the husband's employment was obtained for approximately thirty-three (or about 15 percent of the sample).

5. Heidi Hartmann discusses the issue of men's "material interest in women's continued oppression" within Marxist thought and politics, in "The Unhappy Marriage of Marxism and Feminism: Towards a More Progressive Union," in *Women and Revolution: A Discussion of the Unhappy Marriage of Marxism and Feminism*, ed. Lydia Sargent (Boston: South End Press, 1981). For more on the issue of women's suffrage within the Communist Party, see Joan B. Landes, "Marxism and the 'Woman Question,'" in *Promissory Notes: Women in the Transition to Socialism*, ed. Sonia Kruks et al. (New York: Monthly Review Press, 1989).

6. "El mejoramiento femenino," *El Socialista* 249 (18 August 1917), 3.

7. "La acción de la mujer," *El Socialista* 248 (4 August 1917), 3.

8. "La conferencia femenina—un gran éxito-discurso de Dra. Luisi," *El Socialista* 308 (14 December 1918), 2.

9. Victor Alba, *Politics and the Labor Movement in Latin America*, (Stanford, CA: Stanford University Press, 1968), 119. This meant that there were two thousand party members on paper; the number of active militants was far smaller.

10. "Centro 'Rosa Luxemburgo,'" *Justicia* 541 (12 July 1921), 2. In her study of women and socialism in the United States, Mari Jo Buhle sees the formation of the Communist Party as a dramatic break, separating a more dynamic focus on women associated with the Socialists from an antifeminist backlash in the early years of the Communist Party. In the Uruguayan case, we see more continuity than contrast, perhaps due to the fact that so many former Socialists became Communists. See Mari Jo Buhle, *Women and American Socialism, 1870–1920* (Urbana: University of Illinois Press, 1981), 318–23.

11. Isabel Fernández, "Para las sirvientas," *Justicia* 543 (14 July 1921), 2.

12. "Las mujeres se organizan," *Justicia* 587 (3 September 1921), 2.

13. "A las camaradas sirvientas," *Justicia* 645 (10 November 1921), 1.

14. "Como debe hacerse propaganda entre las mujeres," *Justicia* 840 (1 July 1922), 2.

15. In her study of gender politics in the early years of the Soviet Union, Elizabeth A. Wood has made similar observations, that women were considered to be "citizens-in-training," in need of "remedial" work,

and constant supervision. See Elizabeth A. Wood, "The Trial of the New Woman: Citizens-in-Training in the New Soviet Republic," *Gender and History* 13, no. 3 (November 2001): 524–45.

16. Julia Arévalo, "Vengan a luchar," *Justicia* 842 (4 July 1922), 2.
17. "La propaganda entre las mujeres," *Justicia* 856 (20 July 1922), 2.
18. In *The Eighteenth Brumaire of Louis Bonaparte*, Marx compared the French peasantry to "potatoes in a sack." "The small peasants," he wrote, "form a vast mass, the members of which live in similar conditions, but without entering into manifold relations with one another." (Robert C. Tucker, ed., *The Marx-Engels Reader* (New York: W. W. Norton and Co., 1978), 608. Many may have seen housewives and domestic servants as occupying a similar category. In a 1926 report on the Passaic textile strike in New Jersey, Communist organizer Albert Weisbord criticized those (presumably members of his own party) who characterized women (especially housewives) as "backward peasants" (Online Archives of Albert and Vera Weisbord at *www.weisbord.org*).
19. "El programa de la Alianza U. de Mujeres," *Justicia* 1312 (14 January 1924), 2.
20. "Alianza U. de Mujeres: breve réplica," *El Siglo*, 16 January 1924. PL-AGN, Box 252, Folder 1, 19.
21. On July 30, 1911, for example, an article appeared in *El Socialista* titled "El Feminismo y el proletariado intelectual," in which it was argued that the entry of women into the professions, and the pressure that placed on the so-called intellectual proletariat exercised a radicalizing influence that could act to make this group, more than the working class, the vanguard of revolutionary change.
22. "A propósito de una réplica," *Justicia* 132 [sic] (23 January 1924), 6.
23. The parallel to the CCF in the United States Communist Party (CPUSA) was the United Council of Working Class Women (also United Council of Working Class Housewives), which also organized women workers and the wives and female family members separately from men. And these women, it seems, did "women's work" in supporting labor activism. See the on-line Archives of Albert and Vera Weisbord, *www.weisbord.org*). Many thanks to Van Gosse for making this connection.
24. "Tribuna femenina," *Justicia* 1408 (7 May 1924), 2.
25. Elizabeth Waters, "In the Shadow of the Comintern," in Kruks et al., *Promissory Notes*, 45.
26. Alba, *Politics and the Labor Movement*, 122–25.
27. Isabel Fernández, interview with Fernando López D'Alesandro,

Montevideo, August 1991.
28. "De la propaganda entre las mujeres," *Justicia* 2921 (15 April 1929), 2.
29. "De Villa del Cerro," *La Batalla*, 18 March 1923, 2. Traditional Uruguayan labor histories focus a good deal on the workers in the *frigoríficos*, but the implication has been that workforce was exclusively male. See, for example, Francisco Pintos, *Historia del movimiento obrero del Uruguay* (Montevideo: n.p., 1960); Germán D'Elía and Armando Miraldi, *Historia del movimiento obrero en el Uruguay: desde sus orígenes hasta 1930* (Montevideo: Ediciones de la Banda Oriental, 1984).
30. "La mujer y la política," *Justicia* 1463 (10 July 1924), 1.
31. "Las mujeres y los niños desplazan a los hombres," *Justicia* 3167 (1 February 1930), 4; "Que ha se hecho [sic] para cumplir el plan de Emulación," *Justicia* 3579 (6 June 1931), 2.
32. "Por la organización de las obreras en los frigoríficos," *Justicia* 2973 (27 June 1929), 2.
33. For more on the history of Jewish immigration to Uruguay, see Teresa Porzecanski, "Vida privada y construcción de la identidad: inmigrantes judíos el Uruguay," in *Historias de la vida privada en el Uruguay: El nacimiento de la intimidad*, ed. José Pedro Barrán (Montevideo: Ediciones Santillana, 1996), 289–322; Daniela Bouret et al. *Entre la Matzá y el Mate: La inmigración judía en el Uruguay: una historia de construcción*, (Montevideo: Ediciones de la Banda Oriental, 1997); Clara Aldreghi et al., *Antisemitismo en Uruguay: raíces, discursos, imágenes (1870–1940)* (Montevideo: Ediciones Trilce, 2000).
34. "A.C. Femenina en el sur de la ciudad," *Justicia* 2915 (8 April 1929), 2.
35. "En el barrio sur," *Justicia* 2921 (15 April 1929), 2.
36. Porzecanski, "Vida privada y construcción de la identidad," 296.
37. "La sección femenina del partido tomó importantes resoluciones en la asamblea de jueves," *Justicia* 3196 (8 March 1930), 5.
38. "Los derechos políticos de la mujer," *Justicia* 3098 (12 November 1929), 1.
39. Manuel Caballero, *Latin America and the Comintern, 1919–1943* (Cambridge: Cambridge University Press, 1986), 57. Secondary literature on this conference makes no mention of discussions about ways to integrate women into the Communist movement, but it seems unlikely that the subject was not discussed, given the importance it seemed to carry in the *Carta Abierta*.
40. "Discusión de la Carta Abierta," *Justicia* 3109 (25 November 1929), 3.
41. "Discusión de la Carta Abierta," *Justicia* 3115 (2 December 1929), 3.
42. "Discusión de la Carta Abierta," *Justicia* 3121 (9 December 1929), 3.

43. Isabel Fernández, Interview with Fernando López D'Alesandro, 1991.
44. Ibid.
45. For more on women and the Communist Party in the United States during this era, see Dorothy Healy and Maurice Isserman, *Dorothy Healy Remembers: A Life in the American Communist Party* (New York: Oxford University Press, 1990), esp. 66–67.
46. "Los curas y el voto femenino," *Justicia* 3848 (24 December 1932), 4.
47. See Heidi Tinsman, *Partners in Conflict: The Politics of Gender, Sexuality, and Labor in the Chilean Agrarian Reform, 1950–1973* (Durham, NC: Duke University Press, 2002), 117–127. Also see the introduction to Margaret Power, *Right-Wing Women in Chile: Feminine Power and the Struggle against Allende, 1964–1973* (University Park, PA: The Pennsylvania State University Press, 2002).

Conclusion

1. Servicio Paz y Justicia Uruguay, *Uruguay Nunca Más: Human Rights Violations, 1972–1985* (Philadelphia: Temple University Press, 1989), 325.
2. Margaret Power, *Right-Wing Women in Chile: Feminine Power and the Struggle against Allende, 1964–1973* (University Park, PA: The Pennsylvania State University Press, 2002). See also Heidi Tinsman, *Partners in Conflict: The Politics of Gender, Sexuality, and Labor in the Chilean Agrarian Reform, 1950–1973* (Durham, NC: Duke University Press, 2002).
3. See, for example, Gisela Bock and Pat Thane, *Maternity and Gender Policies: Women and the Rise of European Welfare States* (London and New York: Routledge, 1991); Seth Koven and Sonya Michel, eds., *Mothers of a New World: Maternalist Politics and the Origins of Welfare States* (London and New York: Routledge, 1993); Susan Pedersen, *Family, Dependence, and the Origins of the Welfare State: Britain and France, 1914–1945* (Cambridge and New York: Cambridge University Press, 1993); Alisa Klaus, *Every Child a Lion: The Origins of Maternal and Infant Health Policy in the United States and France, 1890–1920* (Ithaca, NY: Cornell University Press, 1993); Julia O'Connor, Sheila Shaver, and Ann Orloff, *States, Markets, and Families: Gender, Liberalism and Social Policy in Australia, Canada, Great Britain and the United States* (Cambridge and New York: Cambridge University Press, 1999).
4. Koven and Michel, *Mothers of a New World*, 24.
5. This framework has been criticized as overly simplistic, even for Europe itself. See, for example, Theda Skocpol, *Protecting Soldiers and Mothers:*

The Political Origins of Social Policy in the United States (Cambridge: Harvard University Press, 1992), esp. 36–37. Linda Clark offers a corrective to the frameworks delineated by both Koven and Michel and Alisa Klaus, who argue different forms of the strong state/weak state thesis: that "strong states" have experienced comparatively weaker feminist movements, arguing that state formation itself acts as a sort of demobilizer for women. Koven and Michel, *Mothers of a New World*; Alisa Klaus, *Every Child a Lion: The Origins of Maternal and Infant Health Policy in the United States and France, 1890–1920* (Ithaca, NY: Cornell University Press, 1993); Linda L. Clark, "Feminist Maternalists and the French State: Two Inspectresses General in the Pre–World War I Third Republic," *Journal of Women's History* 12, no.1 (Spring 2000), 32–33.

6. For more on the FBPF and professional women, see June Hahner, *Emancipating the Female Sex: The Struggle for Women's Rights in Brazil, 1850–1940*, (Durham, NC: Duke University Press, 1990), 148; and Francesca Miller, *Latin American Women and the Search for Social Justice* (Hanover, NH: University Press of New England, 1991), 88.

7. Karin Alejandra Rosemblatt, *Gendered Compromises: Political Cultures and the State in Chile, 1920–1950* (Chapel Hill: University of North Carolina Press, 2000), 103.

8. Rosemblatt, *Gendered Compromises*, 112.

9. Ibid., 131.

10. See Shirlene Soto, *Emergence of the Modern Mexican Woman: Her Participation in Revolution and Struggle for Equality, 1910–1940* (Denver, CO: Arden Press, 1990), esp. 61–63.

11. Jerry Dávila, *Diploma of Whiteness: Race and Social Policy in Brazil, 1917–1945* (Durham, NC: Duke University Press, 2003). See also Alejandro De la Fuente, *A Nation for All: Race, Inequality, and Politics in Twentieth-Century Cuba* (Chapel Hill: University of North Carolina Press, 2001); Richard Graham, ed., *The Idea of Race in Latin America, 1870–1940* (Austin: University of Texas Press, 1990).

12. Anne S. MacPherson, "Citizens v. Clients: Working Women and Colonial Reform in Puerto Rico and Belize, 1932–1945," *Journal of Latin American Studies* 35 (May 2003), 291.

13. Sandra McGee Deutsch, *Las Derechas: The Extreme Right in Argentina, Brazil, and Chile, 1890–1939* (Stanford, CA: Stanford University Press, 1999), 289.

Bibliography

Archival Sources

Unless otherwise noted, archives located in Montivideo, Uruguay.

Archivo Nacional de la Imagen, Archivo Paulina Luisi, Archivo General de la Nación, Particulares (PL-AGN)

Archivo Paulina Luisi, Biblioteca Nacional (PL-BN)

Consejo National de Mujeres del Uruguay, Private Archives (Conamu Private Archives)

Consejo Patronato Delincuentes y Menores, Archivo General de la Nación (CPDM-AGN)

Latin American Labor Newspapers Collection, Bunche Library, University of California, Los Angeles, California

Ministerio de Educación y Cultura, Dirección General del Registro de Estado Civil

Ministerio de Educación y Cultura, Registro de Personerías Jurídicas

Papers of the Asociación "La Bonne Garde"

Papers of Carrie Chapman Catt, New York Public Library, New York, NY

Private Archives of Oscar Padrón Favre, Durazno, Uruguay

Archives of Albert and Vera Weisbord, on line at *www.weisbord.org*

Índices de la personería jurídica, Archivo General de la Nación, Montevideo, Uruguay

Periodicals and Government Publications

Unless otherwise noted, published in Montevideo, Uruguay.

Acción Cívica (Tacuarembó)

Acción Femenina

La Batalla

Boletín de la Asistencia Pública Nacional

Boletín del Instituto Intenacional Americano de la Protección a la Infancia

Caras y Caretas (Buenos Aires, Argentina)

La Democracia

El Día

Diario de sesiones de la H. Cámara de Representantes

El Eco de la Liga de Damas Católicas del Uruguay

Feminismo Internacional (New York)

Bibliography

Ideas y Acción
Justicia
El Liberal
London Times -Latin America Supplement (London)
Mundo Uruguayo
Nuestra Causa (Buenos Aires)
Oficina del Trabajo; Boletín
Página Blanca
Colección Legislativa de la República Oriental del Uruguay, *Registro Nacional de Leyes y Decretos*, 1900–1933.
El Socialista
El Sol
La Voz de la Mujer

Interviews

Luce Fabbri, interview with the author, 7 June 1995.
Amalia Polleri, interview with the author, 17 March 1995.
Isabel Fernández, interview with Fernando López D'Alesandro, August 1991.

Books, Articles, and other Printed Materials

Abella de Ramírez, María. *Ensayos Feministas*. Montevideo: El Siglo Ilustrado, 1965.
Abramowitz, Mimi. *Regulating the Lives of Women: Social Welfare Policy from Colonial Times to the Present*. Boston: South End Press, 1988.
Accampo, Elinor A., et al., eds. *Gender and the Politics of Social Reform in France, 1870–1914*. Baltimore: Johns Hopkins University Press, 1995.
Ackelsberg, Martha A. *Free Women of Spain: Anarchism and the Struggle for the Emancipation of Women*. Bloomington: Indiana University Press, 1991.
Adams, Julia, and Tasleem Padamsee. "Signs and Regimes: Rereading Feminist Work on Welfare States." *Social Politics* 8, no. 1 (2001): 1–23.
Alba, Victor. *Politics and the Labor Movement in Latin America*. Stanford, CA.: Stanford University Press, 1968.
Aldrighi, Clara, et al. *Antisemitismo en Uruguay: raíces, discursos, imágenes (1870–1940)*. Montevideo: Ediciones Trilce, 2000.
Alexander, Ruth M. *The Girl Problem: Female Sexual Delincuency in New York, 1900–1930*. Ithaca, NY: Cornell University Press, 1995.
Alianza Uruguaya y Consejo de Mujeres. *La mujer uruguaya reclama sus derechos políticos*. Montevideo: Editorial Apolo, 1929.
Allen, Ann Taylor. "Feminism and Eugenics in Germany and Britain,

1900–1940: A Comparative Perspective." *German Studies Review* 23, no. 3 (October 2000): 477–505.

———. "Reproductive Rights and Responsibilities? Feminism and Eugenics in Germany and Britain, 189–1940." Paper presented at the University of Louisville Faculty Forum, September 26, 2003.

Álvarez, Sara Rey. "Los derechos civiles de la mujer." *Ideas y Acción* suplemento No.3. Montevideo: n.p., 1939.

Álvarez, Sonia E. *Engendering Democracy in Brazil: Women's Movements in Transition Politics.* Princeton, NJ: Princeton University Press, 1990.

Ardão, María Julia. *La creación de la Sección de Enseñanza Secundaria y Preparatoria para Mujeres en 1912.* Montevideo: Editorial Florensa y Lafon, 1962.

Arena, Domingo. *La presunción de legitimidad: Comentario á los artículos 190 y 196 del Código Civil.* Montevideo: Imp.de Lagomarsino y Vilardebó, 1910.

Arrom, Silvia Marina. "De la caridad a la beneficiencia? Las reformas de la asistencia pública desde la perspectiva del Hospicio de Pobres de la ciudad de México, 1856–1871." *Ciudad de México: Instituciones, actores sociales y conflicto político, 1774–1931.* Zamora, Michoacán.: Colegio de Michoacán, 1996.

———. *Containing the Poor: The Mexico City Poor House, 1774–1871.* Durham, NC: Duke University Press, 2000.

Asociación Pro-Matre. *Memoria correspondiente al ejercicio social 1915–1916.* Montevideo: El Siglo Ilustrado, 1916.

Barrán, José Pedro. *Amor y transgresión en Montevideo, 1919–1931.* Montevideo: Ediciones de la Banda Oriental, 2001.

———. *Historia de la sensibilidad en el Uruguay.* 2 vols. Montevideo: Ediciones de la Banda Oriental, 1991–1992.

———. *Iglesia Católica y burguesia en el Uruguay de la modernización (1860–1900).* Montevideo: Universidad de la Republica, Facultad de Humanidades y Ciencias, 1988.

———. *Medicina y sociedad en el Uruguay del novecientos.* 3 vols. Montevideo: Ediciones de la Banda Oriental, 1993–1995.

Barrán, José Pedro, and Benjamin Nahum. *Batlle, los estancieros y el imperio británico.* 8 vols. Montevideo: Ediciones de la Banda Oriental, 1979–1985.

———. *Historia rural del Uruguay moderno.* 5 vols. Montevideo: Ediciones de la Banda Oriental, 1967–1977.

Barrios Píntos, Aníbal. *Los barrios de Montevideo.* 2 vols. Montevideo: Nuestra Tierra, 1971.

———. *El Silencio y la voz: Historia de la mujer en el Uruguay.* Montevideo: Linardi y Risso, 2001.

Bauzá, Julio A. "Mortalidad infantil en la República del Uruguay en el decenio 1901–1910." *Revista Médica del Uruguay* 16, no. 2 (February 1913): 45–81.

Beaumont, J. A. B. *Viajes por Buenos Aires, Entre Rios y la Banda Oriental (1826–1827).* Buenos Aires: Librería Hachette, 1957.

Becerro de Bengoa, Miguel. *Los problemas de la Asistencia Pública.* Montevideo: El Siglo Ilustrado, 1922.

Bell, E. Moberly. *Storming the Citadel: The Rise of the Woman Doctor.* London: Constable and Co., 1953.

Berkovitch, Nitza. *From Motherhood to Citizenship: Women's Rights and International Organizations.* Baltimore: Johns Hopkins University Press, 1999.

Bernstein, Laurie. "Fostering the Next Generation of Socialists: Patronirovanie in the Fledgling Soviet State." *Journal of Family History* 26, no. 1 (January 2001): 68–89.

Besse, Susan K. *Restructuring Patriarchy: The Modernization of Gender Inequality in Brazil, 1914–1940.* Chapel Hill: University of North Carolina Press, 1996.

Bethell, Leslie, ed. *Latin America Economy and Society, 1870–1930.* New York: Cambridge University Press, 1989.

Black, Gregory D. *The Catholic Crusade against the Movies, 1940–1975.* Cambridge: Cambridge University Press, 1998.

Bliss, Katherine Elaine. *Compromised Positions: Prostitution, Public Health, and Gender Politics in Revolutionary Mexico City.* University Park, PA: Pennsylvania State University Press, 2001.

———. "The Science of Redemption: Syphillis, Sexual Promiscuity, and Reformism in Revolutionary Mexico City." *Hispanic American Historical Review* 79, no. 1 (February 1999): 1–40.

Bock, Gisela. *Women in European History.* Oxford: Blackwell, 2002.

Bock, Gisela, and Pat Thane. *Maternity and Gender Policies: Women and the Rise of European Welfare States.* London and New York: Routledge, 1991.

Borges, Dain. "'Puffy, Ugly, Slothful and Inert': Degeneration in Brazilian Social Thought, 1880–1940." *Journal of Latin American Studies* 25, no, 2 (May 1993): 235–56.

Bouret, Daniela, et al. *Entre la Matzá y el Mate: La inmigración judía en Uruguay: una historia de construcción.* Montevideo: Ediciones de la Banda Oriental, 1997.

Bridal, Tessa. *The Tree of Red Stars*. Minneapolis, MN: Milkweed Press, 1997.
Broder, Sherri. *Tramps, Unfit Mothers, and Neglected Children: Negotiating the Family in Nineteenth-Century Philadelphia*. Philadelphia: University of Pennsylvania Press, 2002.
Brum, Baltasar. *Los derechos de la mujer: Reforma a la legislación civil y política del Uruguay*. Montevideo: Peña Hermanos, 1925.
Buela, Juana Rouco. *Historia de un ideal vivido por una mujer*. Buenos Aires: Editorial Reconstruir, 1964.
Buhle, Mari Jo. *Women and American Socialism, 1870–1920*. Urbana: University of Illinois Press, 1981.
Burke Janet M., and Margaret C. Jacob. "French Freemasonry, Women, and Feminist Scholarship." *Journal of Modern History* 68, no. 3 (September 1996): 513–49.
Caballero, Manuel. *Latin America and the Comintern, 1919–1943*. Cambridge: Cambridge University Press, 1986.
Caetano, Gerardo. *La República Conservadora*. 2 vols. Montevideo: Fin de Siglo, 1992–1993.
Caetano, Gerardo, ed. *Los uruguayos del centenario: nación, ciudadanía, religión y educación (1910–1930)*. Montevideo: Taurus, 2000.
Caetano, Gerardo, and Roger Geymonat. *La secularización uruguaya (1859–1919), Tomo 1: Catolicismo y privatización de lo religioso*. Montevideo: Ediciones Santillana, 1997.
Caetano, Gerardo, and Raúl Jacob. *El nacimiento del terrismo (1930–1933)*. 3 vols. Montevideo: Ediciones de la Banda Oriental, 1989–1991.
Caetano, Gerardo, and José Rilla. *Historia contemporánea del Uruguay moderno: de la colonia al Mercosur*. Montevideo: CLAEH/Fin de Siglo, 1994.
Cámara de Representantes, *Leglislación referente a la mujer*. Montevideo: División Información y Antecedentes Legislativos, 1986.
Cánova, Virginia. *Por una Fortuna una Cruz y Los orígenes del feminismo en Uruguay*. Montevideo, Biblioteca Nacional, 1998.
Carey, Hillary. *Truly Feminine, Truly Catholic: A History of the Catholic Women's League in the Archdiocese of Sydney, 1913–1987*. Sydney: New South Wales University Press, 1987.
Carlson, Marifran. *Feminismo!: The Woman's Movement in Argentina from Its Beginnings to Eva Perón*. Chicago: Academy Chicago Publishers, 1988.
Carnoy, Martin. *The State and Political Theory*. Princeton, NJ: Princeton University Press, 1984.
Carreras de Bastos, Laura. *Acción social de la mujer ante el divorcio absoluto*. Montevideo: Imp. de la buena prensa, 1909.

———. *Las espigas de Ruth.* Montevideo: Barreiro y Ramos, 1922.
———. *Feminismo Cristiano.* Montevideo: Imp. de la buena prensa, 1907.
Cassina de Nogara, Alba G. *Las Feministas.* Montevideo: Instituto Nacional del Libro, 1989.
———. *Hacia una democracia integral: Apuntes para una historia del feminismo en Uruguay.* Montevideo: Consejo Nacional de Mujeres del Uruguay, 1990.
———. "Una revista Uruguaya: Acción Femenina." *Boletin del EUBCA,* No.14 (Montevideo, 1978).
Castellanos de Etchepare, Delia. *Mariposas.* Montevideo: Claudio García, 1921.
Caulfield, Sueann. *In Defense of Honor: Sexual Morality, Modernity, and Nation in Early-Twentieth-Century Brazil.* Durham, NC: Duke University Press, 2000.
Caulfield, Sueann, and Martha de Abreu Esteves. "Fifty Years of Virginity in Rio de Janeiro: Sexual Politics and Gender Roles in Juridical and Popular Discourse, 1890–1940." *Luso-Brazilian Review* 30, no. 1 (Summer 1993): 47–74.
Chambers, Sarah C. *From Subjects to Citizens: Honor, Gender, and Politics in Arequipa, Peru, 1780–1854.* University Park, PA: Pennsylvania State University Press, 1999.
Chaney, Elsa. *Supermadre: Women in Politics in Latin America.* Austin: Unversity of Texas Press, 1979.
Chasteen, John Charles. *Heroes on Horseback: The Life and Times of the Last Gaucho Caudillos.* Albuquerque: University of New Mexico Press, 1995.
———. "Fighting Words: The Discourse of Insurgency in Latin American History." *Latin American Research Review* 28, no.3 (Summer 1993).
Cherpak, Evelyn M. "The Participation of Women in the Wars for Independence in Northern South America, 1810–1824." *Minerva: Quarterly Report on Women and the Military* 11, no.3 (December 1993): 11–28.
Clark, Linda L. *The Rise of the Professional Woman in France: Gender and Public Administration Since 1830.* Cambridge and New York: Cambridge University Press, 2000.
———. "Feminist Maternalists and the French State: Two Inspectresses General in the Pre–World War I Third Republic." *Journal of Women's History* 12, no.1 (Spring 2000): 32–59.
Collier, David, and Ruth Berins. *Shaping the Political Arena: Critical Junctures, The Labor Movement, and Regime Dynamics in Latin America.* Princeton, NJ: Princeton University Press, 1991.

Consejo Nacional de Higiene, *Nómina de los doctores y licenciados en medicina y cirugía (farmacéuticos, dentistas, parteras, veterinarios, practicantes y flebótomos) hasta el 30 de diciembre de 1922.* Montevideo: El Siglo Ilustrado, 1923.

Cortinas, Laura. *Teatro del amor.* Barcelona: Ed. Juventud, 1930.

Cuadernos del ITU. *La Iglesia en el Uruguay.* Montevideo: Instituto Teológico del Uruguay, 1978.

Dames de Charité Française. *Rapport sur l'oeuvre des Dames de Charité Française de Montevideo Juin 1892 a Juin 1893.* Montevideo: Imp. Latina, 1893.

Dávila, Jerry. *Diploma of Whiteness: Race and Social Policy in Brazil, 1917–1945.* Durham, NC: Duke University Press, 2003.

De la Fuente, Alejandro. *A Nation for All: Race, Inequality, and Politics in Twentieth-Century Cuba.* Chapel Hill: University of North Carolina Press, 2001.

De la Fuente, Ariel. *Children of Facundo: Caudillo and Gaucho Insurgency during the Argentine State-Formation Processs (La Rioja, 1853–1870).* Durham, NC: Duke University Press, 2000.

De Letre, María, *La masonería y la mujer.* México DF: Editorial Herbasa, n.d.

D'Elía, Germán, and Armando Miraldi. *Historia del movimiento obrero en el Uruguay: desde sus orígenes hasta 1930.* Montevideo: Ediciones de la Banda Oriental, 1984.

Di Liscia, María Herminia, and José Maristany, eds., *Mujeres y estado en la Argentina: educación, salud y beneficencia.* Buenos Aires: Editorial Biblos, 1997.

Dore, Elizabeth, and Maxine Molyneux, eds. *Hidden Histories of Gender and the State in Latin America.* Durham, NC: Duke University Press, 2000.

DuBois, Ellen Carol. "Women Suffrage and the Left: An International Socialist-Feminist Perspective." *New Left Review* 186 (March/April 1991): 19–45.

Dumenil, Lynn. *Freemasonry and American Culture, 1880–1930.* Princeton, NJ: Princeton University Press, 1984.

Edwards, Rebecca. *Angels in the Machinery: Gender in American Party Politics from the Civil War to the Progressive Era.* New York: Oxford University Press, 1997.

Ehrick, Christine. "*Madrinas* and Missionaries: Uruguay and the Pan-American Women's Movement." *Gender and History* 10, no. 3 (November 1998): 406–24.

Elwitt, Sanford. *The Third Republic Defended: Bourgeois Reform in France,*

1880–1914. Baton Rouge: Louisiana State University Press, 1986.

Fabregat, Julio T. *Elecciones Uruguayas (Febrero de 1925 a Noviembre de 1945).* Montevideo: Corte Electoral, 1948.

Farnsworth-Alvear, Ann. *Dulcinea in the Factory: Myths, Morals, Men and Women in Colombia's Industrial Experiment, 1905–1960.* Durham, NC: Duke University Press, 2000.

Ferreira, Mariano. "La mujer Uruguaya en la Beneficiencia Pública." *Revista del Instituto Histórico y Geográfico del Uruguay* 1 (1920): 99–116.

Filguiera, Nea, et al. *La mujer en el Uruguay: ayer y hoy.* Montevideo: Ediciones de la Banda Oriental, 1983.

Finch, Henry. *A Political Economy of Uruguay since 1870.* New York: St. Martin's Press, 1982.

Findlay, Eileen J. Suárez. *Imposing Decency: The Politics of Sexuality and Race in Puerto Rico, 1870–1920.* Durham, NC: Duke University Press, 1999.

Fiol-Matta, Licia. *A Queer Mother for the Nation: The State and Gabriela Mistral.* Minneapolis: University of Minnesota Press, 2002.

Fitzgibbon, Russell H. *Uruguay: Portrait of a Democracy.* London: Allen and Unwin, 1956.

Forment, Carlos A. *Democracy in Latin America, 1760–1900:* Volume I: *Civic Selfhood and Public Life in Mexico and Peru.* Chicago: University of Chicago Press, 2003.

Foucault, Michel. *The Birth of the Clinic: An Archaeology of Medical Perception.* New York: Pantheon, 1973.

———. *Power/Knowledge: Selected Interviews and Other Writings, 1972–1977.* New York: Pantheon, 1980.

Fox Piven, Frances, and Richard Cloward. "Welfare Doesn't Shore Up Traditional Family Roles: A Reply to Linda Gordon." *Social Research* 55, no. 4 (Winter 1988): 631–47.

Frega, Ana. "Redentores, amos y tutores: La concepción dominante sobre el papel de la mujer en el Uruguay a comienzos del siglo XX." Montevideo: GRECMU, 1990. Photocopy.

French, John D., and Daniel James, eds. *The Gendered World of Latin American Women Workers: From the Household and Factory to the Union Hall and Ballot Box.* Durham, NC: Duke University Press, 1997

Frugoni, Emilio. *La mujer ante el derecho.* Montevideo: Editorial Indo-americana, 1940.

———. *Obras de Emilio Frugoni.* 8 vols. Montevideo: Ediciones de la Banda Oriental, 1987–1989.

Fuchs, Rachel G. *Abandoned Children: Foundlings and Child Welfare in*

Nineteenth-Century France. Albany: State University of New York Press, 1984.

Fuchs, Rachel G., and Leslie Page Moch. "Pregnant, Single, and Far from Home: Migrant Women in Nineteenth-Century Paris." *American Historical Review* 95, no. 4 (October 1990), 1007–31.

Gallardo, Ricardo. *Divorcio, separación de cuerpos y nulidad del matrimonio en las naciones latino-americanas*. Madrid: n.p., 1957.

Gish, Clay. "Rescuing the 'Waifs and Strays' of the City: The Western Emigration Program of the Children's Aid Society." *Journal of Social History* 33, no.1 (Fall 1999): 121–42.

Godio, Julio. *Historia del movimiento obrero latinoamericano*, Vol. 1: *Anarquistas y Socialistas, 1850–1918*. San José, Costa Rica: Editorial Nueva Sociedad, 1985.

González, Luis E. *Political Structures and Democracy in Uruguay*. Notre Dame, IN: University of Notre Dame Press, 1991.

González Laurino, Carolina. *La construcción de la identidad uruguaya*. Montevideo: Ediciones Santillana, 2001.

González Sierra, Yamandú. *Del hogar a la fábrica: deshonra o virtud?*. Montevideo: Ed. Nordan, 1996.

———. "Mujeres de los sectores populares: Obreras, madres o prostitutas?" Montevideo: GRECMU, n.d. Photocopy.

Gordon, Linda. *Pitied but Not Entitled: Single Mothers and the History of Welfare, 1890–1935*. New York: Free Press, 1994.

———. "What Does Welfare Regulate?" *Social Research* 55, no. 4 (Winter 1988): 609–30.

———. ed. *Women, the State, and Welfare*. Madison: University of Wisconsin Press, 1990.

Gosse, Van. "'To Organize in Every Neighborhood, in Every Home': The Gender Politics of American Communists between the Wars." *Radical History Review* 50 (1991): 109–41.

Graham, Richard, ed. *The Idea of Race in Latin America, 1870–1940*. Austin: University of Texas Press, 1990.

Grompone, Romeo. *Divorcio*. Montevideo: Edina, 1946.

Gustafson, Melanie. *Women in the Republican Party, 1854–1924*. Urbana: University of Illinois Press, 2001.

Gustafson, Melanie, Kristie Miller, and Elisabeth Israels Perry, eds., *We Have Come to Stay: American Women in Political Parties, 1880–1960*. Albuquerque: University of New Mexico Press, 1999.

Guy, Donna J. *White Slavery and Mothers Alive and Dead: The Troubled Meeting of Sex, Gender, Public Health, and Progress in Latin*

America. Lincoln: University of Nebraska Press, 2000.

———. "The Pan-American Child Congresses, 1916 to 1942: Pan-Americanism, Child Reform, and the Welfare State in Latin America." *Journal of Family History* 23, no.3 (July 1998), 272–91.

———. "The Politics of Pan-American Cooperation: Maternalist Feminism and the Child Rights Movement, 1913–1960." *Gender and History* 10, no. 3 (November 1998): 449–69.

———. *Sex and Danger in Buenos Aires: Prostitution, Family, and Nation in Argentina*. Lincoln: University of Nebraska Press, 1990.

Hahner, June. *Emancipating the Female Sex: the Struggle for Women's Rights in Brazil, 1850–1940*. Durham, NC: Duke University Press, 1990.

Hanson, Simon G. *Utopia in Uruguay: Chapters in the Economic History of Uruguay*. New York: Oxford University Press, 1938.

Harmann, Heidi. "The Unhappy Marriage of Marxism and Feminism: Towards a More Progressive Union." In *Women and Revolution: A Discussion of the Unhappy Marriage of Marxism and Feminism*, ed. Lydia Sargent. Boston: South End Press, 1981.

Haslip-Viera, Gabriel. *Crime and Punishment in Late Colonial Mexico City, 1692–1810*. Albuquerque: University of New Mexico Press, 1999.

Headings, Mildred J. *French Freemasonry under the Third Republic*. Baltimore: Johns Hopkins University Press, 1949.

Healy, Dorothy, and Maurice Isserman. *Dorothy Healy Remembers: A Life in the American Communist Party*. New York: Oxford University Press, 1990.

Horne, Janet R. *A Social Laboratory for Modern France: The Musée Social and the Rise of the Welfare State*. Durham, NC: Duke University Press, 2002.

Hudson, W. H. *The Purple Land*. New York: Dutton, 1916.

Hugarte, Renzo Pi. *Los indios del Uruguay*. Montevideo: Ediciones de la Banda Oriental, 1998.

Hume, Blanca. *La unidad de la moral*. Buenos Aires: Imprenta Levinsky, 1919.

Hutchison, Elizabeth Quay. "Add Gender and Stir?: Cooking up Gendered Histories of Modern Latin America." *Latin American Research Review* 38, no. 1 (2003), 267–87.

———. *Labors Appropriate to Their Sex: Gender, Labor, and Politics in Urban Chile, 1900–1930*. Durham, NC: Duke University Press, 2001.

———. "From 'La Mujer Esclava' to 'La Mujer Limón': Anarchism and the Politics of Sexuality in Early-Twentieth-Century Chile." *Hispanic American Historical Review* 81, nos. 3–4 (August/November 2001): 519–53.

Instituto Teológico del Uruguay. *La Iglesia en el Uruguay: Libro conmemorativo en el primer centenario de la erección del obispado del Montevideo, primero en el Uruguay, 1878–1978.* Montevideo: Instituto Teológico del Uruguay, 1978.

International Council of Women. *Women in a Changing World: The Dynamic Story of the International Council of Women since 1888.* London: Routledge and K. Paul, 1966.

Iriarte, Tomás de. *Memorias: El Sitio de Montevideo*, Vol. 11. Buenos Aires: Editorial Goncourt, 1969.

Kane, Paula M. "The Willing Captive of Home?: The English Catholic Women's League, 1906–1920." *Church History* 60, no. 3 (September 1991): 331–55.

Kaplan, Temma. *Anarchists of Andalusia, 1868–1903.* Princeton, NJ: Princeton University Press, 1977.

———. *Red City, Blue Period: Social Movements in Picasso's Barcelona.* Berkeley: University of California Press, 1992.

Kertzer, David I. *Italian Infant Abandonment and the Politics of Reproductive Control.* Boston: Beacon Press, 1993.

Klaus, Alisa. *Every Child a Lion: The Origins of Maternal and Infant Health Policy in the United States and France, 1890–1920.* Ithaca, NY: Cornell University Press, 1993.

Klubock, Thomas Miller. *Contested Communities: Class, Gender, and Politics in Chile's El Teniente Copper Mine, 1904–1951.* Durham, NC: Duke University Press, 1998.

Koven, Seth, and Sonya Michel, eds. *Mothers of a New World: Maternalist Politics and the Origins of Welfare States.* London and New York: Routledge, 1993.

Kruks, Sonia et al., eds. *Promissory Notes: Women in the Transition to Socialism.* New York: Monthly Review Press, 1989.

Kruse, Hermán C. "Las damas de la caridad y los caballeros de la filantropía: Un estudio sobre caridad, filantropía y beneficencia en el Uruguay del Siglo XIX." Master's thesis, University of the Republic, Montevideo, Uruguay, 1994.

Kunzel, Regina G. *Fallen Women, Problem Girls: Unmarried Mothers and the Professionalization of Social Work, 1890–1945.* New Haven, Conn: Yale University Press, 1993.

Lacey, Kate. *Feminine Frequencies: Gender, German Radio, and the Public Sphere, 1923–1945.* Ann Arbor: University of Michigan Press, 1996.

Ladd-Taylor, Molly. "Toward Defining Maternalism in U.S. History." *Journal of Women's History* 5, no. 2 (Fall 1993): 110–13.

Lauderdale Graham, Sandra. *House and Street: The Domestic World of Servants and Masters in Nineteenth-Century Rio de Janeiro*. Austin: University of Texas Press, 1988.

Lavrin, Asunción. "Paulina Luisi: Pensamiento y escritura feminista." In *Estudios sobre escritoras hispanoaméricanas en honor de Georgina Saban Rivero*, ed. Lou Charnon-Deutsch. Madrid: Editorial Castalia, 1992.

———. *Women, Feminism, and Social Change in Argentina, Chile, and Uruguay, 1890–1940*. Lincoln: University of Nebraska Press, 1995.

Lerena, Andrés. *Investigación de la paternidad: Alegato presentado en el juzgado letrado departamental del Rio Negro*. Montevideo: n.p., 1920.

Liga de Damas Católicas del Uruguay. *Conferencias pronunciadas bajo los auspicios de la Liga de Damas Católicas durante el año 1907*. Montevideo: Imp. de la buena prensa, 1908.

Liga de Damas Católicas, Comité departamental de Paysandú. *Estatutos de la Sociedad Femenina de Socorros Mutuos*. Montevideo: Tip. Uruguaya de M. Martínez, 1909.

Little, Cynthia Jefress. "Moral Reform and Feminism: A Case Study." *Journal of Inter-American Studies and World Affairs* 17, no. 4 (November 1975): 386–97.

Lockhart, Washington. *Vida de dos caudillos: Los Galarza*. Montevideo: Ediciones de la Banda Oriental, 1968.

Londres, Albert. *The Road to Buenos Ayres*. Translated by Eric Sutton. New York: Blue Ribbon Books, 1928.

López-Alves, Fernando. *Between the Economy and the Polity in the River Plate: Uruguay, 1811–1890*. London: University of London Institute of Latin American Studies, 1993.

———. *State Formation and Democracy in Latin America, 1810–1910*. Durham, NC: Duke University Press, 2000.

López D'Alesandro, Fernando. *Historia de la izquierda Uruguaya*. 3 vols. Montevideo: Nuevo Mundo/Vintén, 1988–1992.

Luisi, Paulina. *Algunas ideas sobre eugenía*. Montevideo: El Siglo Ilustrado, 1916.

———. *Un crimen social: la trata de blancas*. Buenos Aires: Tribuna Libre, 1918.

———. *Enseñanza sexual*. Montevideo: El Siglo Ilustrado, 1916.

———. *La escuela al aire libre y la acción del cuerpo médico escolar en al lucha contra la tuberculosis*. Montevideo: El Siglo Ilustrado, 1918.

———. *La lucha contra el alcoholismo y el sufragio femenino*. Buenos Aires: Revista Argentina de Ciencias Políticas, 1918.

———. *Una moral única para ambos sexos*. Buenos Aires:Tribuna Libre, 1920.
———. *Movimiento Sufragista*. Montevideo: El Siglo Ilustrado, 1919.
———. *Otra voz clamando en el desierto*. Montevideo: n.p., 1948.
———. *Para una mejor descendencia*. Buenos Aires: Juan Perrotti, 1919.
———. *El problema de la prostitutción: Abolicionismo o Reglamentarismo?* Montevideo: Sindicato Médico del Uruguay, 1925.
———. *Proyectos sobre moralidad*. Buenos Aires: J. Perrotti, 1919.
Machado Bonet, Ofelia. "Sufragistas y poetisas." *Enciclopédia Uruguaya* 38. Montevideo: Editores Reunidos y Editorial Arca, 1969.
MacPherson, Anne S. "Citizens v. Clients: Working Women and Colonial Reform in Puerto Rico and Belize, 1932–1945." *Journal of Latin American Studies* 35 (May 2003): 279–310.
Marshall, T. H. *Class, Citizenship and Social Development*. New York: Anchor Books, 1965.
Martin, Franklin. *South America from a Surgeon's Point of View*. New York: Fleming H. Revell, 1922.
Martínez-Vergne, Teresita. *Shaping the Discourse on Space: Charity and its Wards in Nineteenth-Century San Juan, Puerto Rico*. Austin: University of Texas Press, 1999.
Matos Rodríguez, Félix V. *Women and Urban Change in San Juan, Puerto Rico, 1820–1868*. Gainesville: University of Florida Press, 1999.
McCreery, David. "'This Life of Misery and Shame': Female Prostitution in Guatemala City, 1880–1920." *Journal of Latin American Studies* 18, no. 2 (November 1986): 333–53.
McGee Deutsch, Sandra. *Counterrevolution in Argentina, 1900–1932: The Argentine Patriotic League*. Lincoln: University of Nebraska Press, 1986.
———. *Las Derechas: The Extreme Right in Argentina, Brazil, and Chile, 1890–1939*. Stanford, CA: Stanford University Press, 1999.
———. "Gender and Sociopolitical Change in Twentieth-Century Latin America." *Hispanic American Historical Review* 71, no. 2 (May 1991): 259–306.
Mead, Karen. "Gendering the Obstacles to Progress in Positivist Argentina, 1880–1920." *Hispanic American Historical Review*. 77, no. 4 (November 1997): 645–75.
———. "Oligarchs, Doctors, and Nuns: Public Health and Beneficence in Buenos Aires, 1880–1914." Ph.D. diss., University of California Santa Barbara, 1994.
Méndez Vives, Enrique. *La tiza y el sable: Vida cotidiana en el Uruguay de Varela y Latorre*. Montevideo: Fin de Siglo, 1993.
Miller, Francesca. *Latin American Women and the Search for Social Justice*.

Hanover, NH: University Press of New England, 1991.

Miranda, Cesar. *Constatación judicial de la paternidad ilegítima y leyes de investigación de la paternidad e hijos naturales del Uruguay, España, Portugal, Argentina, Honduras, Bélgica y Francia.* Montevideo: El Siglo Ilustrado, 1926.

Molyneux, Maxine. "Mobilization without Emancipation? Women's Interests, The State, and Revolution in Nicaragua. *Feminist Studies* 11 (Summer 1985): 227–54.

———. "No God, No Boss, No Husband: Anarchist Feminism in Nineteenth Century Argentina." *Latin American Perspectives* 13, no. 1 (Winter 1986): 119–45.

Montaño, Oscar. *Yeninyanya (Umkhonto II): historia de los afrouruguayos.* Montevideo: Organizaciones Mundo Afro, 2001.

Montevideo social, 1919–20. Montevideo: Agencia Della Croce, 1919.

Morantz-Sánchez, Regina. *Sympathy and Science: Women Physicians in American Medicine.* New York: Oxford University Press, 1985.

More, Ellen S. *Restoring the Balance: Women Physicians and the Profession of Medicine, 1850–1995.* Cambridge, MA: Harvard University Press, 1999.

Moses, Claire Goldberg. *French Feminism in the Nineteenth Century.* Albany: State University of New York Press, 1984.

Moya, José C. *Cousins and Strangers: Spanish Immigrants in Buenos Aires, 1850–1930.* Berkeley: University of California Press, 1998.

Nahum, Benjamín. *Manual de Historia del Uruguay.* 2 vols. Montevideo: Ediciones de la Banda Oriental, 1997–1998.

Nery, Carlos. "La Escuela de Nurses: Su organización y métodos." *Primer Congreso Médico Nacional, Montevideo 9–16 Abril 1916*, Tomo 4. Montevideo: El Siglo Ilustrado, 1917, 367–68.

O'Connor, Julia, Sheila Shaver, and Ann Orloff. *States, Markets, and Families: Gender, Liberalism and Social Policy in Australia, Canada, Great Britain and the United States.* Cambridge and New York: Cambridge University Press, 1999.

O'Dogherty, Laura. "Restaurarlo todo en Cristo: Unión de Damas Católicas Mejicanas, 1920-1926." *Estudios de historia moderna y contemporanea de Mexico* 14 (1991): 129–58.

Offen, Karen. *European Feminisms, 1700–1950: A Political History.* Stanford, CA: Stanford University Press, 2000.

Orloff, Ann. "Gender in the Welfare State." *Annual Review of Sociology* 22 (1996): 51–78.

Ortíz de Terra, María del Carmen, and Rosario Quijano, "Las mujeres durante la revolución lavallejista de 1832." *Hoy es Historia* 4, no. 23 (September-

October 1987): 20–29, and 5, no. 26 (March-April 1998): 17–25.

Padrón-Favre, Oscar. *Durazno: Bases para una identidad y un destino.* Durazno, Uruguay: Imprenta ABC, 1988.

———. *Durazno Antiguo*, Tomo 1. Durazno: Mlm Pesce, 1991.

Pan-American Union. *The First Conference of the Inter-American Commission of Women.* Washington D.C.: Pan American Union, 1930.

Panizza, Francisco. "Late Institutionalisation and Early Modernisation: The Emergence of Uruguay's Liberal Democratic Political Order." *Journal of Latin American Studies* 29 (October 1997): 667–91.

———. *Uruguay, batllismo y después: Pacheco, militares y tupamaros en la crisis del Uruguay batllista.* Montevideo: Ediciones de la Banda Oriental, 1990.

Pateman, Carole. *The Disorder of Women: Democracy, Feminism, and Political Theory.* Stanford, CA: Stanford University Press, 1989.

Peck, Marie J. "Antecedentes de la lucha por los derechos de la mujer en el Río de la Plata, 1790–1910." Montevideo, Uruguay: Instituto del Libro, Sala de la Mujer, n.d. Photocopy.

Pedersen, Susan. *Family, Dependence, and the Origins of the Welfare State: Britain and France, 1914–1945.* Cambridge and New York: Cambridge University Press, 1993.

Pendle, George. *Uruguay.* 3d ed. London: Oxford University Press, 1963.

Penyak, Lee M. "Safe Harbors and Compulsory Custody: Casas de Depósito in Mexico, 1760–1885," *Hispanic American Historical Review* 79, no. 1 (February. 1999): 83–99.

Pereda Valdés, Ildefonso. *El negro en el Uruguay: pasado y presente.* Montevideo: Instituto Histórico y Geográfico del Uruguay, 1965.

Pereira, Antonio N. *Cosas de antaño: Bocetos, perfiles y tradiciones interesantes y populares de Montevideo.* Montevideo: El Siglo Ilustrado, 1893.

Perujo, Carlos. *Filiación natural.* Montevideo: Imprenta La Idea, 1879.

Pinto de Vidal, Isabel. *El Batllismo precursor de los derechos civiles de la mujer.* Montevideo: n.p., 1951.

Pintos, Francisco. *Historia del movimiento obrero del Uruguay.* Montevideo: n.p., 1960.

Plano aerofotgráfico de Montevideo. Buenos Aires: Aerofotos Lda, Intendencia Municipal de Montevideo, Servicio de fotográmetria, 1926.

Poppino, Rollie E. *International Communism in Latin America: A History of the Movement 1917–1963.* London: Collier-Macmillan Limited, 1964.

Porzecanski, Teresa. "Vida privada y construcción de la identidad: inmigrantes judios el Uruguay." In *Historias de la vida privada en el Uruguay*, ed. José Pedro Barrán. Montevideo: Ediciones Santillana, 1996.

Power, Margaret. *Right-Wing Women in Chile: Feminine Power and the Struggle against Allende, 1964–1973*. University Park, PA: The Pennsylvania State University Press, 2002.

Rama, Carlos M. "Obreros y anarquistas." *Enciclopédia Uruguaya* 32. Montevideo: Editores Reunidos y Editorial Arca, 1969.

Rivanera Carles, Federico. *Las escuelas judías en Argentina: documentación secuestrada por la policía*. Buenos Aires: Biblioteca de Formación Política, 1986.

Rocha Imaz, Ricardo. *Los blancos: Breviario de hombres y hechos del Partido Nacional, 1836–1966*. Montevideo: Ed. Cerno, 1978.

Rock, David, and Fernando López-Alves, "State Building and Political Systems in Nineteenth-Century Argentina and Uruguay." *Past and Present* 167 (May 2000): 177–202.

Rodríguez, Blanca, and Cielo Pereira, eds. *Mujeres uruguayas: El lado femenino de nuestra historia*. 2 vols. Montevideo: Alfaguara, 1997–2001.

Rodríguez Díaz, Universindo. *Los sectores populares en el Uruguay del novecientos*. 2 vols. Montevideo: Compañero, 1989–1994.

Rodríguez Villamíl, Silvia. "La historia de las mujeres en el Uruguay." *Hoy es Historia* 9 (July-August 1992): 5–14.

———. ed. *Mujeres e historia en el Uruguay*. Montevideo: GRECMU, 1992.

Rodríguez Villamíl, Silvia and Graciela Sapriza. "Feminism and Politics: Women and the Vote in Uruguay." In *Retrieving Women's History: Changing Perceptions of the Role of Women in Politics and Society*, ed. S. Jay Klienberg. New York: Oxford University Press, 1988.

———. *Mujer, estado y política en el Uruguay del siglo XX*. Montevideo: Ediciones de la Banda Oriental, 1984.

Rosemblatt, Karin Alejandra. *Gendered Compromises: Political Cultures and the State in Chile, 1920–1950*. Chapel Hill: University of North Carolina Press, 2000.

Ruggiero, Kristin Hoffman. "Honor, Maternity and the Disciplining of Women: Infanticide in Late Nineteenth-Century Buenos Aires." *Hispanic American Historical Review* 72, no. 3 (August 1992): 353–73.

———. "Wives on 'Deposit': Internment and the Preservation of Husbands' Honor in Late-Nineteenth Century Buenos Aires." *Journal of Family History* 17, no. 3 (1992): 253–70.

Rupp, Leila J. *Worlds of Women: The Making of an International Women's Movement*. Princeton, NJ: Princeton University Press, 1997.

Ryan, Mary P. *Cradle of the Middle Class: The Family in Oneida County, New York, 1790–1865*. New York: Cambridge University Press, 1981.

Sábato, Hilda. *The Many and the Few: Political Participation in Republican Buenos Aires.* Stanford, CA: Stanford University Press, 2001.

Sala de Tourón, Lucía, and Rosa Alonso Eloy. *El Uruguay comercial, pastoríl y caudillesco,* Tomo 2: *Sociedad, Política e Ideología.* Montevideo: Ediciones de la Banda Oriental, 1991.

Salgado, José. *Las damas orientales en la beneficiencia pública.* Montevideo: Impresora L.I.G.U., 1942.

Salvatore, Ricardo D., and Carlos Aguirre, eds., *The Birth of the Penitentiary in Latin America: Essays of Criminology, Prison Reform, and Social Control, 1830–1940.* Austin: University of Texas Press, 1996.

Sapriza, Graciela. *Memorias de rebeldía: siete historias de vida.* Montevideo: Puntosur, 1988.

Sárraga, Belén de. *Conferencias sociológicas y de crítica religiosa.* Santiago de Chile: La Razón, 1913.

Sarti, Odile. *The Ligue Patriotique des Françaises, 1902–1933: A Feminine Response to the Secularization of French Society.* New York: Garland, 1992.

Scarone, Arturo. "Dra. Paulina Luisi: Datos biográficos del libro Uruguayos Contemporáneos hasta 1937." Montevideo: n.p., 1948.

———. *Uruguayos Contemporáneos: Nuevo diccionario de datos biográficos y bibliográficos.* 2d ed. Montevideo: Barreiro y Ramos, 1937.

Schell, Patience. "An Honorable Avocation for Ladies: The Work of the Mexico City Unión de Damas Católicas Mexicanas, 1912–1926." *Journal of Women's History* 99, no. 10 (Winter 1999): 78–103.

Schneider, William. "Toward the Improvement of the Human Race: The History of Eugenics in France." *The Journal of Modern History* 54, no. 2 (June 1982): 268–91.

Schulkin, Augusto I. *Historia de Paysandú: Diccionario biográfico,* Tomo 3. Buenos Aires: Ed. Van Roosen, 1958.

Secco Illa, Joaquín de. *Tres Años de Periodismo: Ideas Sueltas.* Montevideo: Vita Hermanos, 1908.

Servico Paz y Justicia Uruguay. *Uruguay Nunca Más: Human Rights Violations, 1972–1985.* Philadelphia: Temple University Press, 1989

Skocpol, Theda. *Protecting Soldiers and Mothers: The Political Origins of Social Policy in the United States.* Cambridge: Harvard University Press, 1992.

———. *Social Policy in the United States: Future Possibilities in Historical Perspective.* Princeton, NJ: Princeton University Press, 1995.

Soto, Shirlene. *Emergence of the Modern Mexican Woman: Her Participation in Revolution and Struggle for Equality, 1910–1940.*

Denver, CO: Arden Press, 1990.

Steinmetz, George. *Regulating the Social: The Welfare State and Local Politics in Imperial Germany*. Princeton, NJ: Princeton University Press, 1993.

Stepan, Nancy Leys. *The Hour of Eugenics: Race, Gender, and Nation in Latin America*. Ithaca, NY: Cornell University Press, 1991.

Stern, Alexandra Minna. "Responsible Mothers and Normal Children: Eugenics, Nationalism, and Welfare in post-Revolutionary Mexico, 1920–1940." *Journal of Historical Sociology* 12, no. 4 (December 1999): 369–97.

Stern, Steve J. *The Secret History of Gender: Women, Men and Power in Late Colonial Mexico*. Chapel Hill: University of North Carolina Press, 1995.

Stone, Judith F. *The Search for Social Peace: Reform Legislation in France, 1890–1914*. Albany: State University of New York Press, 1985.

Stoner, K. Lynn. *From the House to the Streets: The Cuban Woman's Movement for Legal Reform, 1898–1940*. Durham, NC: Duke University Press, 1991.

Stuart, Robert. "Whores and Angels: Women and the Family in the Discourse of French Marxism, 1882–1905." *European History Quarterly* 27, no. 3 (1997): 339–69.

Szurmuk, Mónica. *Women in Argentina: Early Travel Narratives*. Gainesville: University Press of Florida, 2000.

Taylor, Philip. "The Uruguayan Coup d'Etat of 1933." *Hispanic American Historical Review* 32, no. 3 (August 1952): 301–20.

———. "Uruguay: The Costs of Inept Political Corporatism." In *Latin American Politics and Development*, ed. Howard Wiarda and Harvey F. Kline. Boulder, Co.: Westview Press, 1985.

Tinsman, Heidi. *Partners in Conflict: The Politics of Gender, Sexuality, and Labor in the Chilean Agrarian Reform, 1950–1973*. Durham, NC, Duke University Press, 2002.

Tong, Rosemarie Putnam. *Feminist Thought*. 2d ed. Boulder, CO: Westview Press, 1998.

Trochon, Yvette, and Beatríz Vidal. *Bases documentales para la historia del Uruguay contemporáneo (1903–1933)*. Montevideo: Ediciones de la Banda Oriental, 1998.

Tucker, Robert C, ed. *The Marx-Engels Reader*. New York: W. W. Norton and Co., 1978.

Turenne, Augusto. *El Aborto criminal es un grave problema nacional*. Montevideo: Sindicato Médico del Uruguay, 1926.

———. *La Protección a la Madre Soltera*. Montevideo: Consejo de Salud Pública, 1932.

Twinam, Ann. *Public Lives, Private Secrets: Gender, Honor, Sexuality, and Illegitimacy in Colonial Spanish America*. Stanford, CA: Stanford University Press, 1999.

United States Bureau of Labor Statistics. *Labor Legislation of Uruguay*. Washington: U.S. Government Printing Office, 1929.

Valenzuela, Erika Maza. "Liberals, Radicals, and Women's Citizenship in Chile, 1872–1930." Kellogg Institute for International Studies, Working Paper no. 245, November 1997.

Vanger, Milton. *José Batlle y Ordoñez of Uruguay: The Creator of His Times, 1902–1907*. Cambridge, MA: Harvard University Press, 1963.

———. *The Model Country: José Batlle y Ordoñez of Uruguay, 1907–1915*. Hanover, NH: University Press of New England, 1980.

———. *Reforma o Revolución?: La polémica Batlle-Mibelli, 1917*. Montevideo: Ediciones de la Banda Oriental, 1989.

Vaughan, Mary Kay. *Cultural Politics in Revolution: Teachers, Peasants, and Schools in Mexico, 1930–1940*. Tucson: University of Arizona Press, 1997

Vaz Ferreira, Carlos. *Sobre Feminismo*. Buenos Aires: Editorial Losada, 1945.

Verba, Ericka Kim. "Catholic Feminism and *acción social femenina* [Women's Social Action]: The Early Years of the Liga de Damas Chilenas, 1912–1924." Ph.D diss., University of California Los Angeles, 1999.

———. "The *Círculo de Lectura* [Ladies' Reading Circle] and the *Club de Señoras* [Ladies' Club] of Santiago: Middle- and Upper-Class Feminist Conversations (1915–1920)." *Journal of Women's History* 7, no. 3 (Fall 1995): 6–33.

Verdesio, Gustavo. *Forgotten Conquests: Rereading New World History from the Margins*. Philadelphia: Temple University Press, 2001.

Verdisco, Aimee. "Between Accountability and '*Reivindicación*': Development and Intra-National Differentiation in Uruguay." Ph.D. diss., State University of New York, Buffalo, 1996.

Waelti-Walters, Jennifer, and Steven C. Hause, eds. *Feminisms of the Belle Epoque: A Historical and Literary Anthology*. Lincoln: University of Nebraska Press, 1994.

Walsh, Frank R. *Sin and Censorship: The Catholic Church and the Motion Picture Industry*. New Haven, CT: Yale University Press, 1996.

Weinstein, Martin. *Uruguay: Democracy at the Crossroads*. Boulder. CO.: Westview Press, 1988.

Bibliography

Weir, Margaret, Ann Orloff, and Theda Skocpol, eds. *The Politics of Social Policy in the United States*. Princeton, NJ: Princeton University Press, 1988.

Wilson, Elizabeth. *Women and the Welfare State*. London: Tavistock Publications, 1977.

Wood, Elizabeth A. "The Trial of the New Woman: Citizens-in-Training in the New Soviet Republic." *Gender and History* 13, no. 3 (November 2001): 524–45.

Zubillaga, Carlos. "El Batllismo: Una experiencia populista." *Cuadernos del CLAEH* 24 (1984): 29–57.

Zubillaga, Carlos, and Jorge Balbis. *Historia del movimiento sindical Uruguayo*. 4 vols. Montevideo: Ediciones de la Banda Oriental, 1985–1992.

Zubillaga, Carlos, and Mario Cayota. *Cristianos y cambio social en el Uruguay de la modernización (1896–1919)*. Montevideo: CLAEH/Banda Oriental, 1988.

Zum Felde, Alberto. *Proceso histórico del Uruguay*. Montevideo: ARCA, 1967.

Index

Abella de Ramírez, María, 58–59, 61, 63, 67
Abramovich de Dubinsky, Sara, 196
Acción Femenina, 112, 132, 134, 145, 151, 152
Acción social de la mujer ante el divorcio absoluto, 51
Agrupacíon Socialista Femenina, 65
Alianza Uruguaya por el Sufragio Femenino (Alianza), 17, 128, 134, 135, 142–46; Communist Party and, 192–93, 206; founding, 137–40, 178; political action, 157–58; social views, 149; split with Conamu, 151, 167; working women, 154–56, 192, 208
Allen, Ann Taylor: "Eugenics and Feminism," 237n. 31
"alto de Viera", 83, 161, 205
Álvarez, Sara Rey, 138, 148
Álvarez, Sonia, 11
Álvarez de Amézaga, Celia, 112
Álvarez Vignoli (de Demichelli), Sofía, 167, 178
Amor y transgresión en Montevideo, 1919–1931 (Barrán), 218n. 18
anarchists, 34, 39–42; Chile, 41; feminism and, 40; mobilization of women and, 42–44
"An Honorable Avocation for Ladies" (Schell), 227n. 31
anticlericalism, 37–39, 98, 106, 161; associations, 30, 44–45, 47, 53, 156, 180; feminism and, 57–60, 62, 64, 66; politics and, 67

APN. *See Asistencia Pública Nacional* (APN)
Arévalo, Julia, 65, 136, 181, 191–92, 196; *Centro Socialista Femenino*, 130, 185–86; political activism, 202
Argentina, 22, 47; feminist movement, 12
Argos, El, 38
Arias, José, 120
Arrom, Silvia: *Containing the Poor*, 239n. 58
Asilo Buen Pastor, 113
Asilos Maternales, 114*i*
Asistencia Pública Nacional (APN), 71, 110–11, 118, 123; Bonne Garde and, 118–20
Asociación de Damas Liberales (Damas Liberales), 53–58
Asociación de Señoras Cristianas, 37
Asociación Femenina "Emancipación", 62–64, 66
Asociación Pro-Matre, 92, 111, 111–12
Association of Liberal Propaganda, 53
Aurora, La, 39, 41–42

Banda Oriental, 6–7, 28, 35
Barrán, José Pedro: *Amor y transgresión en Montevideo, 1919–1931*, 218n. 18
Barrán, José Pedro and Benjamin Nahum: *Batlle, los estancieros y el imperio británico*, 245n. 6
Bastos, Juan José, 49
Batlle y Ordóñez, José, 1–2, 17,

275

Index

71–72, 73i, 74–77; *El Día* and, 74; first presidency, 44–46, 61–62; second presidency, 62, 70; "shield of the weak," 71–72; "woman question" and, 85–86, 105, 112, 139, 146, 219

Batllismo, 2, 4, 206–7; "compensation politics," 207; democratic reform and, 206; European immigration and, 226; ideology and policy, 2; Jewish immigrant community and, 196; liberal feminism and, 55, 107, 123, 129, 156–57, 207; paternalism and, 7–8, 80–82, 86; secularism and, 29; social reform, 70–72, 70–74, 184; women, politicization of, 13, 45, 47, 55, 66–67, 74–75

Becerro de Bengoa, Miguel, 71
Berbesé, Dolores, 24
Berkovitch, Nitza: *From Motherhood to Citizenship*, 88
Besse, Susan: *Restructuring Patriarchy*, 9–10
Bettembourg, Father, 49
Bien Público, El , 46
Blanco (National) Party, 23, 48, 82, 102, 162–64. See also political parties
Bliss, Katherine: *Compromised Positions*, 237n. 34
Bock, Gisela, 14
Bolten, Virginia, 61, 63, 65
Bonne Garde, La , 111, 113–20
Brazil, 47, 209–10; *Federacão Brasileira pelo Progresso Feminino* (FBPF), 210; "modernization of patriarchy," 3
Brum, Baltasar, 84–87, 134; *Los derechos de la mujer* , 85
Buela, Juana Rouco, 61

Buen Amor (Cortinas), *El* , 120–21
Buhle, María Jo: *Women and American Socialism 1870–1920*, 249n. 10
Butler, Josephine, 101
Butler, Kim: *Freedoms Given, Freedoms Won*, 218n. 20
"Butterfly," 190–91, 192, 193

Caetano, Gerardo, 7, 87–88
Carreras de Bastos, Laura, 30, 49–52, 117
Carrió de Polleri, Fanny, 128, 141i, 148, 158; letters, 138, 144, 151, 157; Liga de Damas Católicas del Uruguay and, 166; "Para Nosotras," 140
Casal y Canda, María, 64
Castellanos de Etchpare, Delia (*pseud.* Madre): *Mariposas*, 172–73
Catholic Church, 27–29, 37
"Catholic Feminism and *acción social femenina* [Women's Social Action]" (Verba), 246n. 14
Catholic Ladies' League. See *Liga de Damas Católicas*
Cerro region, 26, 197
Chile, 4, 12, 16, 96, 202, 210–11; anarchism, 41; Catholic Ladies' League, 47; Damas Católicas, 213; feminism and, 210; International Women's Council, 97; Liga, 168; "modernization of patriarchy," 3–4; *Movimiento pro Emancipación de la Mujer Chilena*, 210; Popular Front, 16; socialism, 208
Cibils, Jaime, 48
Cibils de Jackson, Petrona, 48
Clark, Linda L., 14–15; "Feminist Maternalists and the French

State," 221–22n. 42
Colegiado proposal, 82
Collazo, María, 61, 62i, 63
Colorado Party, 15–16, 21, 23–28, 35, 38, 82–83; Batllismo and, 1, 139, 178; Riveristas and, 134. See also political parties
Comintern, 194–95, 198
Comisión de Beneficencia, 27
Comité de Vigilancia Económica, 86–87
Communist Party, 10, 18, 181, 182, 189, 208; *Agrupación de Mujeres Comunistas*, 189–90; Arévalo and, 191–92; *Carta Abierta*, 198–99; *Centro Femenino Clara Zetkin*, 197; *Comité Central Femenino* (CCF), 193–94; domestic servants and, 190–91, 202–3; European immigrant Jews and, 196–97, 202; Liga de Damas Católicas del Uruguay and, 181–83; Rosa Luxemburg Center, 189; *Sección Femenina de la Agrupación Lituana*, 198; *Sección Femenina del Club Húngaro*, 198; Third International and, 189; "Tribuna Femenina," 190–91; Union of Servants, Maids and Affiliates, 190; "women's issues," 183–84; women's participation in, 191–92, 194, 195–97; Women's Section, 197–98; women's suffrage, 198–201
"compensation feminism," 4, 17, 72–75, 77, 79–80, 85
Compromised Positions (Bliss), 237n. 34
Compte y Riqué, Enriqueta, 133
Conamu. See Consejo Nacional de Mujeres del Uruguay (Conamu)
Congreso Femenino Internacional (Buenos Aires, 1910), 59–60
Consejo Nacional de Mujeres del Uruguay (Conamu), 17, 36, 94, 131, 135i, 145; Constitutional Convention (1916-1917), 130–31, 134; founding, 83, 97, 128, 144; ladies' committees, 132–33; leadership, 133; suffrage and, 130–31
Constitutional Convention (1916-1917), 82–84, 129, 129–31, 133, 185–86
Constitution of 1917, 83
Containing the Poor (Arrom), 239n. 58
Cortinas, Laura, 121i; *El Buen Amor*, 120–21
Cott, Nancy, 10–11
coup d'état of 1933, 3, 87–88
Crime and Punishment in Late Colonial Mexico (Haslip-Viera), 239n. 60
Cuestas de Nery, Carmen, 112, 117, 133

damas de caridad, 8
Damas de Durazno, 38
Damas Liberales. *See Asociación de Damas Liberales*
de la Fuente, Ariel, 6
de la Sierra de Sánchez, Margarita, 119, 133
De María de Prat, Berta, 133
Democracy in Latin America (Forment), 218n. 16
Derecho a la Vida, 40–41
Devita, Maria, 142, 155
Día, El, 24–25, 60, 64, 74, 77, 81
Díaz, Eloísa, 97–98
divorce law of 1913, 79–80
Domínguez, Luisa, 95

277

Dore, Elizabeth, 6
Durazno, 26, 38, 57–58

Earle, Rebecca, 6
Eco, El, 48, 53
Edwards, Rebecca, 11–12
El Socialista, 65, 186–87
Emergence of the Modern Mexican Woman (Soto), 219n. 24
Escuela de Aplicación de Señoritas, 78i
Estrázulas de Piñeyrúa, Dolores, 133
"Eugenics and Feminism" (Allen), 237n. 31
European Feminisms (Offen), 228n. 49

Fabbri, Luce, 87
Federación Obrera Regional Uruguaya (FORU), 43
Federación Rural, 82, 83
feminism, 2, 9; "individualistic," 10, 72, 140; Marxism and, 65; "relational," 10–11, 34, 206; secularism and, 29; three poles of, 66–67. *See also* liberal feminism
feminism, Uruguayan: qualities, 9
Feminismo Cristiano, 49, 51i
"Feminist Maternalists and the French State" (Clark), 221–22n. 42
Fernández, Isabel, 190, 192, 195, 198–201
Findlay, Eileen, 3
First Latin American Communist Conference, 198–99
Fitzgibbon, Russell, 205; *Uruguay: Portrait of a Democracy*, 16
Forment, Carlos: *Democracy in Latin America*, 218n. 16
Fragoso, Carmen, 26
Fragoso de Rivera, Bernardina, 25–26, 27
France, 15, 231n. 2

Freedoms Given, Freedoms Won (Butler), 218n. 20
freemasonry, 30, 37–38, 225n. 10
From Motherhood to Citizenship (Berkovitch), 88

Galarza, General Pablo, 57, 59i
Galeano, Eduardo, 2
García Gómez de Secco Illa, Faustina, 48, 164
García Lagos de Hughes, María, 164–65, 176
Gendered Compromises (Rosemblatt), 210, 221n. 35
Gómez, General Leandro, 48
González Sierra, Yamandú, 41
Gosse, Van, 195; "To Organize in Every Neighborhood, in Every Home.," 248–49n. 3
Gota de leche, 109i
Graham, Sandra Lauderdale, 8
Grierson, Cecilia, 97, 131
Guerra Grande, 26–28
Guy, Donna: *Sex and Danger in Buenos Aires*, 235n. 15

Haslip-Viera, Gabriel: *Crime and Punishment in Late Colonial Mexico*, 239n. 60
Horne, Janet, 15
Hutchison, Elizabeth, 11, 41; *Labors Appropriate to Their Sex*, 230n. 86

Instituto de Ciegos, 112
International Catholic Women's Union, 169
International Council of Women, 106
International Freethinkers' Conference, 58
International Women's Suffrage Alliance, 106, 243n. 36
Internato Normal para Señoritas, 36

"investigation of paternity" legislation, 80–82
Iriarte, Tomás de, 24, 27

Jackson, Juan D., 48
Jacob, Raúl, 87–88
Jewish immigrants, 196–97, 202

Koven, Seth, 10, 209
Kruse, Hermán, 27

labor movement, 34, 41–42
Labors Appropriate to Their Sex (Hutchison), 230n. 86
Ladd-Taylor, Molly: "Toward Defining Maternalism in U.S. History," 220n. 27
"ladies' committees," 8, 110, 113–14, 124
"ladies of charity," 15–16
Lanteri Renshaw, Julieta, 59, 148
Latin American Women and the Search for Social Justice (Miller), 232n. 12
Latorre, Colonel Lorenzo, 35
Lavalleja, Juan Antonio, 22, 25
Lavrin, Asunción, 12; "Paulina Luisi," 236n. 25; *Women, Feminism, and Social Change in Argentina, Chile, and Uruguay, 1890–1940*, 4–5, 236n. 23, 236n. 25, 241n. 8
Law of Common Education, 35
League of Nations, 106
Lerner, Gerda, 7
Liberal, El, 54, 55, 57, 59, 60
liberal feminism, 8–10, 15–16, 36, 39, 61, 127–58; Batllismo and, 55, 107, 123, 129, 156–57, 207; social class and, 92–93, 122–24; Socialism and, 193; state formation and, 209–10. *See also* Asociación de Damas

Liberales (Damas Liberales); Luisi, Paulina (*pseud.* Ananké,); *specific feminist leaders*
Liberal Party, 16
Liga de Damas Católicas del Uruguay (Liga), 10–11, 16–18, 44, 161–62, 176–78, 201–2; activities, 168–76; Alianza Uruguaya por el Sufragio Femenino and, 167, 169; anti-Semitism and, 174; Comité de Vigilancia Económica, 173–74; committees, 52–53; Communist Party and, 167–68; formation, 5, 46–50, 161; influence, 54–55; labor movement and, 182–83, 191, 194; leadership, 162–65; *Liga pro-trabajadores de la tierra*, 169; men and, 67; "paladin of Catholicism," 173–76; political rivalries, 165–68; Pro-Illiterates Committee, 169–70; "Radio Jackson," 171; Student Association, 167; theatricals and film productions and, 170–71; US imperialism and, 174–75; women's suffrage, 166–67, 169
Liga Nacional de Mujeres Librepensadores, 58–59
Liga Patriótica de Damas Católicas del Uruguay. See *Liga de Damas Católicas del Uruguay* (Liga)
literacy, 35
Little, Cynthia Jeffress: "Moral Reform and Feminism, 236n. 25
López-Alves, Fernando, 6–7
Lucha Obrera, La, 41
Luisi, Angel, 30

Luisi, Clotilde, 45, 75, 95
Luisi, Inés, 95
Luisi, Josefa, 30
Luisi, Luisa, 95
Luisi, Paulina (*pseud.* Ananké,), 4–5, 14, 17, 30, 45, 58, 97*i*; education, 95–96; eugenic thought, 98–104; Liga de Damas Católicas del Uruguay and, 166; National Women's Council of Uruguay (Conamu) and, 94, 130–32; parents, 94–95; *Primer Congreso Femenino* and, 96; "Sobre el voto femenino," 103–4; socialism and, 105–8, 136; Women's Suffrage Alliance and, 94
Lutz, Bertha, 210, 221n. 39

Mann, Horace, 35
Mariposas (Etchepare), 172–73
Martínez de Williman, Carmen, 117
Matos Rodríguez, Félix, 8; *Women and Urban Change in San Juan, Puerto Rico*, 222n. 47, 239–40n. 60, 241n. 75
Mauthone Falco, Rosa, 167
McGee Deutsch, Sandra, 213
Melián Lafinur, Luis, 77–78
Mexico, 211–12, 213; Law of Family Relations, 211; "modernization of patriarchy," 3; Revolution, 211
Michel, Sonya, 10, 209
Miller, Francesca, 12–13; *Latin American Women and the Search for Social Justice*, 232n. 12
"modernization of patriarchy," 3–4
Monterroso de Lavalleja, Ana, 25–26, 27
"Moral Reform and Feminism (Little), 236n. 25
Mujer Cristiana, La , 48–49

Mundo Uruguayo, 69, 127, 128
Muñoz de De María, Bernardina, 117

National Assistance Law. *See Asistencia Pública Nacional* (APN)
National Public Assistance, 71
National University, 76
National Women's Council of Uruguay. *See Consejo Nacional de Mujeres del Uruguay* (Conamu)
Normal School for Girls, 95
Nuestra Causa, 84
Nueva Senda, La , 61

Offen, Karen, 10–11; *European Feminisms*, 228n. 49
Oribe, Manuel, 22, 26
Orloff, Ann, 3

Página Blanca, 117–18
Pan American Federation, 61–63, 66–67
Panizza, Francisco, 5–7
Parodi, Alfredo, 38
patriarchy, 3, 8, 40, 88
"Paulina Luisi" (Lavrin), 236n. 25
Pérez, Francisco, 81–82
Pernet, Corinne, 12
Philanthropic Society of Oriental Ladies. *See Sociedad Filantrópica de Damas Orientales*
Pinto de Vidal, Isabel, 133, 135
political parties, 21, 23–27, 37, 38; immigration and, 29–30. *See also specific parties*
Polleri, Amalia, 102, 130, 142, 149, 154–55, 205
Polleri, Félix, 128, 157
Power, Margaret: *Right Wing Women in Chile*, 208–9
Protecting Soldiers and Mothers

(Skocpol), 221n. 41
Puerto Rico, 8, 212, 226; "modernization of patriarchy," 3
Puig de Turenne, Elena, 111

Quintana, Catalina, 24

racial discourses, 212
Radio Jackson, 171
Ramírez, Félix, 199
República Oriental del Uruguay, 22
Resistance Societies, 42
Right Wing Women in Chile (Power), 208–9
Río de la Plata, 22, 23, 28
Rivera, Fructuoso, 22, 25–27
Riverista Colorados, 82–83, 84
Rodríguez,de Morató, Adela, 133
Rodríguez, Villamíl, Silvia, 74
Rodríguez de Morató, Adela, 133
Rodríguez Larreta, Aureliano, 102
Rosemblatt, Karin, 3; *Gendered Compromises*, 210, 221n. 35

Santos de Bosch, Teresa, 112
Sapriza, Graciela, 74
Sarmiento, Domingo, 35
Sárraga. Belén, 30, 54, 55–56, 56*i*, 57, 229n. 60, 230n. 86
Schell, Patience: "An Honorable Avocation for Ladies," 227n31
schoolteachers, 13–14
Schultze, Otilia (de Bournasell, de Galarza), 59*i*, 95, 230n. 79
Seccíon de Enseñanza Secundaria y Preparatoria. See Universidad de Mujeres
Secco Illa, Joaquín de, 46, 48, 164, 174
Señoras Cristianas, 164
Sex and Danger in Buenos Aires (Guy), 235n. 15
Skocpol, Theda: *Protecting Soldiers and Mothers*, 221n. 41
Socialist Party, 10, 18, 60–61, 64–65, 82, 98, 184; Alianza and, 142; *Centro Socialista Femenino*, 185–86; Communism and, 189, 193; domestic servants and, 185; Dubinsky and, 196; elections, 134; immigrants, 144; labor movement, 186; Luisi and, 104–5, 107, 136, 150; women's participation, 186–89; women's suffrage, 130, 185–86
Sociedad Filantrópica de Damas Orientales, 27
Soler, Archbishop Mariano, 37, 47, 51
Soto, Shirlene: *Emergence of the Modern Mexican Woman*, 219n. 24
Stagnero de Munar, María, 36
state monopolies, 87
Stepan, Nancy: *The Hour of Eugenics*, 235–36n. 22
Stern, Steve: *The Secret History of Gender*, 239n. 59
Stuart, Robert: "Whores and Angels," 248n. 2
subvención, 111

telefonistas (telephone operators), 150–53, 192–95, 205
Terra, Gabriel, 87
The Hour of Eugenics (Stepan), 235–36n. 22
The Secret History of Gender (Stern), 239n. 59
"The Trial of the New Woman" (Wood), 249–50n. 15
Times (London), 75
Tinsman, Heidi, 202
"To Organize in Every Neighborhood, in Every Home." (Gosse), 248–49n. 3

281

"Toward Defining Maternalism in U.S. History" (Ladd-Taylor), 220n. 27
Tribuna Libertaria, 42
Turenne, Augusto, 111, 118, 172

Unión Cívica, 163, 164, 174
Unión de Obreros en Cigarillos, 42
Universidad de Mujeres, 76–78, 79i
University of the Republic, 95
Uriarte, Margarita (de Heber Jackson, de Herrera), 37, 163–64, 165i, 176
Uruguay: Portrait of a Democracy (Fitzgibbon), 16

Vanger, Milton, 27
Varela, José Pedro, 35–37
Vaughan, Mary Kay, 3
Vaz Ferreira, Carlos, 17, 72–73, 80, 85
Verba, Ericka Kim, 168; "Catholic Feminism and *acción social femenina* [Women's Social Action]," 246n. 14
Verdad, La , 40
Viera, Feliciano, 83
Voz de la Mujer, La , 43

Weisbord, Albert and Vera, 250n. 18
"Whores and Angels" (Stuart), 248n. 2

Williman, Claudio, administration, 70
Women, Feminism, and Social Change in Argentina, Chile, and Uruguay, 1890–1940 (Lavrin), 4–5, 236n. 23, 241n. 8; Women, Feminism, and Social Change in Argentina, Chile, and Uruguay, 1890–1940, 236n. 25
Women and American Socialism 1870–1920 (Buhle), 249n. 10
Women and Urban Change in San Juan, Puerto Rico (Matos Rodríguez), 222n. 47, 239–40n. 60, 241n. 75
Women's Assembly of the Civic Union, 176
Women's Section of the Brotherhood of San José, 27
women's suffrage, 18, 87; Liga de Damas Católicas del Uruguay and, 166–67; Socialist Party and, 130
Women's Suffrage Alliance. *See* Alianza Uruguaya por el Sufragio Femenino
Wood, Elizabeth: "The Trial of the New Woman," 249–50n. 15
working women, 208

"Zoraída," 192–93

HQ 1236.5 .U8 E47 2005
Ehrick, Christine, 1967-
The shield of the weak

AUG 1 1 2005